Dear Daniel,
I thank God that God has woven you in
the fabric of my life.
Peace be with you,
Deborah

now owned by ~~[illegible]~~

The Weavings
Reader

The Weavings Reader

*Living with God
in the World*

John S. Mogabgab
Editor

UPPER ROOM BOOKS
Nashville

The scripture quotations identified in the text are used by permission: RSV from the Revised Standard Version of the Bible, copyright 1946, 1952, and © 1971 by the Division of Christian Education of the National Council of the Churches of Christ in the United States of America; TEV from the *Good News Bible, The Bible in Today's English Version*, copyright © by The American Bible Society, 1966, 1971, 1976; JB from *The Jerusalem Bible*, copyright © 1966 by Darton, Longman & Todd, Ltd., and Doubleday Co., Inc.; NEB from *The New English Bible*, © The Delegates of the Oxford University Press and The Syndics of The Cambridge University Press 1961, 1970; NRSV from the New Revised Standard Version of the Bible, copyright © 1989 by the Division of Christian Education, National Council of the Churches of Christ in the United States of America.

Passages designated AT are the author's translation.

"Becoming Bearers of Reconciliation" reprinted by permission from *To Pray and to Love: Further Conversations with the Early Church* by Roberta C. Bondi, copyright © 1991 Augsburg Fortress.

"The Booty of the Dove" (*Weavings*, Nov/Dec 1991) reprinted by permission of Mary Rose O'Reilly. An expanded version of this article appears in *The Peaceable Kingdom* by Mary Rose O'Reilly published by Boynton/Cook Publishers, Inc. in 1993.

"Desert Wisdom" by Abba Poemen reprinted by permission from *The Sayings of the Desert Fathers*, ed. by Benedicta Ward, S.L.G. (Kalamazoo, MI: Cistercian Pubns., 1975).

"Silent Story" by Maureen Noworyta reprinted from *The Journal of Women and Religion*, vol. 8, 1989, by permission of the Center for Women and Religion, Graduate Theological Union, 2400 Ridge Road, Berkeley, CA 94709.

"Waging Spiritual Warfare with the Powers" reprinted by permission from *Engaging the Powers* by Walter Wink, copyright © 1992 Augsburg Fortress.

"The Wild Geese" from *The Country of Marriage*, copyright © 1971 by Wendell Berry, reprinted by permission of Harcourt Brace & Company.

Cover and interior design: Nelson Kane
Library of Congress Catalog Card Number: 92-61443
ISBN 0-8358-0680-4
First printing: July 1993 (10)

Printed in the USA.

"*There is nothing more praiseworthy*

in friendship than loyalty,

which seems to be its

nurse and guardian."

—Aelred of Rievaulx, *Spiritual Friendship*

Dedicated with gratitude
to the loyal authors, artists,
and readers of *Weavings*

Contents

Discerning

Responding

Foreword

WRITING THIS PREFACE for *The Weavings Reader* is like writing a thank-you letter to a teacher who has touched my life. *Weavings*, the journal that first published the essays in this book, has been teaching me about faith since its inception in 1986. Under the gifted editorship of John Mogabgab (who has also been a special mentor of mine), *Weavings* has consistently given voice to the kind of Christianity that we most need in our time—passionately committed to the light that is in us, radically open to the diverse ways that the light gets refracted in our world, and unabashed by the fact that light and shadow are always found side by side.

Many of the writers in this volume have been my mentors through the written word, and some have been my mentors in person: Tilden Edwards, Henri Nouwen, Elaine Prevallet, Douglas Steere, Marjorie Thompson, and Walter Wink. Though I have not always been able to embody their teachings, their words are written in my heart—as they may soon be written in yours.

Several years ago, when I was working on the staff of a Christian retreat center, we met for hours trying to identify the qualifications that people needed to possess if they were to lead programs for us. As our list of criteria became more and more ludicrous (embracing not only faith, hope, and charity, but charisma, low fees, and popularity as well), I finally blurted out my bottom line: "I'll settle for anyone who doesn't make it embarrassing to be a Christian!"

I have thought a lot about that little outburst. I realize that in the Christian life there is a kind of embarrassment that comes with the territory—as in being a "fool for Christ." But that is different from simply being a fool, the kind of fool that religion sometimes breeds, a fool who rides roughshod in the name of God over the difficulties of being human and over the modesty we must feel when we speak of sacred things. Though you will find "fools for Christ" in these pages, you will not find fools of the other kind. I have read *Weavings* faithfully from the beginning, and I have yet to encounter a writer who would be excluded from leading a retreat by my slight but stringent standard—with the occasional exception of myself.

"Living with God in the World," the theme of this volume, is a phrase that captures the heart of *Weavings* and of the faith in which it is rooted. We live *in* this world, and so, praise be, does God. Faith is not a flight from the world. It is a way of entering into daily experience with confidence that we can meet God there—no matter how modest or how difficult our day may be.

In these pages we are taken on a journey of faith. We move from desiring God, to waiting upon God, to discerning God's presence, to responding to God's call. Then, of course, the journey starts again! This endless journey has its solitary passages, but it also requires good companions on the way. Those companions are present in these pages—as are glimpses of the God who always travels with us, whether we are with friends, in an alien crowd, or all alone.

Parker J. Palmer

Introduction

WIND RIFFLED THE SURFACE of the small lake as I slowed my pace along the path to peer into the murky shallows for signs of life. Would a stirring of decayed leaves or a drifting cloud of mud signal the presence of a turtle or a fish foraging here where land and water meet? Yet my gaze was at the same time an inward one, scanning my own inner landscape for hints of spiritual vitality. A small group of us had come to this rural retreat center to explore the theme of personal holiness and public justice, two worlds often separated but in truth no less bound together than water and land. What was stirring in this holy place where soul and society meet?

Some in our company confronted afresh their deep distress at the inexplicable tenacity of injustice. Others noticed their preference for gentle, predictable holiness and their wariness in the face of the wildness of God. Most of us recognized with alarming clarity that when you spend time with God, you are in over your head. As we wrestled with the discrepancies between our actual lives and the vision of life to which God was calling us, our leader offered healing wisdom. The way to a more faithful life, he said, is not gained by haranguing oneself. Nor is the way found through the example of others, important though these are. Neither the insistent voice of conscience nor the inspiring lives of the saints are sufficient to sustain our commitment. No, the path to a life in accord with God's design for creation opens before us as we keep before our eyes the utterly sublime beauty of the Lord. Hearing this, I realized that such a vision could not be impersonal, abstract, or only aesthetic. My mind recalled the emphatic connection between beholding God's beauty and dwelling with God throughout a lifetime (Psalm 27:4). Only this intensely personal yet socially transfiguring relationship can lead us to the days envisioned by the psalmist, when the needy will be delivered from oppression and violence, there will be abundance of food for all, and people will "blossom in the cities like the grass of the field" (Psalm 72).

A faithful life is formed by living with God in the world. That is the word I took with me at the conclusion of our retreat day. Yet this word is not exactly an answer to the questions that accompany our life with God. Indeed, it may serve only to deepen the confusion, heighten the frustration, or intensify the pain in that most mysterious of all human relationships. A generation ago the distinguished Quaker spiritual writer Howard Thurman voiced a sentiment that expresses the feeling of many today: "What we most want to know about God is whether He is present in the commonplace experiences of ordinary living, available to ordinary people under the most garden variety of circumstances."[1]

God's availability may be uncertain for a variety of reasons. We live in a period of intense theological ferment similar in some respects to the early centuries of the Christian era. Long-held convictions about the relation between God and the world, the person and work of Jesus Christ, and the nature of the church are being critically reevaluated and even overturned. Eastern religious traditions as well as "New Age" religious philosophies have brought unfamiliar concepts and disciplines to the contemporary quest for holiness. In view of this sometimes disorienting situation, it is not surprising that for some seekers, living with God in the world is complicated by questions about whether God is immanent or transcendent, personal or impersonal, spirit or force, loving or indifferent.

For other pilgrims the problem may not be how to conceive of God but rather where to find God. Anthony Bloom, the Russian Orthodox priest and spiritual writer, once described God as "extremely sensitive, vulnerable, and shy."[2] Precisely because God loves us so profoundly and with such abandonment there is a certain discriminating restraint in God's ways with us. God's approach, more often than not, is indirect, concealed in a burning bush, a pillar of cloud, a still small voice, a carpenter from Nazareth. The question asked of Jesus by the disciples of John the Baptist is one addressed again and again to the shy God who hides: "Where do you dwell?" (John 1:38, AT).

Our perplexity over God's whereabouts is not always a matter of God's reticence, however. Sometimes the living God seems encased in familiar liturgical forms and theological formulas, preserved for posterity like some great shaggy ice-bound beast of ancient days. Sometimes God seems obscured from our eyes by the heaving distress of a planetary environment in crisis, the blazing

---

[1] Howard Thurman, *Deep Is the Hunger* (Richmond, IN: Friends United Press, 1951), p. 147.

[2] Anthony Bloom, *Beginning to Pray* (New York: Paulist Press, 1970), p. 25.

14

torment of ethnic and tribal strife, the gnawing shame of home-lessness and poverty, the corrosive legacy of abuse and abandon-ment, the numbing exile of loneliness and hopelessness. Job's anguished search for God sears the heart of many a person of faith today: "If I go forward, [God] is not there; or backward, I cannot perceive him; on the left he hides, and I cannot behold him; I turn to the right, but I cannot see him" (Job 23:8-9, NRSV).

These words gather up and express the pain of living in the world with almost everything but God. The siege of suffering within and around us cocoons our lives within a thousand filaments of anxious waiting, cramped yearning, restless striving in a gritty land of parched hope where God is not. This is the desert land of bewilderment and spiritual struggle. It was from this land that Abba Alonius, one of the early desert monks, wrested the insight that, "If a [person] does not say in his [or her] heart, in the world there is only myself and God, [that person] will not gain peace."[3] There is an enormous transposition of experience here. Living in the world with many things, people, and events ropes our sense of identity to these ever-changing realities, causing it to blow hither and yon like the tail of a kite. Living alone with God in the world anchors us in a relationship with One who was before even the founda-tions of the world were laid. So unwaveringly faithful is this mys-teriously vulnerable God, so surely woven from the costly cords of divine love is this relationship, that it has the flex to encompass the whole world. That is why the great nineteenth century Russian spiritual guide Seraphim of Sarov could say, "Learn to be peaceful and thousands around you will find salvation."[4] This peace of which Abba Alonius and Father Seraphim speak is not a static, other-worldly tranquillity. Like the mud Jesus smeared on the eyes of the man born blind (John 9:1-12), this peace shares the often unex-pected, usually messy, but always healing character of living more and more intimately with God in the world.

Weavings, the journal from which this collection of writings has been drawn, was created seven years ago to explore the drama of this deepening intimacy with God. The journal's text, design, and art (some of which appears in these pages) all conspire to help read-ers see more clearly where God's life and human lives are being woven together in love. Throughout its history *Weavings* has tried

[3] Benedicta Ward, S.L.G. (ed.), *The Sayings of the Desert Fathers* (Kalamazoo, MI: Cistercian Publications., 1975), Alonius #1, p. 30.

[4] Valentine Zander, *St. Seraphim of Sarov* (Crestwood, NY: St. Vladimir's Seminary Press, 1975), p. x.

to encourage a contemplative sensibility that refrains from pat religious answers to the hard questions of life and invites seekers to join the incarnate God in the tumult, ambiguity, and aching beauty of human existence. What this interweaving of the most holy and the most human looks like is the substance of this book. The four parts of THE WEAVINGS READER—Desiring, Waiting, Discerning, Responding—point to a basic pattern repeated in varying textures and colors throughout the years of our living with God in the world.

DESIRING

"The soul's greatest desire," remarks Bernard of Clairvaux, "is to see goodness."[5] Here Bernard echoes the sentiment of the psalmist: "As a deer longs for flowing streams, so my soul longs for you, O God. My soul thirsts for God, for the living God. When shall I come and behold the face of God?" (Psalm 42:1-2, NRSV). Just as the thirsting woodland creature can smell water before it is within sight, so a relentless undertow of yearning draws us toward God in the company of a whole creation groaning for complete immersion in the divine life (Romans 8:19-24). Our lives resemble the sign of the covenant God made with Noah—a multihued arc of desire stretched across our days, a desire whose origins lie behind the horizon of our birth and whose complete fulfillment remains hidden beyond the final crest of our brief span here.

WAITING

It is our desire that makes the waiting necessary and difficult. God's time and our time flow differently (Psalm 90:4). God's perceptions rarely match our own (Isaiah 55:8). There are stretches of loneliness and incomprehension in our relationship with this most unusual and often difficult life partner. Like a barren winter tree, whose spindly torso eagerly awaits the adornment of spring, our naked desire waits to be clothed with the grace of God's presence. This waiting is not for the irresolute or the passive; it asks for strength and courage (Psalm 27:14), and draws both from trust: "I believe that I shall see the goodness of the LORD in the land of the living" (Psalm 27:13). Alert waiting hones our inner eye and so prepares us to recognize what we desire when it finally comes.

[5] Bernard of Clairvaux, *Sermons on Conversion*, trans. and intro. by Marie-Bernard Said, O.S.B. (Kalamazoo, MI: Cistercian Pubns., 1981), p. 171.

DISCERNING

"To walk on the earth is something anyone can do," writes the early Syriac Father Babai, "but to walk along a knife edge is something only a mature soul can do."[6] To discern God's goodness amidst the recurring tempests of hope and despair that criss-cross the land of the living requires just the kind of surefooted insight Babai's words evoke. Noticing the constant currents of divine purpose around us and recognizing within us the beckoning whispers of the Lover of souls—these are sensibilities tuned to greater precision as we practice the artful attentiveness of a discerning heart. Paradoxically, our capacity to recognize God in ordinary affairs, unlikely places, uncertain conditions, and improbable people increases the more closely we live with God in the world. "He comes to us as One unknown," observes Albert Schweitzer, "without a name, as of old, by the lakeside. . . . And to those who obey Him, whether they be wise or simple, He will reveal Himself in the toils, the conflicts, the sufferings which they shall pass through in His fellowship, and as an ineffable mystery, they shall learn in their own experience Who He is."[7] Discerning and responding belong together and indeed are inseparable in a life committed to friendship with God.

RESPONDING

In his *Tales of a Magic Monastery*, Theophane the Monk tells the following story about someone who went to the monastery on retreat:

> *I asked each of the monks I met this question: "What great blunder have you made?"*
>
> *One answered, "There was a stone in my room, and I did not love it."*
>
> *Another said, "They called me a Christian, but I did not become Christ."*
>
> *I asked the first, "What do you mean? I don't understand. You didn't love that stone. . . ."*
>
> *"I just didn't love it. I was so close to redeeming the whole world, but I looked down on that stone."*

---

[6] Babai, "Letter to Cyriacus," in *The Syriac Fathers on Prayer and the Spiritual Life*, trans. and intro. by Sebastian Brock (Kalamazoo, MI: Cistercian Pubns., 1987), p. 162.

[7] Albert Schweitzer, *The Quest of the Historical Jesus* (New York: The Macmillan Co., 1950), p. 403.

I asked the second, "You did not become Christ? Is one supposed to become Christ?"

"I kept putting distance between myself and him—by seeking, by praying, by reading. I kept deploring the distance, but I never realized that I was creating it."

"But," I insisted, "is one supposed to become Christ?"
His answer: "No distance." [8]

It was this distance that tormented us on that retreat day in the country. It was our renewed awareness of how much God wants to share life with us that sent us back into the world with a resolute spirit. You are about to join a circle of God's friends who have struggled with the distance. Perhaps in their company and with their encouragement you will discover that God is closer than you think.

John S. Mogabgab

---

[8] Theophane the Monk, *Tales of a Magic Monastery* (New York: Crossroad, 1989), p. 33.

Contributors

ELLEN ANTHONY is a poet who works at Wellfleet Public Library on Cape Cod. Besides writing, she designs eggs and lamps. Most recently she performed in "Why Can't I Be Everywhere?" her experimental work at the Academy in Orleans.

KEITH BEASLEY-TOPLIFFE is a United Methodist pastor serving six small churches in south-central Pennsylvania. He and his wife, who pastors four churches, are the parents of a daughter. *Weavings* readers are familiar with him as a writer and reviewer.

WENDELL BERRY is an educator and author of numerous books of poetry and essays. He makes his home in Kentucky.

JEAN M. BLOMQUIST is a writer whose work focuses primarily on spirituality and contemporary religious issues. She is a frequent contributor to *Weavings*. She and her husband live in Berkeley, California.

ROBERTA C. BONDI is Professor of Church History at Candler School of Theology at Emory University in Atlanta. She has a particular interest in the spirituality of early monasticism and is currently working on a book entitled *Memories of God: Theological Reflections on a Life*, to be published by Abingdon Press.

ELIZABETH J. CANHAM, an Episcopal priest, is director of Stillpoint Ministries, a retreat center in Black Mountain, North Carolina. Dr. Canham leads workshops and retreats, teaches in two seminaries, and acts as a local church consultant. She is the author of *Pilgrimage to Priesthood, Praying the Bible,* and *Journaling with Jeremiah* and coauthor of *Where Love and People Are.*

MARY CONROW COELHO holds an M.Div. degree from Union Theological Seminary in New York City. She studied the life and works of St. Teresa of Avila while at Fordham University, where she completed her Ph.D. in theology in May 1990. Ms. Coelho worked for five years at General Theological Seminary in New York, becoming codirector of the Programs in Spiritual Direction at the Center for Christian Spirituality. She is the author of several articles and coauthor of *Writings in Spiritual Direction by the Great Christian Masters.* By avocation, Mrs. Coelho is a watercolorist. She lives with her husband in New York City and is active in a Quaker Meeting there.

ESTHER DE WAAL lives in Wales, having grown up in an Anglican country vicarage on the borders of Wales. She writes, travels, gives lectures and retreats on monastic and Celtic spirituality. Her most recent book is *Every Earthly Blessing: Celebrating a Spirituality of Creation* published by Servant Publications in Ann Arbor, Michigan. She is married and the mother of four sons.

TILDEN EDWARDS is executive director of the Shalem Institute for Spiritual Formation in Washington, D.C. He is an Episcopal priest, retreat leader, and author or editor of six books, including *Sabbath Time, Spiritual Friend,* and *Living in the Presence.*

DAVID M. GRIEBNER is a United Methodist pastor currently serving Riverside United Methodist Church in Columbus, Ohio. He received an M.Div. from Duke University and was trained in spiritual guidance at Shalem Institute for Spiritual Formation in Washington, D.C. He and his wife, Sande, have three daughters.

GUSTAVO GUTIÉRREZ is a professor in the department of theology and social sciences in the Catholic Pontifical University in Lima, Peru. He became internationally known in the 1970s with the publication of his first major book *Teología de la liberación.* He is the author of several other books and numerous articles and essays. Ordained as a priest in 1959, he has been the featured speaker at many conferences in South America, North America, Europe, Asia, and Africa.

GEORGE HUNSINGER teaches systematic theology at Bangor Theological Seminary. Educated at Stanford, Harvard, and Yale Universities, he has lived in Bedford Stuyvesant, where he taught in a storefront school. He also served as a tutor of the Riverside Church Disarmament Program in New York and continues to be active in the antinuclear and anti-interventionist movements. He is the author of *How to Read Karl Barth: The Shape of His Theology* and is married and the father of two children.

SUSAN MANGAM, S.T.R., is an artist and hermit residing at Christ in the Mountain Hermitage in upstate New York. She is a solitary in the Episcopal diocese of Albany, New York.

MAUREEN NOWORYTA is a writer; spiritual guide; and teacher of workshops in journal writing, Celtic spirituality, and contemporary images of Mary. She holds a master's degree in religious studies and a Doctor of Creative Ministry from Graduate Theological Foundation.

20

HENRI J. M. NOUWEN is a Roman Catholic priest of the Diocese of Utrecht, Holland. He is a spiritual director of Daybreak, the L'Arche community near Toronto, Canada. Widely known as a speaker and retreat leader, he has a special interest in Latin America and has made several trips to that region. He is the author of numerous books, most recently *The Return of the Prodigal Son*.

MARY ROSE O'REILLEY teaches English at the University of St. Thomas in St. Paul, Minnesota, where she lives with her two children. Dr. O'Reilley is author of *The Peaceable Classroom: Essays Toward a Pedagogy of Nonviolence* to be published in summer 1993. She is a member of the Twin Cities Friends Meeting and leads occasional retreats at Pendle Hill, Wallingford, Pennsylvania, on aspects of the contemplative life.

PARKER J. PALMER is a writer, teacher, and activist who works independently on issues in education, community, spirituality, and social change. He serves as senior associate of the American Association of Higher Education. His most recent book is *The Active Life: A Spirituality of Work, Creativity, and Caring*.

ELAINE M. PREVALLET, S.L., is director of Knobs Haven Retreat Center on the grounds of the Motherhouse of the Sisters of Loretto at Nerinx, Kentucky. Previously she taught at Pendle Hill and at Loretto Heights College in Denver. She holds a doctorate in religious studies from Marquette University.

ELIZABETH ROONEY manages a family farm and cave sightseeing business with her husband in Blue Mounds, Wisconsin. She is a member of the Episcopal women's lay order of the Society of the Companions of the Holy Cross. Her poetry has appeared in many journals and in the anthology *A Widening Light*. She and her husband have four grown children.

DON E. SALIERS is a professor of worship and theology at Candler School of Theology at Emory University in Atlanta, Georgia. A member of the *Weavings* advisory board, he is a contributing editor of *Worship* and is the author of *Worship and Spirituality*.

JOAN SAURO, C.S.J., is a sister of St. Joseph of Carondelet who lives and writes in Syracuse, New York. She is the author of *Inner Marathon: The Diary of a Jogging Nun* and *Whole Earth Meditation: Ecology for the Spirit*.

J. BARRIE SHEPHERD is pastor of The First Presbyterian Church in the city of New York. A graduate of Yale Divinity School, he is a widely published poet and the author of several books, most recently *Faces at the Manger*.

JUDITH E. SMITH is associate general secretary for interpretation of The United Methodist Board of Higher Education and Ministry. She is a clergy member of the Oregon-Idaho Annual Conference and is a frequent contributor to *Weavings*.

DOUGLAS V. STEERE was the T. Wistar Brown Professor of Philosophy at Haverford College, Haverford, Pennsylvania, where he taught for thirty-six years prior to his retirement. An authority on the centered and contemplative spiritual life, his books include *Door into Life, Together in Solitude, Quaker Spirituality*, a translation of Søren Kierkegaard's *Purity of Heart*, and *Gleanings*.

MARJORIE J. THOMPSON is a writer, spiritual director, and retreat leader who lives in Nashville, Tennessee. A Presbyterian clergywoman, she is on the adjunct faculty of Vanderbilt Divinity School and teaches in The Upper Room's Academy for Spiritual Formation. She is the author of the book, *Family: The Forming Center*.

JOHN W. VANNORSDALL is President Emeritus of the Lutheran Theological Seminary in Philadelphia and now resides in Orange, Massachusetts, with his wife Patricia. He was university chaplain at Yale University and a preacher on the Lutheran Series of the Protestant Hour from 1976 to 1990.

WALTER WINK is professor of biblical interpretation at Auburn Theological Seminary in New York. He is the author of *The Bible in Human Transformation, Naming the Powers: The Language of Power in the New Testament,* and *Unmasking the Powers: The Invisible Forces That Determine Human Existence*

WENDY M. WRIGHT is on the faculty of Creighton University in Omaha, Nebraska, and previously taught at Weston School of Theology in Cambridge, Massachusetts. Her most recent book is *The Vigil: Keeping Watch in the Season of Christ's Coming.* She is married and has three children.

FLORA SLOSSON WUELLNER is a former adjunct faculty member of the Pacific School of Religion in Berkeley, California. She is an ordained minister in the United Church of Christ and a frequent leader of retreats. She is the author of several books on prayer, most recently *Prayer, Fear, and Our Powers* and *Heart of Healing, Heart of Light*.

Desiring

DAVID KLEIN

Transformation

OUR FEAR, OUR LONGING

by Flora Slosson Wuellner

WHAT MAKES US HESITATE to respond to that invitation to our school reunion? Don't we want to walk down those halls, see the old classrooms, talk with the old friends and enemies? Somewhere I have read that only the very rich and the very thin actually *want* to attend their school reunions!

Perhaps we are paradoxically afraid both that we *have* changed and yet we *haven't* changed. The outer changes are obvious and disconcerting: gray hair, wrinkles, expanded waistlines; grandfathers and grandmothers in place of those young friends; dull jobs and domestic routines in place of all the bright expectations of doing something new and startling in the world. Underlying these dramatic changes is a bittersweet homesickness, a nostalgia for the way things were, the way we were. We know we cannot go back.

But are we not in equal fear that we have *not* changed? Will we find ourselves, reflected in the eyes of our classmates, still caught in the old categories that defined us? Are we in a panic that we will still find ourselves as the shy one, the unpopular one, the class clown, the "loser," last to be chosen in dance or sports, the one who was never elected to any class office, or perhaps the one always elected and expected to do all the work? Are we still that ugly duckling who somehow never evolved into the swan? And won't the old friends see that the minute they lay eyes on us?

In every great transition of our lives—graduation, marriage, promotion, moving to a new home, parenthood, old age—we encounter a two-headed fear. The first is the anxious question: "Where is the life I am used to?" I think many of us feel a strange depression and lethargy as we face a new experience. The old familiar routine is gone forever. We will become a strange new person. But at the same moment we are struck by the second, equally terrifying question: "But will I ever really move an inch? Will I be up against the same old 'me,' caught in the same old habits? Will I ever really change at all?" Surprisingly, many of those who seem the most successful in the eyes of the world are besieged by this question. No matter how far they advance in promotion and wealth and influence, they still feel that "if others really knew what sort of person I really am, they would see me for the incompetent loser I know myself to be. And at any moment I will make some awful mistake that will prove to everyone (including me) that I haven't and never will change."

Many of us wonder if in old age we will look back at our lives and say sadly to ourselves: "Everything changed, and yet... *nothing* changed. I don't know which is sadder!"

CHANGE OR TRANSFORMATION

THE UNDERLYING FEAR and sadness is that of powerlessness. There is so much in our lives over which we seem to have little or no control. We did not choose the family into which we were born. We could not control our genetic, inherited tendencies. We had no power over the way we were raised as children. We could not control changes in the lives and choices of those nearest us. We have felt powerless in the face of so much that threatens our air, water, earth, neighborhoods, cities, world. We cannot stop the inevitable advance of old age and death. The biblical promise "We shall all be changed" (1 Corinthians 15:51, RSV) sometimes sounds more like a threat than a promise!

We are surrounded, overwhelmed, battered, swept along by outer change. The inner self adapts, adjusts, survives, but too often does not undergo any deep transformation. We have *reacted* rather than acted.

There are many forms of both spirituality and relationship that anesthetize our sense of powerlessness. Sometimes we are tempted to join a faith or enter a relationship that invites us to surrender our identity, to relinquish our freedom and responsibility of choice, and to merge ourselves with the identity of others. Sometimes, on the other hand, we are invited into spiritualities or relationships in which we are offered total control. We are taught methods of manipulative power over everything and everybody.

These extremes and their various adaptations do not enable us to face the deep challenge of change: "While all events and persons around me change, am I able to change with power *from my center* rather than be swept along helplessly?"

This is the great, grave distinction between change and transformation. Change refers to adaptation, reaction, without necessarily involving any *newness of being*. Transformation involves much more than mere adaptation to outer manipulation. Transformation implies new being, a new creative energy flowing from the center that acts with creative power upon surrounding events.

When Jesus spoke of the kingdom of God, he used many symbols of transformation: growing plants; the action of the yeast within the dough; marriage; the act of birth; the action of fire, light, and wind. When Paul spoke of our rebirth in Christ, he spoke of the transformation as a new creation: "If anyone is in Christ, there is a new creation: everything old has passed away; see, everything has become new" (2 Corinthians 5:17, NRSV).

This is what is offered by God through Christ: transformation, new creation rather than change, growing from our deep center, expanding our empowered freedom even in the midst of the power of outer events. When our inner selves waken, stretch, stand up, move out, make choices, our terror of change becomes the hunger, thirst, and ecstasy of growing.

Vivid in my memory is instruction given me thirty years ago when pregnant with my first child. Our instructor in the new, exciting methods of childbirth told us: "If you think of the process of birth labor as a rope *dragging* you to a cliff's edge and doom while you struggle and resist, you will be filled with terror and anger. But if you think of your birth labor as *pulling* on the rope to bring forth something you long for... desire unutterably to see, your work and your bodily groans will be filled with excited purpose and deep determination."

I have remembered this offered transformation of attitude, this offered power and energy flowing from the center, when I read Paul's vision of the whole universe: "We know that the whole creation has been groaning in travail together until now; and not only the creation, but we ourselves, who have the first fruits of the Spirit, groan inwardly as we wait" (Romans 8:22-23, RSV). In this vision of promise we see, on a larger scale, the process of transformation no longer as overwhelming assault from the outside, but as ecstatic (though often painful) unfolding from within.

God's promise of transformation is not a demand: "Clean up your act... pull yourself together... I want to see your room spotless from now on... You'd better produce a decent report card..." God's promise is the ecstatic invitation of lover to beloved: "Come, join yourself to me, and from our togetherness there will come forth the new creation!" Note how often the wedding feast is used in scripture as the supreme symbol of the transformation that occurs when God and the human being unite.

GOD'S WAY OF TRANSFORMATION

I SEE FOUR MAJOR characteristics of God's way of transformation, as contrasted with enforced change from outside forces.

The first of these is the scriptural witness that God's transformation of us does not deny our humanity or wipe out our identity. There are, unfortunately, some forms of spirituality that teach that God is not concerned with our needs, longings, or unique identities, and that spiritual growth consists of denying our humanness. But in both the Old and New Testaments we see a very different thrust. We see God's passionate interest in and concern for our human condition.

A wise student said to me recently: "We are not human beings trying to become spiritual. Rather, we are spiritual beings trying to become human." The scriptures witness that God loves humanity, has called it good (in spite of all problems and failings), and has faith in it and purpose for it. In the second century the great church father Irenaeus of Lyons put it this way: "The glory of God is the fully alive human being."

This understanding might be termed *incarnational spirituality*. In this way of spiritual experience, we are invited more deeply into the rich challenge of the flesh, the earth, and the human personality. The transformation God brings us is seen supremely in Jesus, always involved with the encounter, healing, and release of our full humanity.

As we unite with God, we are invited into bonding rather than bondage. Nothing that has been created is to be enslaved or destroyed. God did not create us as amusing toys to be manipulated and then swept off the board. We are given life, guided, transformed through ecstasy and anguish unspeakable, by love immeasurable, for cosmic purpose unimaginable.

Second, God's transformation of us unites us with our deepest longings. We are told that God says: "I make all things new" (Revelation 21:5, RSV), but though the inner unfolding indeed feels surprising, it also feels strangely and poignantly familiar. It feels like coming to a home we had long forgotten or like waking from confused dreams to see the sunshine and a loved face near ours. God's transformation at work within us brings us increasingly closer to the person we have always (perhaps subconsciously) longed to be. How could it be otherwise if, indeed, "the kingdom of God is in the midst of you" (Luke 17:21, RSV)?

One of the deepest, clearest ways to discern the will of God for our lives is to ask: "What is my longing?" We will probably think of some activity, some profession, some person, some possession, some way of living. Then we can look deeper and ask: "What is the longing that underlies *that*?" If we keep asking this question, each time deeper, longing below longing, we begin to understand who we are and for what purpose we were created. We begin to know that we long for this purpose because it already exists within us, far below the surface, at our very core. We begin to know that God, even more than we, longs for this fulfillment to unfold within us.

I talked recently with a woman struggling to discern God's will for her life. "What do you most love to do?" I asked her.

"I love to do things with my hands," she answered quickly. "I love to paint, to sew, to garden."

"What longing underlies that love?" I asked.

This took more thought, and her answer came more slowly: "I really want to feel that I am making something beautiful and that I have become part of that beauty."

"What longing lies beneath *that*?" I probed. "Try to *feel*, to sense that longing at your deepest core."

She closed her eyes, and there was a long silence. Then she answered softly: "I want to be part of God while God creates. My whole body, my whole self wants to be part of that power, part of that mighty river. It feels very fierce, very joyous."

She opened her eyes. "Is this really what God wants for me too? I've always been a bit ashamed that what I really liked to do was material and physical. I never thought that was spiritual enough. Perhaps my hands knew it before I did—that God made me to be a creator in my own way. Maybe I'll begin to see other ways, too, in which I can create."

A third manifestation of God's transformation within us is that it always involves our deep healing. Frequently we experience blocks, plateaus, even partial regressions in our inner growing. Why do we keep falling back into the old patterns? This can be discouraging when we see what exciting possibilities lie within us. Even though we know we have grown in many wonderful ways, still there are parts within us that are untransformed, childish, full of fear and anger.

Is this part of the meaning in that strange last book of the Bible, the vision of John of Patmos recounted in the Book of Revelation? In the final chapters John sees the fulfilled Heavenly City, the redeemed, the transformed, full of light, love, new life. But he also sees lying outside those gates of life the fiery pain, the shapes of fear and falsehood, the devastation of darkness. Is this an insight into our own human hearts, communal as well as individual? There *is* within us the water of life, the new signs of growth, the sense of God's light and closeness. But there are also the dark, unreconciled vortices within us.

I recently visited a man recovering from a life-threatening illness. All his life he had been a compulsive perfectionist, a driven person, neglecting his own needs, ignoring his body in order to accomplish the rigid tasks he set for himself. With tears in his eyes he told me that he envisioned a new way of living that would include respect and love for his body and his needs, new ways of claiming rest and re-creation. But within just a few weeks after leaving the hospital, he began staying up half the night, grimly replacing all the wallpaper in his home! His vision of a new life and his determination were not enough to reach the dark compulsiveness.

What does this mean? There is deep, unencountered woundedness, perhaps passed on for generations, that blocks our inner growing. Deep unhealed fear, anger, grieving, loneliness, brought about by the assaults, lovelessness, and manipulation of much of the life around us have made us resistant to trust and love. Often it is difficult to discern that we *are* wounded and blocked by unhealed pain. We have become so used to deep pain and defensive/offensive reaction that it has become part of the air we breathe. We can learn to listen to our pain by attentiveness to our negative side: our tendency to worry, hair-trigger anger, compulsive overcontrol, inertia and procrastination, manipulating or closing off to others, constant broken resolutions.

Too often in some forms of spiritual teaching we have been told to denounce or ignore our faults, merely confessing them as sins, and then using willpower to increase our positive aspects. But if we learn to listen attentively to our faults (which is not the same as condoning or giving in to them), they can teach us as much about our pain and needs as our longings can teach us about the gifts that lie beneath them.

For example, if we have a tendency always to be worried and anxious and that does not seem to change no matter how much we pray about it, no matter how many good resolutions we make; we can dialogue with our worry, asking ourselves: "What are you afraid of?" We should ask this question with sincere respect, a genuine desire to know, not with contempt or scorn. And then we can ask it again and keep asking, each time at a deeper level. Perhaps we will discover that for some reason, all our lives, we have felt like a target. We have always felt that accidents, traumas, illnesses, nasty surprises are sneaking up on us from behind or will suddenly leap out to confront us. Did some such traumas actually occur to us or to people close to us? Do we feel powerless, helpless much of the time? Is this chronic worry a signal given to us by our deep self that there is a child within us who feels helpless and frightened? A child whose time for healing has come?

Such a condition is not reached by mere confession of sins. Such a condition cannot be overcome by resolutions and willpower. There is a child in there who needs healing. We begin to understand something of the compassion God has for us. We begin to share with others what we really feel. We begin to release these inner hurt and frightened children into God's hands for healing.

Why is this central pain, which has for so long blocked our growth, not automatically, spontaneously healed by God's love without our awareness and asking? Much of it is, of course. In many ways we are healed at subconscious levels without consciously knowing it. But apparently there are some forms of inner pain whose healing needs our intentional consent. God's *love* always surrounds us, our unreconciled areas as well as our light-filled areas. But God's full *healing* seems to wait for our longing and consent. Is this because we are not helpless puppets but created to be children, heirs, spouses, partners, cocreators with God, our free consent a crucial part of the creative wisdom of growing?

The fourth great sign I see of God's way of transformation, and perhaps this is the greatest, is that our inner unfolding rises from a living relationship with God rather than from laws and commands. Somewhere I have read that the Sermon on the Mount is not a series of orders but rather a description of what begins to happen as we grow closer to God through Christ.

> *Abide in me, and I in you. As the branch cannot bear fruit by itself, unless it abides in the vine, neither can you, unless you abide in me.*
>
> —John 15:4, RSV

This is said by the living Christ to our hearts. We cannot bring forth the full fruits of the Christian life unless we are rooted and growing in the Source of that life. This was expressed with power in a famous little spiritual classic written in the last century by the

Quaker spiritual leader, Hannah Whitall Smith:

> *We all know that growing is not a thing of effort, but is the result of an inward life principle of growth. All the stretching and pulling in the world could not make a dead oak grow; but a live oak grows without stretching... The essential thing is to get within you the growing life... "hid with Christ in God," the wonderful divine life of an indwelling Holy Ghost.... Abide in the Vine. Let the life from Him flow through all your spiritual veins.*[1]

The further we are from this living relationship with the Christ, the more lifeless, the less exciting and transforming becomes our Christianity. How do we most deeply bond with the Living One? Just as each identity is unique, so is each relationship. But those who have lived the longest and most profoundly with the Christ tell us to let our very breathing become the breathing of God's breath of life. They show us the healing power of sharing each need, each hurt, each longing with the Christ who walks with us each moment of the day. They witness to us that all that is within us is loved compassionately and searched for passionately by the Risen One who only asks our consent to "come quickly" with the healing water and light (Revelation 22:20, K J V).

For some of us the great transformation from the inside out comes gradually. For some of us it comes swiftly. But for *all* of us it comes inevitably as we unite more closely to the One who brings the yeast, salt, wind, and fire of the new creation—the deep self we have always longed to be.

---

[1] Hannah Whitall Smith, *The Christian's Secret of a Happy Life* (Westwood, NJ: Fleming H. Revell Co., 1952), Chapter 14, p. 183.

Prospects

by J. Barrie Shepherd

October is a stained-glass world,

a mellow organ with a distant choir

that fades too speedily beyond the heavy doors.

This over-ripened year

falls fast now forward to the early chill

of frosty death. There is no way

to stay here, to arrest

the plunging calendar, rejoice forever

in the glowing palace of the maple trees,

among the longer glancing shafts of amber light.

Days flutter past like foliage

or flocks of birds toward the time of starkness.

We remain, at least for now,

to search among the bitter evergreens

for wood enough to warm a winter hearth

or even build a cradle for this yearning

that lives on beyond the burning of the leaves

into a cold, austere, yet cleansing winter light.

The Company *of* God's Friends

by Douglas V. Steere

I ONCE VISITED the parsonage of John Frederick Oberlin (1740–1828), the old Alsatian pastor for whom Oberlin College was named. I found a large rack that was still full of three-by-five-inch sheets that were by then well browned by over a century of exposure. On each of these he had printed with his own printing press a compelling Bible verse. His biographers tell how, when he prepared himself to call on a parishioner, he picked with great care a text that he thought might be especially suitable for the person's needs at this point in his or her life and left this slip with the parishioner as a little gift. How often God speaks to us through the printed word! Some luminous line in a book may be freighted with precisely the answer to some long-delayed decision. You may recall Walt Whitman's word about his first reading of Emerson. He said, "I was simmering, and he brought me to a boil." Sometimes some providential happening brings us to a boil and makes us hungry, fiercely hungry, to read and know what this experience means for our life, or terribly eager to see if others have had the same experience and what they did about it.

I remember what happened to Thomas Kelly, whose *Testament of Devotion* many of you have read, after his transforming experience in the autumn of 1937 after a tragedy kept him from getting the Harvard doctorate for which he had slaved seven years and dragged his family through many hardships. After his deep acceptance of the pain, there came the sense of the overwhelming presence of God. He followed this by digging into the writings of the Christian mystics with a whole new passion to see if they could help him understand what he had been through and to see if their experience checked out with his own! Anyone who is entrusted with the guidance of others in the spiritual life knows that the gift of sharing with them the right book at the right time may be of critical importance in the person's spiritual growth. Teresa of Avila tells us in the introductory pages of her autobiography that if you want to grow in openness to God, you ought to seek the company of

God's friends. And this good counsel certainly includes friends of God who lived in centuries other than our own. In fact, if we are to believe T. S. Eliot, after a long search we may find that our closest friend is not among our contemporaries at all. This friend may be hidden away in some other century, and we may come into his or her presence through some devotional book or biography. T. S. Eliot found a contemporary of Shakespeare and of James I, a bishop named Lancelot Andrewes, to be nearer to him than anyone living in his own time. T. S. Eliot lived with Lancelot Andrewes through the medium of his *Private Devotions*, a day-book that was found after Bishop Andrewes's death "slubbered with his tears" and his daily handling. Such books are rare, but they do exist, and to be able to put into the hands of another a book that speaks to his or her condition is to give a gift indeed. Into these books of devotion some friend of God may have put a word that will be a gate into the inner company of God's friends and a blessing beyond measure.

TESTED GUIDES

PERHAPS IT MIGHT BE USEFUL to take a few tested books of devotional literature and see some of the flashes of spiritual nurture that are hidden in them. Baron von Hügel testifies to the fact that for over forty years he spent a quarter of an hour each day reading the New Testament, Augustine's *Confessions*, and the *Imitation of Christ* and found that he never tired of them. The first nine books (as those chapters are called) of Augustine's *Confessions* are an example of the power of a great devotional classic to hold the mirror up to our own lives as he pictures his own persistent postponement of obedience to the divine whisper—his "Save me O Lord, but not yet." This book has moved how many million hearts by its relentlessly honest description of their own condition! His words pierce our defenses. "My heart is restless until it finds its rest in Thee," or "I was collected from the dispersion in which I turned from Thee, the One, and was vainly divided." Again he tells of the dissolving powers of his mother's prayers; of the way he was led step by step to part with the opposition to taking the final step into Christian commitment; by his recovery of the spiritual treasures of Neo-Platonism that ate away his skepticism and opened to him the discovery of a reality that drew him beyond his surface self. There is no concealing the bitter by the sweet. He tells of his immense admiration of Ambrose, the Bishop of Milan, which is followed by a painful account of Ambrose's insensitivity as he sat in his public study in the Milan cathedral absorbed in his reading while Augustine, moved by Ambrose's preaching and ready to take the next step, stood at the open grille longing to be asked in so that he might pour out his heart to him, but too shy to interrupt him! Then there is the story of the final stroke in his conversion, when both his sin and his forgiveness interpenetrate each other as God speaks to his condition through a passage from the Bible and his heart of stone is finally melted into a heart of flesh.

There is something so authentic about his quietly continuing his lectures in rhetoric after his conversion in order to finish out the term that closed at the grape harvest season, when he would leave this role forever. He leaves us to imagine the facade of those lectures being given just as before, whereas the one giving them had been completely changed! How many of us are still giving the same lectures, flying the same external flag, but knowing we are actually no longer in the grip of this former life posture and knowing that our grape harvest exit too, is clearly marked on our life calendar. Finally, there is in the whole of mystical literature almost nothing to exceed the scene on the porch at Ostia where Monica, his mother, and Augustine experience the mystical communion that lights up the ninth book of the *Confessions*. How these incidents illumine our own lives, and how many lives have found this classic to be decisive in the inward transformations that it has brought about during the 1600 years since it was written in A.D. 382!

In the third century the Desert Fathers witnessed to a fresh dimension of spiritual life that has fascinated this generation. Helen Wadell's classic book, *The Desert Fathers*, is still a suitable gate by which to enter. Two centuries after Augustine the classical form of western monasticism was laid down in Benedict's *Rule*, which has been a guide through all the centuries that followed. It is most readable, and its wisdom and sanity and spiritual focus make it exciting reading. Sabatier's *Francis of Assisi* is still a happy way to make acquaintance with one who was called "the thirteenth disciple." Meister Eckhart's *Sermons* journey into the mystical insights of this tested guide and are full of ageless spiritual counsel.

Next to the Bible, the *Imitation of Christ* is still the most republished book of devotion in the Christian world. It actually appeared in the first quarter of the fifteenth century under the name of Thomas à Kempis. Whether he actually wrote it, copied it out, or drew it together has long been debated. For us it is sufficient to know that the book came out of the spirituality of what began as a lay group—the Dutch Brethren of the Common Life, guided by their founder, the Dutch mystic Gerard Groote.

The word *imitation* is not especially acceptable in this generation. A more suitable synonym has appeared in one modern translation of this book that projects Christ's words "follow me," and it becomes *The Following of Christ*. What such following requires, what it costs, and some of the tests of the following are eloquently witnessed to in this remarkable little book that was equally precious to Ignatius of Loyola and John Wesley. Great lines appear in it which, like snatches from the Psalms and the Gospels, come back to us in critical moments of our lives: "Blessed are those who are glad to hear the pulses of the divine whisper"; "Blessed are those who are glad to have time to spare for God"; "He in whom the eternal word speaks is delivered from many opinions"; "No man should speak unless he is able to hold his peace"; "No man should leave his chamber but he who can willingly abide in it."

People find a devotional book speaking differently to them at different periods in their lives. I was first drawn to the *Imitation* when I found it on my bed table in a British home where I was a guest. It searched me and I read it again and again, having been given a copy of the book by my hostess. Later I laid it aside as too ascetic for one living in the world as I was, but I returned to it again and it spoke to me with penetrating power. There are few books for all seasons. But a really great book speaks often to more than one season of our lives.

The *Theologia Germanica* and the *Cloud of Unknowing* appeared in Germany and in Britain, respectively, in this same fourteenth to fifteenth-century period—both as anonymous spiritual gems. There is an inward tone to them both. For the *Theologia Germanica*, heaven and hell were states of the human spirit, and we live in them in this present life as well as beyond it. It declares, "The only thing that shall burn in hell is self-will," and there is some evidence that self-will is able to be considerably transformed in this life. In its depiction of our Christian outreach to the needs of others, it cries out, "I fain would be to the Eternal Goodness, what a man's hand is to a man!"

The *Cloud of Unknowing* is a deeply spiritual essay that accents the mystery of God and the futility and the impossibility of reason's being able ever to prove God's existence or of our being able to snug up our faith by any outward means. Faith for it is "the bird that sings in the darkness that preludes the dawn." The loving God that Christ revealed is hidden in the *Cloud of Unknowing* and can only be reached by the soul's deepest intent: by "the sharp dart of love."

For that reason comes the gentleness of the assurance that "When thou comest before the all-merciful judge, He will not ask thee, what thou *wast* or what thou *art*, but what thou *wouldst be*!" Ira Progoff, who issued an edition some years ago of the *Cloud of Unknowing*, was drawn to it as a psychotherapist. He saw in it a profound account of the ascent of the human spirit by nonrational means. William Johnson, the Irish Jesuit who wrote *Christian Zen* a decade ago, produced a beautiful edition of the *Cloud of Unknowing*. He was drawn to it as a bridge between Christianity and Zen Buddhism and to Asiatic thought, which is most reluctant to conceptualize the ultimate ground of being. He saw that for the Asiatic the *Cloud of Unknowing,* with its accent on love as the only vehicle to penetrate the innermost mystery of God's being, might turn out to be one of the most moving books in all Christian history. The *Cloud* commends imageless prayer and regards prayer as the prime gift that God has given us to use, for it points out that all of our other activities will ultimately at death be swept away. But prayer is something that, if we learn how to do it here, we may continue forever. A companion essay that came out of the same school of thought as the *Cloud* expresses the hiddenness of God and God's precious nearness by saying, "Silence is not God; and speaking is not God. Fasting is not God; and eating is not God. Solitude is not God; and company is not God. But [God] hid between them."

The great Roman Catholic Renaissance treasures of Christian exploration into the interior life found in the works of Teresa of Avila and John of the Cross are not for all, but Teresa's *Life* and John of the Cross's *Dark Night of the Soul* must be cited among the great classics of all time in the matter of spiritual wisdom.

Francis de Sales's *Introduction to the Devout Life* is the fruit of a quarter of a century of spiritual direction of souls. Written for lay people living in the world, it is one of the first pocket guides whose plain sense about the life of inward abandonment lived in the midst of the world of our time is both authentic and sound. His definition of devotion must suffice as a citation: "Devotion is simply the promptitude, fervor, affection, and agility which we have in the service of God." The book is given over to the cultivation of this devotion, and its thrust cuts across all denominational lines.

Pascal's *Thoughts* is another book that is not meant for all. But it was this book, along with the New Testament, that was most often carried in the knapsacks of French soldiers in World War I. A man of "two books," the Bible and Montaigne's *Essays*, Pascal's brilliance glittered even in a century of scientific genius. He is an example of a genius become apostle who depicts the human condition with a scalpel that opens us to ourselves. Every great writer tends to have some heart metaphor within which his or her own master blade is sheathed. Pascal's metaphor was a scene in the Gospels where Jesus returned three times from his bloody sweat in the Garden of Gethsemane only to find each time that his disciples, whom he had charged to stay awake, had lapsed again into sleep. Pascal saw his task in the *Pensées* to wake up the sleeper in us all and to compel us to know our options and to choose among them.

The seventeenth century is alive with devotional classics like Lancelot Andrewes's *Private Devotions*, Jeremy Taylor's *Holy Living and Holy Dying*, Thomas Traherne's *Centuries of Meditation*, to say nothing of the great poets and writers like John Donne, George Herbert, and the so-called metaphysical poets like Robert Herrick that crowd the pages of the *Oxford Book of Mystical Verse*, a most precious book to own and to read. George Fox's *Journal* is a power-drenched record of inward illumination. It is authentic and has had its readers in each generation up to our own day. It was Fox who drew the Quakers together, and he had a colleague in witness and suffering in that century, Isaac Pennington, whose *Letters* are among the choicest fruits of one who among the Quakers might be called a first-generation guide of souls. He has two especially telling lines. The first, "The greatest as well as the least must be daily taught of the Lord both in ascending and in descending, or they will miss the way." The second, "There is that near you which will guide you, O wait for it and be sure that you keep to it." Coming to the end of the seventeenth century, Fénelon's *Letters to Men* and *Letters to Women* are full of jewels like "The wind of God is always blowing, but you must hoist your sail."

In the eighteenth century John Woolman's *Journal* and William Law's *A Serious Call to a Devout and Holy Life* are classics. This book of William Law's had a profound influence on John Wesley. Woolman's *Journal* gives us that rare and wonderful girding of a spiritually-rooted life available for use in carrying out, in the midst of earning a living and supporting a family, a social concern to liberate the slaves a century before this country took the issue seriously. In eighteenth-century France there were two Jesuits whose writings on the spiritual life have been translated and widely read in the past generation: Père Caussade's *Abandonment to Divine Providence* and Père Grou's *Manual for Interior Souls*.

In the nineteenth century a Danish prophet appeared named Søren Kierkegaard, whose works have been translated into English only in my generation. *Purity of Heart* is one of his gems, and it is still available. The book uses Søren Kierkegaard's root metaphor taken from the western Danish province of Jutland, where the soil is so sandy that the brush is stunted and no one could ever hide there. Kierkegaard's work is to strip us of our masks of double-mindedness and let us see ourselves as we are before God, where there can be no hiding place. Few writers have ever had deeper insight into the nature of our masks, our hideouts, and have more effectively helped us to face and to remove them.

Another nineteenth-century classic is Leo Tolstoy's *Twenty-Three Tales*, for Tolstoy belongs to this great company of God's friends who seem to have lived to nurture us. Stark in their simplicity, these simple stories tear open the heart and leave it open for the heavenly rain.

When it comes to the present century, there are, of course, many books to mention. Among those which I have found especially helpful are Von Hügel's *Letters to a Niece*; Evelyn Underhill's *Letters*; Simone Weil's *Waiting on God*; Dag Hammarskjöld's *Markings*; Mark Gibbard's *Prayer and Contemplation*; Anthony Bloom's *Beginning to Pray*; Alan Eccleston's *Yes to God*; and a book of Tilden Edwards called *Living Simply Through the Day*, which many have found very stirring.

READING SPIRITUAL CLASSICS

GOD DOES INDEED speak to us through books. To read a book and to discover a great line that speaks to our condition, to copy it out and put it in our day-book, makes it really belong to us and is a long step beyond confining ourselves to the anthologies of others.

There are a few obvious footnotes to any word about the use of devotional classics in the nurture of the spiritual life. In the first place readers must be warned about overfastidiousness. Some parts of almost every one of these books may not seem just irrelevant but even repulsive to a contemporary reader. It is important to learn that in reading spiritual classics, you are not being asked whether you accept every detail of the ecclesiastical presuppositions in the historical period in which the book was written. Rather, you are reading this book to find whether anything in it speaks to you and calls out your personal response to it. Phillips Brooks once explained that when he was served a fish for dinner, he did not have to eat it, bones and all, but that he carefully separated out the bones and, laying them to one side of the plate, he went on to eat the flesh and was grateful for it.

Closely related to this is a second reminder, that a devotional book is not to be read with the prosecuting attorney's frame of mind but rather with a mood of receptivity and openness that is asking, "What may God be saying to me through this book?" This frame of mind obviously means reading the book slowly, not intent on finishing a chapter or a section of the book itself, but learning to read reflectively and to stop and ponder over the personal thrust that some line has opened to you. The *lectio divina* (holy reading) that was learned and practiced in the early monasteries did not commend the speedreading that is advertised in our day but precisely the opposite. Yet it is not easy to reverse the moods of the time in which we live. A hard-driven mother with a sizable brood of children is said to have asked a shopkeeper if he might possibly have some breakfast cereal that could *sap* their energy! To learn to read reflectively reverses the whole mood of seeking techniques to finish a book in an hour! In reflective reading the line becomes hair-thin between reading and meditating or reading and praying in the course of moving through a devotional classic. It is interesting to note how the Coptic monks, after some four years of living in a monastery with others, are then liberated to live alone (if they wish to undertake it) in the nearby desert in Egypt and to spend their time largely in reading slowly and prayerfully from the Bible and the great Christian spiritual classics. In the course of time this literally becomes their life of prayer. But the mood of reading that we are talking about does not require either a monastery or a hermitage to validate it. Until we have learned something of its genius, we shall be denying ourselves a principal spiritual aid.

Reading regularly some devotional classic may serve as an effective means of beginning a season of private prayer. To take up such a book is to break with the swift, ordinary pace of life. It serves as a Muslim's prayer rug or a Jew's prayer shawl or a Roman Catholic's rosary, which remind us that life's whirl is not all there is, but that there is another dimension of life that we are now longing to enter.

Often from years of spiritual reading certain wonderful passages that we have come across cling to our minds and become part of our mental treasury, coming back to us in all kinds of situations in life. Gerald Heard, a spiritual guide of a generation ago who meant much to those who were close to him, knew well over fifty great passages from the Bible and from devotional writings by heart. As he entered prayer or lay on his bed at night, these drew him into that center where instead of praying we find ourselves being prayed in. How often a devotional classic can supply us with just such a staff to center us down and support us as we lay the book aside and follow it with a season of prayer.

Two final remarks need to be made about spiritual reading. There is such a thing as overreading! Reading a devotional book before a season of prayer can be overdone and can take up the whole time we have available for prayer. Veterans of prayer know well enough how acute this temptation may often be. At retreats visitors may be found humped over a book throughout the precious hours, when they might have come to some inward renewal had they taken a single insight from a book or a message and opened themselves in silent prayer to what the next steps were in their journey inward that God was asking of them.

The second remark is more delicate to make to those who teach Sunday school classes or are in the active ministry with at least one sermon a week to prepare, who are never entirely free of feeling its urgency. I am referring to the differences between gleaning for others and reading for a word that will speak to one's own condition. The clerical gleaning mind in its eagerness often glazes over an old distinction that Quakers have always had brought firmly to them in the insights that come to them in the course of the silent meeting for worship. The distinction is that God gives us certain insights for ourselves that are not to be publicly communicated at this time but are to be personally worked out. Other messages may well come with a sense that they are to be shared at once with those present. In reading spiritual classics, if the gleaning mind predominates too sharply, the piercing heart of the message for my own life may be lost. It might be noted that great sermons are not a necklace of collected gleanings; they grow out of the costly life-transformations in those that give them. I used the word *delicate* about this second remark, for my own need is so often my neighbor's need as well. Yet it may still be worth pondering if spiritual reading is being considered as an adjunct to the minister's personal prayer life.

Let us, then, remember Teresa of Avila's good counsel that if you want to grow in openness to God, you ought to seek the company of God's friends. These friends of all ages are waiting to share their treasures with us if we will find the time to read of their experiences in the great books that in our time are so readily available.

Desert Wisdom

Do not
  give your
heart to
that
  which
does not
  satisfy
your
  heart.

Abba Poemen

For All *the* Saints

by Wendy M. Wright

BEHIND A LARGE Catholic hospital in Santa Barbara, three blocks from where I once lived, is a meditation garden dedicated to St. Francis of Assisi. When my daughters were small, we would sometimes wander up the hill on a quiet afternoon and sit on a bench beneath the fuchsias or explore the network of irregular paths, sweet with mock orange, that could lead us to one of the several clearings that invited prayer.

At the lower end of the garden near the back hospital entrance we could kneel in a grotto with St. Bernadette Soubirous and climb up the rockery to touch the concrete feet of the apparition of Mary as she appeared at Lourdes. Or we could circle around a moss-lined pond and pause at the space between two intersecting paths where a crucifix stood as a rough-hewn reminder. Occasionally we would venture to the upper level of the garden, where a birdbath served as the focal point of a mandala-like clearing circled by benches and presided over by a smooth white St. Francis, whose arm draped about the neck of a lamb.

Best of all, we could follow a ribbon of stones down to the garden's most interior space, where a rectangle of dahlias emerged from a monumental bronze sculpture of the saint from Assisi. This Francis of green and brown patina was crouched, one knee and the other foot rooted in the soil, his torso arched up to follow the trajectory of arms flung wide. The neck too and the impressionistic face strained up, pulling at the density of the grounded body with the force of longing. From the cup of palms turned over and from the tops of feet protruded the stark tips of driven nails. Here was Francis, ecstatic with love and anguish, receiving the imprint in his own hands and feet of the wounds that had torn the flesh of his Lord.

Circling the dahlias we could view on all sides this figure that hushed me into silence. I knew that Francis was reported to have received the stigmata late in his life at the climax of a retreat taken on Mount Alverna in the Umbrian Hills. I also knew that this mysterious episode, shaped here in bronze, was expressive of the profound identification with Jesus that was at the core of the Italian saint's life: that everything Francis did and said from the time of his youthful conversion was done and spoken in response to the Gospels. Francis read the accounts of Jesus' life with sometimes startling literalness. He stripped himself of all possessions in imitation of the naked, cross-hung Jesus; he publicly disassociated himself from his own father in order to claim sonship with God (as he understood Jesus to have done); he became a begging, itinerant preacher to fulfill his Lord's dictum that his followers should carry nothing with them when they went to preach the good news. The saint's life, permeated with an urgent sense of the call to follow, became at last an embodiment of the mission and the very experience of Jesus, whom he loved.

I also knew, as I eyed this powerful image framed alternately by the seascape horizon and the hills of Santa Barbara dressed in the same flora that dresses the hills of Umbria, that there was another story depicted along with the stories of Francis of Assisi and Jesus of Nazareth. I knew that the sculptor, a Southern California artist, was suffering when he created this particular work. He had lost a son to suicide. When he was commissioned by the Franciscans of Mission Santa Barbara to sculpt their founder-saint, all the anguish of his own loss and his own painful reaching into the dark reserves of faith were chiseled into the substance of that work of art.

Here was a story overlaid with story overlaid with story. And standing with an infant in one arm, watching my lithe five year old hike herself up to the bronze saint's back by means of the stake pinioning his foot, I knew that here was another story: my story. My story mirrors the stories of all of us who hope and who weep, sometimes with authentic passion, sometimes with vague inattention, that our ordinary lives in all their tediousness and real sorrow might become vibrant with a sense of God's presence. I am, as were Jesus and St. Francis and the grieving sculptor, what this bronze statue mutely articulated. We are all firmly rooted in the earth, our lives coterminous with the dahlias and the soil that feeds them. But from the earth itself comes the longing, the extension, the straining out and up to see and experience life vibrantly, to touch the soil and to touch the force that gives it life, to see into the unyielding thickness of human suffering with something like eyes of love. We long to live with arms and hearts so lifted up that God's own life becomes enfleshed in us. That, I think, is what the saints are all about.

ROOTED IN THE EARTH

WHEN ST. FRANCIS WAS DYING, he refused the comfort of the pillowed bed that was urged on him by those who tended him. Instead, he preferred to lie uncushioned on the bare ground. It was not simply that the saint chose austerity rather than ease but that he had always lived in the spirit of the truth proclaimed by Job, "Naked I came from my mother's womb, and naked shall I return" (Job 1:21, RSV). He saw no reason to alter his ways as death approached.

Throughout Francis's life, following Christ meant following the Jesus stripped naked and dying on the cross. From the beginning of Francis's public ministry, when he symbolically renounced his natural father and claimed sonship with God by stripping himself of his clothes in the piazza of Assisi before an assembled crowd, Francis bent his formidable will to following this naked Jesus. Nakedness for him was both literal—without protective clothing, barefoot, unburdened of property, wealth, excessive learning—and interior—without choice or self-protection, empty of all that could separate him from God or God's creation. To be naked meant that he could be utterly surrendered into the arms of the source of life that had made him and to whom he would return.

It was the deep sense of createdness evident in his life of nakedness that was, I think, at the heart of the vision of the saint from Assisi. He knew that he was rooted in the earth. He was part of the vitality that animated his brothers—the sun, wolf, and birds, and his sisters—the moon, stars, and water. Even bodily death he addressed in loving and relational terms, for she too was kin to Francis as she was to all created things.

The Umbrian saint was not merely a lover of nature or a precursor of our contemporary ecological sensibilities (although he has been made official patron of ecology). Francis, with his bare feet callused and dusty from the roads he walked, knew that he was created and that this was deeply blessed. He knew that to be created meant to be part of the rhythms and processes of the earth itself, to flow with water, be warmed by sun, enlightened by fire, slowly consumed by time and the caresses of age and death. He knew that, in living his createdness in a spirit of gratitude and wonder, he gave praise to the one who created him.

While Francis was markedly ascetic in his own life, he did not despise his createdness. He saw it as a gift of the Creator, and he cherished and celebrated the divine source that vitalized all the earth's elemental matter. He knew himself to be part of a whole. His nakedness, his refusal to set himself apart from or erect barriers against his brothers and sisters and his God rooted him firmly in the earth.

I sometimes think we forget how blessed it is to be rooted in the earth. In my own life, it has been those intimations that have arisen from bodily experiences that have plunged me most deeply into God. Conjugal love, pregnancy, birth, and lactation have taught me about the profound communion that exists at the heart of human intimacy, about waiting for God, about new life that comes of giving one's own life, about the love of a nourishing parent. To watch my parents age and struggle with physical limits and loss has initiated me into the mystery that encircles our little lives and calls us back into itself like little children, needing tending and supporting arms.

We do so much to keep ourselves from being naked, to keep ourselves from knowing our createdness. We overdress ourselves in property, wealth, accomplishments, positions, titles, degrees, and skills. We drape our hearts in layers of success, self-sufficiency, pride, or self-loathing. Yet the beginning of our holiness lies, I think, in uncovering a true sense of being rooted in the earth; of being created, along with all the other persons and creatures and growing things; of being a child who, with all the children, is welcomed back into the arms of a creating God. It is blessed to be here. The more we allow ourselves to be naked, to touch and be touched, to be disarmed and tender of others' nakedness, the closer we draw to that naked, cross-hung man whose life was a gift of welcoming others and allowing all that is created, even in its darkest aspects, to touch and open him to the depth of self-giving so that all might live.

LONGING FOR THE FULLNESS OF LIFE

THERE IS A FAMOUS STORY about St. Francis that touches on a paradox at the center of his life. It is the same paradox that Francis perceived in the life of Jesus and the same paradox that exists at the heart of our lives. The story is known by the title "True and Perfect Joy." It recounts how Francis tells one of the friars, Brother Leo, of what true joy consists. It does not consist of knowing that all the great teachers of the universities have entered the Franciscan order or that all the ecclesiastical and civil authorities have adopted the rule of life laid down by the saint. Nor does it consist in the conversion of all nonbelievers to the faith of

Christ. True joy instead is known when Francis returns home from a long trip in the dead of a winter's night. Covered with mud and paralyzed by the cold, he knocks at the door of the friary. A brother answers and, not recognizing Francis, insists that he be on his way. Even when the saint reveals his identity, the surly and sleep-heavy doorkeeper insults him and refuses him entry. Francis tells Leo how, if he had patience and did not become upset, in this there would be true joy.

For most of us this depiction of true joy can on first sight only be ironic. Or perhaps we might interpret it as meaning that we can be joyful only when we are "above" the concerns of most people—when cold, hunger, pain, rejection, and ill treatment no longer ruffle our "spiritual" calm. Neither of these interpretations does justice to the richness of insight found in the parable on true joy. I think Francis is saying that there is in each of us a longing, an intimation of urgency and depth, that cannot be matched by anything that we might achieve or realize by ourselves. Even in the comfort of our homes, surrounded by the warmth of friends and family, fed, clothed, healthy, successfully employed, enjoying the fruits of our creative powers, even then we feel our restless longing for the fullness of life.

To say in a flippant way that *only* God can respond adequately to such longing is to speak a half-truth. For we are made with hearts and arms ready to cherish and embrace each other. We must know and live out the fact that we are firmly rooted in the earth. But our lives have trunks and branches and tendrils as well as roots. And these, with urgent momentum, stretch up and out, climb, surround, and curl beyond all obstacles. The fullness of our lives compels us to expand through and beyond the ordinary daily preoccupations.

Sometimes late in the day in the quiet of my sleeping children's rooms, I am suddenly made aware of the unspeakable beauty of each human life. It is in these rare moments that I am also made aware that I will not experience this forever, that I will die. At these times I feel not only the poignancy and transience of being created; I sense that I have been seized by the "more" that lies at the very core of created being. I have touched the paradox of belonging fully to what is created and yet belonging just as fully to what is uncreated and divine.

I am taken to a place in myself, well beyond my own personal concerns of history, even beyond the history and story I share with others, where some presence lives in me, and in us all, that is much more than me or us. I come to the root level of my person, where

I discover myself in God. Beyond, or perhaps beneath each of our singular dreams and unique psychic configurations we find in ourselves a place where we can no longer call ourselves by name but where we can only speak the name of God. In many ways it is a wordless place where all the explanations, the constructs that contain meaning, and even the questions we cling to, give way. It is the place of the fullest longing of our hearts. It is that place, I think, that the confessing St. Augustine discovered when he cried out, "*You* are the life of the life of my soul!"[1]

There in this inner place, silent and simple, in the depth of our aloneness we are surprised to find ourselves not alone. For it is a place of presence, a presence that most deeply defines who we are and yet is not confined to us. This is a place of presence more real than any perceived in our daily routines. What is most vital about each of us lives most fully there. There is the life of the life of our souls.

There the deepest level of our own story is revealed. There our longing is met. Who we are is made clear. We are the fragments of a creation fashioned by loving hands being gathered back in by the Creator. We are earth made more and more luminous as the divine, which animates it, is allowed to shine through. Earth is lifted up in longing to transcend herself. Divine love reaches out to welcome her home. We are one with that man whose life was stretched out upon a tree. With him our roots drink the blood of earth, and our branches reach out in urgent longing for the fullness of what is and can be. The saints are those among us who know themselves in this way.

SEEING WITH EYES OF LOVE

MY IMPRESSION is that the saints see things differently than most of us do. I think of one of the tales recounted in the *Fioretti*, that delightful collection of word-pictures drawn by the early Franciscans to illustrate the teachings of their beloved brother Francis. It is about the wolf of Gubbio. The small hill town of Gubbio just outside of Assisi was paralyzed with fear because of the maraudings of a ravenous wolf in the region. The beast's hunger had led it to kill not only livestock but also human beings. In terror, the entire town had barricaded itself up within the city walls. Hearing of this, Francis went to the town and offered to go out and meet and subdue the beast. Armed only with faith, Francis approached the snarling wolf and, making the sign of the

---

[1] Augustine of Hippo, *Confessions* (Washington, D.C.: Catholic University Press), 1953.

49

cross, spoke gently to the animal, who we are told lay down at the saint's feet with the docility of a lamb. Francis addressed the wolf as his brother and pointed out to him the seriousness of his crimes. But then he offered him forgiveness and proposed that he, Francis, act as peacemaker between the beast and the people of the town. If the wolf would promise to cease harassing the inhabitants, Francis pledged that he would see that the people not only would not harm the wolf but would tend to his hunger by feeding him. The tale from the *Fioretti* recounts that the wolf gave his promise by offering the saint his paw. The people of Gubbio, in turn, were exhorted to treat the creature with respect and to agree not to harm him. For two years, until the wolf's natural death, the people fed the wolf as it begged from door to door, and both people and animal observed the terms of the peace set forth by Brother Francis.

What moves me deeply about this quaint tale, which is so easy to dismiss as a meaningless fable from a long-ago time when sensibilities were so much "less sophisticated" than our own, is that Francis's seeing, his perception of the situation, was so different from anyone else's. He did not see from the wolf's perspective (if a wolf can be said to "see" in this sense). He was not dominated by sheer need, driven out of biological necessity to kill in order to stay alive. Neither did he see the situation from the perspective of the good people of Gubbio. He did not have eyes clouded by fear that saw only their own survival and the threat to it. Neither did Francis attempt to solve the "conflict" by dealing with the situation in the terms that had been set up: adversaries battling to the death for survival. Instead, Francis saw through the dilemma of the wolf and people of Gubbio with eyes of love. He looked into the hearts of the people and the creature and drew forth their mutual compassion and awakened them to their mutual needs. He showed them how their shared life on this earth could be lived for their mutual enhancement.

There is an art—a truly spiritual art—in learning to see with eyes of love. I do not mean seeing with the rose-colored glasses of sentimentality but seeing with a heart and mind awakened to the other as "self." There is a Buddhist practice that can be translated as something like "benevolent glancing" that involves training the eye to see with compassion. For example, if there has been some disagreement between monks in a Buddhist monastery and they are brought together to achieve some resolution of their conflict, they are expected first to sit silently face to face and gaze benevolently on one another. They are asked to look into the heart of the other as if it were their own heart. This is a giant step beyond simply learning to listen to another's position and reach a compromise. In the experience of seeing differently, the very way that the issue has been constellated—as a conflict between two separate wills—is transformed by the vision of the common humanity of the persons involved.

The saints in all religious traditions are those who have approached this kind of seeing with the eyes of love. I sometimes wonder what it would be like to read the Gospels to one another as stories of a man whose vision so penetrated the opaque fabric of human life that all false vision, all violation of the true and compassionate presence that we are called to be with one another, was laid bare. What kind of seeing was Jesus bringing to bear on his contemporary culture? What kind of seeing have the saints, whose stories once again retell the story of Jesus, brought to their own times?

It is very hard to see one another with eyes of love. For the most part even the most sensitive of us tend to see one another with eyes informed by our own agendas, our own beliefs, and our own needs. In rare moments, when I can slow down enough or when seemingly unsolvable conflicts erupt in my family, I am forced to remember the discipline of benevolent glancing. It has been my habit to look at my children's feet when they are sleeping. This has helped me to cultivate an awareness of their uniqueness, their God-givenness, and to disarm myself of the posture of defensiveness and combativeness that I have created in myself. There are three different sets of feet, each perfect, each expressive of the lifestage and personality of each of my children: the blunt, babyish toes and flat arches that support a tirelessly running body, sturdy enough to use the way a rabbit uses its hind feet in defense; the slightly larger, more graceful toes and heels that are fond of practicing "ballet," feet that often remain tucked up under a frilly skirt that, when the impulse strikes, can run like the wind; the slender feet, half-child's, half-woman's, that kick off their shoes whenever they enter a room, that are alternately decorously placed in a ladylike pose or sprawled out on any and all available pieces of furniture. It is those feet that have taught me the very little I know about seeing with eyes of love.

This kind of perception, I believe, is something for which we all long. Like the citizens of Gubbio, we would prefer not to be walled within the confines of our terrors and self-preoccupations. We can begin to dismantle those walls by learning to look at each other anew, by benevolent glancing. But we must accompany this by learning to look at ourselves anew, by searching the depths of our hearts for our deepest identity, by asking ourselves who we are and waiting for the answer to be uttered in the stillness where we, with St. Augustine, once again exclaim, "*You* are the life of the life of my soul."

I sometimes imagine to myself what the world would look like if we all were saints, if we all were able to see with eyes of love. I picture it as a circle with all the persons, living and dead and as yet unborn, standing on the circle's circumference facing outward. From the initial perspective each woman and man sees only her or himself and the persons nearest by. Further away and really out of sight are all the other seemingly autonomous and unrelated persons. But this initial perspective is limited. It does not discern the reality that exists at the circle's center.

The circle's center is the creative and redemptive life of God, God who is the womb from which the many lives on the circle's edge issue, God who is the voice of dying anguish as those lives stumble and lose their way, God who is the feet and legs that rise again, God who is the loving arms that enfold each life as it returns home: One story of love poured and gathered in again.

The way into this center is through the saints themselves, through the center of each discrete self. The movement inward, in fact, if pursued beyond the narrow boundaries of personal need, leads "outward" through, as it were, the "back" of the self to the circle's center. It leads to the discovery that in fact we are not self-contained but limitless and that at the narrow gate of exit from the limited self we encounter the limitlessness of one another. We are, with God, outside of time where all of us, living, dead, and as yet unborn, share in that one dynamic life that is God's own. We are in the presence of one another as God lovingly fashioned us, knowing our common story, willing to extend a hand and, if need be, to carry one another home.

When our seeing has been thus turned inside out, we come to perceive that our most authentic selves are not the separate selves viewing one another as "other" but the selves that know the mystery of our mutual communion, our shared birth and death with Christ in God.

The saints are those whose seeing has been turned inside out. And the fabric of their being has been transfigured by what they have seen. They have seen and so have *become* what each of us is most authentically. The saints know that we are story overlaid with story overlaid with story. Each of us is a word spoken by God, a part of a greater Word, the story of God's love poured out into creation and welcomed back into waiting arms.

GOD ENFLESHED IN US

S T. BONAVENTURE, a younger contemporary of Francis and his official Franciscan biographer, tells us that when the saint from Assisi made his retreat to the mountains of Alverna, he was at the end of his life. He was spent from his long labors and the ravages of illness. He had labored to follow and to *be* the spirit of the naked Christ. He, like his beloved Jesus, had emptied himself so that God's presence could come alive in him.

It was there—in that mountaintop retreat—that Francis received the stigmata, the wounds on his hands and feet and side, that marked him with the sign of his Lord. Just as God became enfleshed in the body, mind, and heart of Jesus of Nazareth, so Jesus became enfleshed in the body, mind, and heart of the poor man from Assisi. In a striking and visual way, Francis's miracle speaks of a simple truth—that the stories of the saints overlay and continue the story of Christ. Jesus becomes enfleshed over and over again in the missionary zeal of a first-century Jew, in the visionary creations of a twelfth-century abbess, in the outcry of a fourteenth-century Italian laywoman calling a decadent church government to task, in the quest of two eighteenth-century English clergymen to renew their church with the fires of enthusiasm, in the dream of a twentieth-century black man who opposed the evils of racism with the power of love, in the compassion of an American journalist who gave her life in welcome to the poor, in the unnoticed and uncelebrated lives of witness in all ages.

It is, in fact, in *us* that God is born. And that is why I think we are compelled by the stories of saints like Francis. There is something in their stories that speaks to us of our own stories. There is something in both the ordinary and yet extraordinary quality of their lives that speaks to us of where we are and where we feel called to be, of the yearning that we feel to transcend ourselves. The saints are men and women quite like ourselves who have glimpsed (perhaps more keenly or consistently than we have) what it is to see and feel God's quickening presence in the otherwise opaque density of daily events. They are people who have been awakened to the gentle hand of God in the love of family and friends, who have seen the face of the crucified God in the anguish of human suffering. They are people who have known Jesus as the embodiment of their own deepest identity. They have, in fact, so known their own stories to be enlivened by the story of Jesus that the Gospel has, in their own flesh, come off the page and entered into the life stream of history. They are people who have had the imagination and audacity to allow themselves to be remade slowly in the image of the living God, people who have so opened their hearts to God that God's own story is in them once again (yet always uniquely) retold.

I cannot claim to be numbered among the exemplary saints. It would only take testimony from those with whom I am most intimately associated to confirm that fact. Yet I know that in my little life God is born once again in some small way, that as a part of this miraculous creation I am rooted in the stuff of God's self and that, through the longing that I have for the fullness of life, I stretch beyond the confines of my limited self to begin to see and to touch with eyes of real love. You and I and the saints, with Christ, are here to give flesh to God. We do this through the paradox of self-gift, of dying. Just as God labored and gave birth to new life through the body of Jesus, so we labor and spend ourselves in giving birth to our God-given capacity to love with real expansiveness. In doing this we truly become together the body of Christ.

Dusk comes early to the meditation garden of St. Francis Hospital in the winter. Its coming is long delayed during the sultry days of summer. But whenever dusk draws the day to a close, the orange and red of the Santa Barbara sky is always displayed behind the haunting figure of the saint from Assisi. A crimson halo, fading slowly to purple and then to gray, encircles the reaching arms. Fingertips and the nail heads sprouting from the palms become indistinguishable, swallowed by night. The gaunt, bronze body is mute in longing and anguish. The saint waits and watches for dawn.

We, with the saints and with Christ, wait and watch: rooted in the earth, we stretch out in longing; we strain to see into our lives with eyes of love. We long to live with arms and hearts so lifted up that God's life becomes enfleshed in us, so that our own flesh becomes the vessel into which God's own life is poured.

Living *the* Day *from the* Heart

by Tilden Edwards

HOW DO WE SPEAK of the unspeakable—of that which is closer to us than our thoughts? Such is our dilemma when we try to communicate with one another about God's presence and ways with us. Fortunately, the overlapping words and insights of scripture and spiritual tradition help us find some common language about our experience, along with engendering hopefulness about what happens in us at this most intimate level of our being. Even so, the words and insights are often loosely used or interpreted, and understanding their meaning requires some connection with our own experiential awareness. It's that awareness that counts most, and we could use endless words to describe and interpret it. I am going to be using a few key words to describe my own sense of daily contemplative living and understanding. As I do so I suggest that you stay close to your own spiritual awareness and translate my vocabulary into words meaningful for you, wherever that is needed.

Contemplation is the ever-fresh world of the spiritual heart. Noncontemplation is the ever-constricted world of the head, senses, and feelings separated from that heart. The spiritual heart is the true center of our being. It is the placeless place where divine Spirit and human spirit live together. When the great historical spiritual elders of the church advocated keeping the mind in the heart, I believe they were speaking of the need to keep our thoughts, feelings, bodies, actions, wills, and sense of identity connected with our spiritual heart day by day, moment by moment. Our sanity and authentic discernment, love, and delight depend on this connectedness.

RECOGNIZING THE SPIRITUAL HEART

How do we know when we are in our spiritual heart? For me, such words as *childlikeness, intimacy, freedom, spontaneous action, home,* and *obscurity* say a lot about what it's like to be in my spiritual heart. I think much in contemplative tradition, including scripture, would support the awareness I sense behind such words.

I feel a certain childlike simplicity when I'm in touch with my spiritual heart. Like a cared-for child, I feel trusting of a mysterious yet intimate Presence that bears me moment by moment. Rather than experiencing complex, striving, calculating ambition and fear, I feel a certain willingness to be as and where I am, doing what I'm doing with an easeful openheartedness. I accept the humility of not knowing very much in the obscurity of my spiritual heart, because I want to be open for more of God's immediate guiding knowledge. My own cognitive knowledge surrounds and eventually helps to interpret this open center, but it doesn't displace it.

There is an accepting givenness, giftedness, to the moment. This frees me to participate so fully that I feel lightly "inside" whatever is before my eyes, rather than feeling myself as an alienated outsider, projecting all kinds of anxieties and grasping on to what is there. I remember the time when a preschool child whom I did not know stood stock-still and stared at me as I was ascending a staircase in a public building. The child was wide-eyed, obviously without thought, or rather, he was present to me before thought. I felt him inside me as our eyes met. He "knew" me in that moment in an innocent, immediate way.

That was a natural contemplative moment. Such moments can show themselves at any time in the day, with people, nature, work, and objects of all kinds. They leave us touching the incredible intimacy of a shared creation, realizing the way that everything is a unique shaping of the same clay. When we turn this intimacy toward the Shaper of the clay, there is the same potential direct meeting before our thoughts, closer than our thoughts, closer than our breath. The childlike trust of the spiritual heart is crucial for such intimacy. We need the graced trust that our true nature will not be destroyed by such intimacy but rather further revealed in its beauty and distinctiveness. In the intimacy allowed by that trust, our unique nature in the image of God glistens beneath and even through all our confusions and willfulness. We need to pray for that trust and for the removal of the conditioned barriers that may have arisen from betrayal or fear of such trust in our human relationships.

A related mark of the spiritual heart is a loving freedom for the real. We sense a certain capacity to be in touch with what is given before us as it is, without having to grasp for it possessively, skew it, or run away. Since the spiritual heart lives so close to God's heart, it senses nothing encountered within or around us to be completely outside of God's grace. Everything ultimately is redeemable. Thus we are free to be with what is given in any way that may be called for. If, for example, we encounter a coworker who is making life difficult for us in some way, and we are grounded in our spiritual heart, we will find the freedom to be present with a sense of God's compassion and pain for this person. We become capable of a wide range of firm or gentle responses that grow out of our groundedness. Even if this leads to a break in the relationship, it is still done with a sense of God's being continually, lovingly at work in the hearts of both of us, a sense that God does not give up on what God shapes into being and loves.

When we are most purely in our spiritual heart, we bypass a great deal of ego calculation as to what we will gain or lose from a certain decision. We may be aware of what might be gained or lost personally, but this has lost its importance to us. Indeed, the preservation of our physical life itself diminishes as a motive for action, because we sense our true life "hidden with God in Christ," a life not ultimately dependent on our controlling physical protectiveness. We are here in this plane of existence for a period of time, cocreating life forms with the One who lives in our spiritual heart with us. Our identity, our home, is in that larger creative Love more than it is in our individual distinctiveness, and we do not need to cling to this personal form of that Love any longer than called for. We trust that whatever in us is a shaping of that Love will not die.

Thus we are left free for more direct, light, spontaneous actions that flow from the immediate calling of the moment. We are less bound by anything that is not of God's expansive, radiant, reconciling, bearing presence, showing itself right now. Many times, of course, we do feel bound by so much other than this liberating, beckoning presence. We are painfully aware of how dominated we are by our own and others' grasping, fearing ego presence that shows itself when we are separated from our spiritual heart. This raises the crucial question of how we can live out of our spiritual heart more easily through the day.

FREEING THE SPIRITUAL HEART

P ART OF THE GREAT MYSTERY of our being is the fact that even though all I have said may sound wonderful and even natural to our true being, we often find ourselves living far from it in the course of a normal day. We live rather out of our "fallen" nature, fallen away from our true nature in God, trying to create separate empires and frozen security. When our mind separates from our spiritual heart, we see ourselves at bottom as impoverished and anxious, dimly striving for what can preserve and enhance us in our little self-securing sense of reality. Jesus, I believe, is referring to this quality of separation when he says, in effect (in John's Gospel), that the "world" doesn't want or recognize the truth and that we are called with him to be in the world but not of it, called instead to be intimately of God. "Worldliness" is our confused, willful inner orientation that shows itself when we have lost touch with our spiritual heart.

Once we have been graced to become conscious of our spiritual heart, though, we do find ourselves little by little "recognizing" the truth and "wanting" it more and more. The usually long, struggling process of conversion that we call the spiritual life is the process of slowly grounding every dimension of our awareness and action in our spiritual heart, until nothing is left outside its influence. Freeing this heart involves some common dimensions for all of us.

DESIRE

T HE MOST FUNDAMENTAL step I believe we can take toward opening our spiritual heart is to open our longing for God: our yearning for God's fullness in us and the world, through and beyond every desire we may have. That longing is placed deep in us as a reflection of God's wondrous, loving desire to be full in us. God seems to want to cocreate a unique dance with us moment by moment that never before has been, although it is always a variation on the divine eternal theme of enlightened love. This love continually connects our special dance with all the others in creation in mutually serving ways.

When we awaken in the morning and myriad thoughts and feelings pass through our minds, our first spiritual task is to be in touch with our desire for God right through that stream of consciousness. As this happens, we touch into our spiritual heart. There we can let whatever is passing through our minds be very simply opened, offered to God. Our consciousness expands to include God. We can consecrate ourselves then to God's immediately present, pervasive love through all that registers in our minds. Then we are saved from beginning the day on some seemingly autonomous track of worry and driven activity. We begin instead with our trust that God, manifest in Christ's living Spirit, is mysteriously with and for us right now, wanting to share the day. In our freedom, which is part of the nature of love, we can ignore this invitation to collaborate and instead run off on our own, losing the larger consciousness and identity of our spiritual heart. Then we easily find ourselves grasping for control and falling into off-target attitudes and actions, which eventually can lead us to the edge of burnout and spiritual insanity.

REMEMBERING THE DESIRE

SO MUCH INSIDE US and in our culture cultivates this separation from our spiritual heart and its desire that we often need help in reconnecting with our underlying intent for God. The first kind of help can be found in our prayer for it: "Holy One, you know how easily I forget your radiant presence; remind me of it again and again through this day, through all my mental processing and activities; I want to be yielded to your loving truth through all things."

We never know just what that loving truth is until it is shown us as we go through the day from situation to situation. Therefore our hope is not focused on any particular expectations or results; it is more open and available for what we do not know and do not need to know until the time comes. Our hope is that God will be God and help us to be our true selves in the image of God, as the created love-child of God. Such wide-eyed, open hope frees us to be more in touch with what is of God during the day, rather than being in touch only with what we have predetermined by our too controlling and narrow expectations. Contemplative seeing is grounded in such open hope. At its fullest this openness no longer is defining "God," "self," and "world." We are free to live without securing definitions then, free to let what is show itself in all its unity and diversity, unskewed by definitions that separate and categorize. Then we are free as that preschool child who saw "inside" me and became unself-consciously one with the reality that is me,

FURTHER CULTIVATION
OF THE DESIRE

B ESIDES THE FUNDAMENTAL need for prayer to remember our depth and desire in God and for our open hopefulness during the day, we may be drawn to a variety of other aids for living out of the collaborative, delicate place of our spiritual heart. Any of the classical spiritual disciplines for attentiveness to help us remember our intention for God may be included here: praying with scripture; other spiritual reading; worded, imaged, and formless kinds of personal and corporate prayer; journal keeping; icons and other art forms; recollecting interior words, images, and objects that we carry through the day (such as the Jesus Prayer, a phrase of scripture, or a stone in our pockets); and anything else that can help us live in touch with our heart.

Contemplative presence would give special weight to appreciative spaces during the day, times during which we commit ourselves to just being and appreciating what is given, being in communion with God and creation just as an end-in-itself love affair. It is often in such times that we come to realize how far we have tried to go in taking over the day with our plans and how little we have leaned back into the source of all true activity. In that realization we give God an opportunity to free us from the dreary drivenness of the day. We allow the fresh, truly new reality of the moment in God to affect our discernment of what is really called for in our actions as opposed to what is just self-justification or fearful pleasing of others.

These appreciative contemplative spaces consist of not only little external "restings" spread through the day and week but also internal ones. These show themselves when we are able to rest our mind's constant attempt to secure us through its grasping for definition and understanding and instead simply appreciate the open spaces between our thoughts as being full of God. In that spaciousness we may find God wanting to show us great and little wondrous truths that are infinitely beyond the grasp of our minds. We find that we are given a kind of knowing and belonging in our spiritual heart that is too fine for our minds to comprehend, yet profoundly substantial. We are being taught in God's own language, which only the heart can apprehend, and there we are slowly being transformed from the image to the likeness of God, our unique Christ-nature.

These external and internal spaces that help us contact our deep heart in God can be found in solitude or in community. One of the most powerful contemplative practices is sitting mostly in silence with other people who appreciate and yearn for the honest deepening of their spiritual hearts. When one person is floundering out of touch, another's yearning silence can help that person settle down and open to his or her own yearning. If the people in the group work together outside of the silence, their interactions and decisions can be grounded more surely in a common sense of the divine wellspring. As such a given-to-God circle spreads in God's grace through the church, the community, and around the world, we will find ourselves in a much happier, more generous, just, and truly reconciled human family.

We cannot force the circle to enlarge, but we can begin the circle where we are, and where two or three are gathered in Christ's name, in the name of the incarnate loving truth of God, there the Spirit will show itself in open hearts. There we will be in touch with that "holy energy that fills the universe, playing like lightning" (Jan Ruusbroec).[1] The rest will follow, as we dedicatedly live with our minds in our hearts more and more in all our personal, social, and political times, letting God's lightning in on everything.

---

[1] As quoted in Evelyn Underhill, *The Anthology of the Love of God*, eds. Lumsden Barkway and Lucy Menzies (Wilton, CT: Morehouse-Barlow, 1976), p. 33.

Oblation

by Elizabeth Rooney

I hope each day

To offer less to you,

Each day

By your great love to be

Diminished

Until at last I am

So decreased by your hand

And you so grown in me

That my whole offering

Is just an emptiness

For you to fill

Or not

According to your will.

Waiting

A Spirituality
of Waiting

BEING ALERT TO
GOD'S PRESENCE IN OUR LIVES

by Henri J. M. Nouwen

I WANT TO REFLECT on something that has been on my mind during the past few years. It is something I have come to believe is very important for our time: a spirituality of waiting. What would waiting mean in our lives?

In order to explore this question, I would like to look at two aspects of waiting. One is the waiting *for* God, and the other is the waiting *of* God. We are waiting. God is waiting. The first two chapters of Luke's Gospel set the context for my thoughts on the waiting for God. The final chapters of the same Gospel provide the framework for thinking about the waiting of God. On the one hand, the story of Jesus' birth introduces us to a host of people who are waiting—Zechariah and Elizabeth, Mary, Simeon, and Anna. On the other hand, the story of Jesus' death and resurrection reveals to us a God who is waiting.

OUR WAITING FOR GOD

WAITING IS NOT a very popular attitude. Waiting is not something that people think about with great sympathy. In fact, most people consider waiting a waste of time. Perhaps this is because the culture in which we live is basically saying, "Get going! Do something! Show you are able to make a difference! Don't just sit there and wait!" For many people, waiting is an awful desert between where they are and where they want to go. And people do not like such a place. They want to get out of it by doing something.

In our particular historical situation, waiting is even more diffi- cult because we are so fearful. One of the most pervasive emotions in the atmosphere around us is fear. People are afraid—afraid of inner feelings, afraid of other people, and also afraid of the future. Fearful people have a hard time waiting, because when we are afraid we want to get away from where we are. But if we cannot flee, we may fight instead. Many of our destructive acts come from the fear that something harmful will be done to us. And if we take a broader perspective—that not only individuals but whole communities and nations might be afraid of being harmed—we can understand how hard it is to wait and how tempting it is to act. Here are the roots of a "first strike" approach to others. People who live in a world of fear are more likely to make aggressive, hostile, destructive responses than people who are not so frightened. The more afraid we are, the harder waiting becomes. That is why waiting is such an unpopular attitude for many people.

It impresses me, therefore, that all the figures who appear on the first pages of Luke's Gospel are waiting. Zechariah and Elizabeth are waiting. Mary is waiting. Simeon and Anna, who were there at the temple when Jesus was brought in, are waiting. The whole opening scene of the good news is filled with waiting people. And right at the beginning all those people in some way or another hear the words, "Do not be afraid. I have something good to say to you." These words set the tone and the context. Now Zechariah and Mary, Simeon and Anna are waiting for something new and good to happen to them.

Who are these figures? They are representatives of the waiting Israel. The psalms are full of this attitude: "My soul is waiting for the Lord. I count on his word. My soul is longing for the Lord more than watchman for daybreak. (Let the watchman count on daybreak and Israel on the Lord.) Because with the Lord there is mercy and fullness of redemption" (Psalm 129:5-7, GRAIL). "My soul is waiting for the Lord"—that is the song that reverberates all through the Hebrew scriptures.

But not all who dwell in Israel are waiting. In fact we might say that the prophets criticized the people (at least in part) for giving up their attentiveness to what was coming. Waiting finally became the attitude of the remnant of Israel, of that small group of Israelites that remained faithful. The prophet Zephaniah says, "In your midst I will leave a humble and lowly people, and those who are left in Israel will seek refuge in the name of Yahweh. They will do no wrong, will tell no lies; and the perjured tongue will no longer be found in their mouths" (Zephaniah 3:12-13, JB). It is the purified remnant of faithful people who are waiting. Elizabeth and

66

Zechariah, Mary and Simeon are representatives of that remnant. They have been able to wait, to be attentive, to live expectantly.

Now I would like to turn our attention to two things. First, what is the nature of waiting? And second, what is the practice of waiting? How are they waiting, and how are we called to wait with them?

THE NATURE OF WAITING

W AITING, AS WE SEE IT in the people on the first pages of the Gospel, is waiting with a sense of promise. "Zechariah, . . . your wife Elizabeth is to bear you a son." "Mary, . . . Listen! You are to conceive and bear a son" (Luke 1:13, 31, JB). People who wait have received a promise that allows them to wait. They have received something that is at work in them, like a seed that has started to grow. This is very important. We can only really wait if what we are waiting for has already begun for us. So waiting is never a movement from nothing to something. It is always a movement from something to something more. Zechariah, Mary, and Elizabeth were living with a promise that nurtured them, that fed them, and that made them able to stay where they were. And in this way, the promise itself could grow in them and for them.

Second, waiting is active. Most of us think of waiting as something very passive, a hopeless state determined by events totally out of our hands. The bus is late? You cannot do anything about it, so you have to sit there and just wait. It is not difficult to understand the irritation people feel when somebody says, "Just wait." Words like that seem to push us into passivity.

But there is none of this passivity in scripture. Those who are waiting are waiting very actively. They know that what they are waiting for is growing from the ground on which they are standing. That's the secret. The secret of waiting is the faith that the seed has been planted, that something has begun. Active waiting means to be present fully to the moment, in the conviction that something is happening where you are and that you want to be present to it. A waiting person is someone who is present to the moment, who believes that this moment is *the* moment.

A waiting person is a patient person. The word *patience* means the willingness to stay where we are and live the situation out to the full in the belief that something hidden there will manifest itself to us. Impatient people are always expecting the real thing to happen somewhere else and therefore want to go elsewhere. The moment is empty. But patient people dare to stay where they are. Patient living means to live actively in the present and wait there. Waiting, then, is not passive. It involves nurturing the moment, as a mother nurtures the child that is growing in her. Zechariah, Elizabeth, and Mary were very present to the moment. That is why they could hear the angel. They were alert, attentive to the voice that spoke to them and said, "Don't be afraid. Something is happening to you. Pay attention."

But there is more. Waiting is open-ended. Open-ended waiting is hard for us because we tend to wait for something very concrete, for something that we wish to have. Much of our waiting is filled with wishes: "I wish that I would have a job. I wish that the weather would be better. I wish that the pain would go." We are full of wishes, and our waiting easily gets entangled in those wishes. For this reason, a lot of our waiting is not open-ended. Instead, our waiting is a way of controlling the future. We want the future to go in a very specific direction, and if this does not happen we are disappointed and can even slip into despair. That is why we have such a hard time waiting; we want to do the things that will make the desired events take place. Here we can see how wishes tend to be connected with fears.

But Zechariah, Elizabeth, and Mary were not filled with wishes. They were filled with hope. Hope is something very different. Hope is trusting that something will be fulfilled, but fulfilled according to the promises and not just according to our wishes. Therefore, hope is always open-ended.

I have found it very important in my own life to let go of my wishes and start hoping. It was only when I was willing to let go of wishes that something really new, something beyond my own expectations could happen to me. Just imagine what Mary was actually saying in the words, "I am the handmaid of the Lord. . . . let what you have said be done to me" (Luke 1:38, JB). She was saying, "I don't know what this all means, but I trust that good things will happen." She trusted so deeply that her waiting was open to all possibilities. And she did not want to control them. She believed that when she listened carefully, she could trust what was going to happen.

To wait open-endedly is an enormously radical attitude toward life. So is to trust that something will happen to us that is far beyond our own imaginings. So, too, is giving up control over our future and letting God define our life, trusting that God molds us according to God's love and not according to our fear. The spiritual life is a life in which we wait, actively present to the moment, trusting that new things will happen to us, new things that are far beyond our own imagination, fantasy, or prediction. That, indeed, is a very radical stance toward life in a world preoccupied with control.

THE PRACTICE OF WAITING

NOW LET ME SAY something about the practice of waiting. How do we wait? One of the most beautiful passages of scripture is Luke 1:39-56, which suggests that we wait together, as did Mary and Elizabeth. What happened when Mary received the words of promise? She went to Elizabeth. Something was happening to Elizabeth as well as to Mary. But how could they live that out?

I find the meeting of these two women very moving, because Elizabeth and Mary came together and enabled each other to wait. Mary's visit made Elizabeth aware of what she was waiting for. The child leapt for joy in her. Mary affirmed Elizabeth's waiting. And then Elizabeth said to Mary, "Blessed is she who believed that the promise made her by the Lord would be fulfilled" (Luke 1:45, JB). And Mary responded, "My soul proclaims the greatness of the Lord" (Luke 1:46, JB). She burst into joy herself. These two women created space for each other to wait. They affirmed for each other that something was happening that was worth waiting for.

I think that is the model of the Christian community. It is a community of support, celebration, and affirmation in which we can lift up what has already begun in us. The visit of Elizabeth and Mary is one of the Bible's most beautiful expressions of what it means to form community, to be together, gathered around a promise, affirming that something is really happening

This is what prayer is all about. It is coming together around the promise. This is what celebration is all about. It is lifting up what is already there. This is what Eucharist is about. It is saying, "Thanks" for the seed that has been planted. It is saying, "We are waiting for the Lord, who has already come."

The whole meaning of the Christian community lies in offering a space in which we wait for that which we have already seen. Christian community is the place where we keep the flame alive among us and take it seriously, so that it can grow and become stronger in us. In this way we can live with courage, trusting that there is a spiritual power in us that allows us to live in this world without being seduced constantly by despair, lostness, and darkness.

That is how we dare to say that God is a God of love even when we see hatred all around us. That is why we can claim that God is a God of life even when we see death and destruction and agony all around us. We say it together. We affirm it in one another. Waiting together, nurturing what has already begun, expecting its fulfillment—that is the meaning of marriage, friendship, community, and the Christian life.

Second, our waiting is always shaped by alertness to the word. It is waiting in the knowledge that someone wants to address us. The question is, are we home? Are we at our address, ready to respond to the doorbell? We need to wait together to keep each other at home spiritually, so that when the word comes it can become flesh in us. That is why the book of God is always in the midst of those who gather. We read the word so that the word can become flesh and have a whole new life in us.

Simone Weil, a Jewish writer, said, "Waiting patiently in expectation is the foundation of the spiritual life." When Jesus speaks about the end of time, he speaks precisely about the importance of waiting. He says that nations will fight against nations and there will be wars and earthquakes and misery. People will be in agony, and they will say, "The Christ is there! No, he is here!" Everybody will be totally upset, and many will be deceived. But Jesus says you must stand ready, stay awake, stay tuned to the word of God, so that you will survive all that is going to happen and be able to stand confidently (*con-fide*, with trust) in the presence of God together in community (see Matthew 24). That is the attitude of waiting that allows us to be people who can live in a very chaotic world and survive spiritually.

GOD'S WAITING FOR US

IN THE PASSION and resurrection of Jesus we see God as a waiting God. That is the second aspect of waiting that affects our whole spiritual life. So it is to the end of Jesus' life that I want to turn our attention. Let me start with a story.

I was invited to visit a friend who was very sick. He was a man about fifty-three years old who had lived a very active, useful, faithful, creative life. Actually, he was a social activist who had cared deeply for people. When he was fifty he found out he had cancer, and the cancer became more and more severe.

When I came to him, he said to me, "Henri, here I am lying in this bed, and I don't even know how to think about being sick. My whole way of thinking about myself is in terms of action, in terms of doing things for people. My life is valuable because I've been able to do many things for many people. And suddenly, here I am, passive, and I can't do anything anymore." And he said to me, "Help me to think about this situation in a new way. Help me to think about my not being able to do anything anymore so I won't be driven to despair. Help me to understand what it means that now all sorts of people are doing things to me over which I have no control."

As we talked I realized that he and many others were constantly thinking, "How much can I still do?" Somehow this man had learned to think about himself as a man who was worth what he was doing. And so when he got sick, his hope seemed to rest on the idea that he might get better and return to what he had been doing. I realized, too, that this way of thinking was hopeless because the man had cancer and was going to get worse and worse. He would die soon. If the spirit of this man was dependent on how much he would still be able to do, what did I have to say to him?

It was in the context of these thoughts that together we read a book called *The Stature of Waiting* by British author W. H. Vanstone.[1] Vanstone writes about Jesus' agony in the Garden of Gethsemane and the events that followed. I want to draw on this powerful book in what follows. It helped my friend and me struggle together to understand better what it means to move from action to passion.

FROM ACTION TO PASSION

THE CENTRAL WORD in the story of Jesus' arrest is one I never thought much about. It is "to be handed over." That is what happened in Gethsemane. Jesus was handed over. Some translations say that Jesus was "betrayed," but the Greek says, "to be handed over." Judas handed Jesus over (see Mark 14:10). But the remarkable thing is that the same word is used not only for Judas but also for God. God did not spare Jesus, but handed him over to benefit us all (see Romans 8:32).

So this word, "to be handed over," plays a central role in the life of Jesus. Indeed, this drama of being handed over divides the life of Jesus radically in two. The first part of Jesus' life is filled with activity. Jesus takes all sorts of initiatives. He speaks; he preaches; he heals; he travels. But immediately after Jesus is handed over, he becomes the one to whom things are being done. He's being arrested;

---

[1] W. H. Vanstone, *The Stature of Waiting* (Minneapolis: Winston-Seabury Press 1983).

he's being led to the high priest; he's being taken before Pilate; he's being crowned with thorns; he's being nailed on a cross. Things are being done to him over which he has no control. That is the meaning of passion—being the recipient of other people's initiatives.

It is important for us to realize that when Jesus says, "It is accomplished" (John 19:30, JB), he does not simply mean, "I have done all the things I wanted to do." He also means, "I have allowed things to be done to me that needed to be done to me in order for me to fulfill my vocation." Jesus does not fulfill his vocation in action only but also in passion. He doesn't just fulfill his vocation by doing the things the Father sent him to do, but also by letting things be done to him that the Father allows to be done to him, by receiving other people's initiatives.

Passion is a kind of waiting—waiting for what other people are going to do. Jesus went to Jerusalem to announce the good news to the people of that city. And Jesus knew that he was going to put a choice before them: Will you be my disciple, or will you be my executioner? There is no middle ground here. Jesus went to Jerusalem to put people in a situation where they had to say, "Yes" or "No." That is the great drama of Jesus' passion: he had to wait upon how people were going to respond. How would they come? To betray him or to follow him? In a way, his agony is not simply the agony of approaching death. It is also the agony of having to wait. It is the agony of a God who depends on us for how God is going to live out the divine presence among us. It is the agony of the God who, in a very mysterious way, allows us to decide how God will be God. Here we glimpse the mystery of God's incarnation. God became human so that we could act upon God, and God could be the recipient of our responses.

All action ends in passion because the response to our action is out of our hands. That is the mystery of work, the mystery of love, the mystery of friendship, the mystery of community—they always involve waiting. And that is the mystery of Jesus' love. God reveals himself in Jesus as the one who waits for our response. Precisely in that waiting the intensity of God's love is revealed to us. If God forced us to love, we would not really be lovers.

All these insights into Jesus' passion were very important in the discussions with my friend. He realized that after much hard work he had to wait. He came to see that his vocation as a human being would be fulfilled not just in his actions but also in his passion. And together we began to understand that precisely in this waiting the glory of God and our new life both become visible.

THE GLORY OF GOD AND OUR NEW LIFE

RESURRECTION is not just life after death. First of all, it is the life that bursts forth in Jesus' passion, in his waiting. The story of Jesus' suffering reveals that the resurrection is breaking through even in the midst of the passion. A crowd led by Judas came to Gethsemane. "Then Jesus...came forward and said to them, 'Whom do you seek?' They answered him, 'Jesus of Nazareth.' Jesus said to them, 'I am he.' When he said to them, 'I am he,' they drew back and fell to the ground. Again he asked them, 'Whom do you seek?' And they said, 'Jesus of Nazareth.' Jesus answered, 'I told you that I am he; so, if you seek me, let these men go'" (John 18:4-8, RSV).

Precisely when Jesus is being handed over into his passion, he manifests his glory. "Whom do you seek?...I am he," are words that echo all the way back to Moses and the burning bush: "I am the one. I am who I am" (see Exodus 3:1-6). In Gethsemane, the glory of God manifested itself again, and they fell flat on the ground. Then Jesus was handed over. But already in the handing over we see the glory of God who hands himself over to us. God's glory revealed in Jesus embraces passion as well as resurrection.

"The Son of Man," Jesus says, "must be lifted up as Moses lifted up the serpent in the desert, so that everyone who believes may have eternal life in him" (John 3:14-15, JB). He is lifted up as a passive victim, so the cross is a sign of desolation. And he is lifted up in glory, so the cross becomes at the same time a sign of hope. Suddenly we realize that the glory of God, the divinity of God, bursts through in Jesus' passion precisely when he is most victimized. So new life becomes visible not only in the resurrection on the third day, but already in the passion, in the being handed over. Why? Because it is in the passion that the fullness of God's love shines through. It is supremely a waiting love, a love that does not seek control.

When we allow ourselves to feel fully how we are being acted upon, we can come in touch with a new life that we were not even aware was there. This was the question my sick friend and I talked about constantly. Could he taste the new life in the midst of his passion? Could he see that in his being acted upon by the hospital staff he was already being prepared for a deeper love? It was a love that had been underneath all the action, but he had not tasted it fully. So together we began to see that in the midst of our suffering and

73

passion, in the midst of our waiting, we can already experience the resurrection.

If we look at our world, how much are we really in control? Isn't our life in large part passion? Of course, we are active, but the margin in which we are active is much smaller than the margin in which we are acted upon by people, events, the culture in which we live, and many other factors beyond our control. This becomes especially clear when we notice how many people are handicapped, chronically ill, elderly, or restricted economically.

It seems that there are more and more people in our society who have less and less influence on the decisions that affect their own existence. Therefore, it becomes increasingly important to recognize that the largest part of our existence involves waiting in the sense of being acted upon. But the life of Jesus tells us that not to be in control is part of the human condition. His vocation was fulfilled not just in action but also in passion, in waiting.

Imagine how important that message is for people in our world. If it is true that God in Jesus Christ is waiting for our response to divine love, then we can discover a whole new perspective on how to wait in life. We can learn to be obedient people who do not always try to go back to the action but who recognize the fulfillment of our deepest humanity in passion, in waiting. If we can do this, I am convinced that we will come in touch with the glory of God and our own new life. Then our service to others will include our helping them see the glory breaking through, not only where they are active but also where they are being acted upon. And so the spirituality of waiting is not simply our waiting for God. It is also participating in God's own waiting for us and in that way coming to share in the deepest purity of love, which is God's love.

Tapes of this material are available from Ave Maria Press (Notre Dame, IN 46556) or your local religious bookstore.

The Extra Room

by Ellen Anthony

*Let us make a small roof chamber with walls, and put there for
him a bed, a table, a chair, and a lamp, so that whenever he comes
to us, he can go in there.*

—2 Kings 4:10, RSV

I

A long time ago
someone in Shunem
built an extra room
on the roof of her house
for the holy one.

That's what I want to do.
I want to go up
to the roof of my house
where the sky starts
and make this room in case the holy one
needs a place to stay.

A table, a chair,
a bed, and a candle.
I'll work on it
when I can,
weekends maybe
or before breakfast.

II

It's coming along.
I go up there,
work with what I have.
Some wood, some stone.
The chair and table

aren't hard to make,
and I got a candle
from a friend.

But the bed is still stone.
And I know that isn't comfortable.

It's grey
and looks billowy from far off,
like a feather comforter,
but it's stone.

I put my hands on it,
on the faces of the stone.
Questions come up
all about work and what my life is for.
I answer what I can.

We're both getting softer, I think,
but not yet a bed.

III

One day the holy one
stays overnight, asks
What can I do for you?
Nothing, I say. I can't
think of anything I need.
You will have new life,
says the holy one leaving.

Don't lie to me.
Don't lie to me
is what I answer back.
I sit down right there
in the kitchen thinking
What new life?

And why do I think it is a lie
that I will have new life?

IV

Someone is waiting there
in that room upstairs.

Someone is dying.

Someone is holding the river
in their hands.
Someone is letting it go.

Someone is crying.

Someone is getting ready.

Someone wants to be
softer than stone.

Who is it waiting for me
in the extra room?

V

I go up,
open the door.

It's pretty much done.
The room.
All I can do anyway.

I sit in the chair.
Plain square chair.

Look at the table.
Flat relaxed wood.

Strike a match
to the wick of the candle,
see the light
pulling the walls into the glow,
corners going blurry.

Holy chair?
Holy table?
Holy candle, holy walls?
or just extra ones?
I sit in the extra chair
watching the extra walls
wondering if we're holy.

Over there
the stone is taking a long time
becoming a bed.

So am I.

We wait here together.

VI

I wonder what the Shunammite
went through.
Whether hospitality
came easy to her
and the furniture
knew itself right off.

I know that after the holy one
came to her extra room
the Shunammite conceived
and bore a son.

I wonder what my extra room
is for. Who will come
and whether it is holy
the way it is, empty.

VII

Lots of time passes.
Time, time, time.
Life goes on downstairs.

Busy one day
I'm in the kitchen
when the phone rings.
Not thinking I go upstairs.
Why? There's no phone
in the extra room.
But I open the door
and there all over the place
is the sky. Sky, sky, sky.
No edges to it. No sign
of roof ending or sky beginning.
As if Sky is the answer
to this phone call.
All seeing, all hearing.

I want to cry
but it is beyond crying.
This is some phone call.

Lots of time passes differently.
Inside time, I don't know how much.
At some point I go downstairs again.

VIII

I pinch my skin
down in the kitchen.
Testing what's real.
Did that really happen?

What kind of phone call
is all sky on the other end?

What kind of answer holds your feet up,
surrounds your shoulders,
and moves through your hair
leaving you nothing at all
to say?

What if here in the kitchen
I could listen that well?
Pull the sky down
into all my conversations.

I want to do it.
That's the next thing
I want to do.

IX

Well, now I go up there all the time
to the extra room that is definitely holy
waiting for the phone to ring,
wishing the sky would answer me
over and over again without edges.

But it doesn't work that way.

I go up there some days
and all the furniture is dead.
Even the wooden stuff
gone to stone on me.

I want to cry and I do cry
and the bed is no comfort to me.
Why? Why did the table and chair
come so easy and the bed so hard?
Is it about working and resting?
Easy to work but hard to rest?
The in-between times,
when nothing is happening,
can I rest in those?

I touch the old faces
of the stone. Someone is dying,
someone is crying, someone is trying
to become softer than stone.

Trying. Why am I trying?
Is the chair trying?

Is the table trying?
Is the sky trying?
Am I the only one around here
who keeps trying?

Please, phone. Ring again.

    X

In the old story
the woman loses her son,
loses her new life.
And she tears off after the holy one
and grabs those feet, Didn't I say
don't lie to me?

And the holy one goes back
to the room where the son lies dead
and stretches out on that boy,
mouth on his mouth, eyes on his eyes,
hands on his hands. Twice.
And the boy comes back to life.

I want to know what that means,
to lie on someone dead,
to get on top of them
mouth on their mouth, eyes on their eyes,
hands on their hands and lie there
stretched out touching our full lengths
breathing into the dead.

How can I match the dead one
that close, like lovers?
Loving the dead one,
is that what that means?

And could I, just as I am,
climb on top and put my
mouth to their mouth,
eyes to their eyes,
hands to their hands

and believe over and over again
in new life
especially when it is dead?

Who is the dead one?
Is it me?
Is it the room itself
or that stone bed?
Is it someone I know
who has gone dead inside?
Someone I am avoiding
loving dead?

XI

I don't know.
I usually don't know.

I touch the stone bed, kneeling,
and say I don't know
who is waiting or what will happen
from day to day in this extra room.
What my new life is
or when it will die on me.

But I have this extra room,
and I just know that I believe in it.
I believe in the extra room,
in making an extra room,
in the possibility of the holy one's coming,
in making new life, in its sometime dying,
and in constantly watching what sleeps there
as if I were ready for the sky
to come in over and over again without edges.

This place, this extra room,
is where I'm becoming
hollow and ample at the same time.

XII

I won't ask
what your extra room is like.
Or what went on
inside the Shunammite lady.
It's not for me
to know other people's
private stuff.

But I want you to know
that when I say my extra room
is for the holy one,
it means you.
It means whoever
needs an extra room that night.
I can't guarantee
there won't be dead furniture
in there from time to time.
Or that the bed will be comfortable.
But if you ever need
an extra room to stay in,
a place where seeing and hearing
have no edges,
I have this place inside me now,
and you are welcome there.

When Prayer Encounters Pain

by Flora Slosson Wuellner

OUR CHURCH SERVICES usually provide space for the awareness and confession of sin, but seldom do they provide intentional space for the awareness of our wounds. Yet the unhealed suffering of individuals and communities, the untended hurts, are probably responsible for most of the perplexities and agony of this world.

It is not enough to say to individuals and nations, "You have sinned. You need repentance and forgiveness." We must also learn to say, "You are wounded. Face your pain. Let the Healer come to you." Are we afraid to encounter the depths of our personal and communal pain? Suffering is the dark enigma of our life and faith. It is a whole spectrum of experience. We cannot understand why sometimes the worst suffering seems to heal so quickly while other forms of apparently trivial pain can last a lifetime. We are frightened that unhealed suffering can affect and infect generations in the life of a family or a nation.

Perhaps most of all we are frightened by what the existence of our suffering seems to be saying about the nature of God and God's universe! Has God intended, planned, or consented to our pain? If so, how can we trust God for any healing?

The temptation is to rationalize, to "comfort" ourselves and others with such platitudes as: "These things are sent to try us," or "This is a punishment because I have deserved it," or "God is teaching me detachment," or "God must love me very much to send me this pain." But this kind of theology, unfortunately taught for centuries, neither comforts nor heals us.

Before we can grow in trust of God and accept God's healing, we need to look with more clarity and honesty at the major roots and meaning of our pain.

84

SOME MAJOR CAUSES OF OUR SUFFERING

BOTH IN OUR LIVES and in the witness of the New Testament we see five major categories of human suffering. Perhaps they can be designated as the thorn in the flesh, the hunger, the catapult, the cross, and the birth.

THE THORN IN THE FLESH: This is the form of suffering, well described by Paul in 2 Corinthians 12, which is part of our natural, human condition of limitation and mortality. Most illnesses, accidents, disabilities, and natural disasters are the experience of the "thorn." Paul describes it again in Romans 8:22-23 when he speaks of the groaning and travail of the natural universe as it works toward the great release and new creation. As beings deeply embedded in nature as well as spirit, we share the pain and problems of nature.

THE HUNGER: This is the suffering rising out of all forms of deprivation—emotional, spiritual, and physical. Here we find the agony of wounding, broken relationships, loneliness, frustrated energies, loss of identity. Here we find the pain of those who have not been loved enough or for whom love has meant constriction rather than freedom. Here we find the agony of unexpressed gifts and powers. Here we find the bitter truth of that powerful proverb: "Hope deferred makes the heart sick" (Proverbs 13:12, RSV). Here we find the pain of nations and communities who have lived for generations in unfulfilled expectations.

THE CATAPULT: The catapult is the symbol of the traumatic encounter with the shock of evil and injustice that sooner or later besets and affects us all. The momentum of injustice, whether intentional or impersonal, engulfs individuals and communities in both chronic and acute depersonalization and destruction.

These first three causes of suffering are not willed, intended, or caused by God. It is a dangerous yet persistent heresy that God ever sends the fragmenting, depersonalizing pain that tears down, humiliates, deprives, and destroys. We are not told why we live in a universe where these things can happen. I believe that God's gift of freedom to all creation and God's refusal to use force to change our choices is involved with the mystery of these forms of pain. But something that is allowed by God does not mean that God has willed it. Not once in the Gospels does Jesus refuse to try to heal someone because it is "God's will" that they suffer! Indeed, throughout the Gospels we are told that God works with far more longing than we do that the thorn be removed, the hunger be fed, the catapult be deflected.

THE CROSS: The cross that we are summoned to carry is God's invitation to us to enter, share, and lift the burden of suffering for others. It is not the same as illness or disasters that come upon us against our will. We are always given the freedom to accept or reject a cross. If we accept, we enter into the pain of another person or a community with loving, redemptive power as a member of Christ's risen body.

It is essential to remember two main things about accepting and carrying our cross. First, we should prayerfully discern if it is really *our* cross. If it is truly the commitment to which God invites us, there will be joy along with the pain. We will feel the renewal of our strength and energy. We will feel an increasing sense of authenticity. But if we feel decreasing joy, strength, energy, meaningfulness, authenticity over a significant period of time, or if we have accepted the task under compulsion, it may either mean that we have picked up a cross intended for someone else or that God may be calling us out of that commitment.

Second, as we carry our cross of loving commitment, it is essential to know that the living Christ is carrying the ultimate weight and pain. If we try to carry it alone, drawing only on our willpower, our unaided strength, our lonely love, we become quickly vulnerable to exhaustion and burnout. Indeed, we may find our original love has become angry manipulation of others! The words of Jesus "Abide in me, and I in you. As the branch cannot bear fruit by itself, unless it abides in the vine, neither can you, unless you abide in me" (John 15:4, RSV) are the central manna, the central nurture for our cross bearing.

THE BIRTH: This is the suffering caused by the awakening, stretching, and rebirth within our deepest selves. This is the pain of endings and new beginnings, the pain of letting go and taking hold. In the new birth experiences, we bring forth our deepest wounds and our deepest powers for healing and release. With every great creative transition in our lives, we feel the mingling of pain, anxiety, joy, and growth as we explore, choose, assert, reach out, and move out. The pain of new beginnings, of inner healing, of released powers is the pain of creation itself in which God shares.

It is significant that the pain of the cross and the pain of the birth are the forms of suffering to which God invites us (unlike the suffering of the thorn, the catapult, and unfilled hunger). And it is significant that the suffering to which God invites us always includes joy along with the pain and always brings with it the authentic awareness of growth and deepened love as part of its intrinsic nature.

This does not mean that we cannot also experience deepening love and growth within the other forms of suffering. Indeed, we are assured that within the clutch of evil and deprivation, God's loving embrace is around us every moment. And God tells us: "My grace is sufficient for you, for my power is made perfect in weakness" (2 Corinthians 12:9, RSV).

It is often difficult to discern among these forms of suffering, of course. They are often deeply intertwined, one profoundly involving another in both our individual and communal lives. But for the sake of our trust in God and our relationship with God's help and healing, it is essential to have some understanding of our suffering and to learn how to respond with wisdom and power.

Strangely enough, it is often hard to face the fact that we *are* suffering. Sometimes the pain is so chronic that we have grown accustomed to it. Sometimes we are numbed and anesthetized. Sometimes we have pushed ourselves so quickly into a positive response that we do not allow ourselves to feel the pain. Perhaps we try too quickly to forgive and forget or feel that our suffering is trivial or that we have no right to register suffering. Often it is with a sense of shock that we realize we *are* grieving and that we may have been carrying unhealed wounds for a long time. This often happens with those in the helping professions who are so used to themselves in the role of comforter and supporter that they become unaware of their own feelings and needs.

DISCERNING OUR HIDDEN PAIN

IN ORDER TO BRING our pain into our prayer, we need to face the reality of our suffering. With gentle self-questioning in God's presence, we can encounter with honesty the depths of masked pain. Here are some questions for reflection:

1. Has there been some significant change or trauma in my personal life in recent months?

It may be a big change, obvious to others, but which we had not realized was causing deep, chronic pain and grieving. Or it may be a small but symbolically significant change, imperceptible or trivial in the eyes of others, which we had not thought to dignify as a category of real suffering.

2. Has there been some significant change or trauma in my immediate community: family, workplace, church, neighborhood, close friends?

More quickly than we believe possible we internalize the suffering of those around us. Often the heaviest and most painful burdens we bear are those of our communities. Yet because nothing has happened to us personally, we do not always realize that we are deeply involved and suffering.

3. As I look upon my life as a whole, do I realize I have never felt quite satisfied, fulfilled, or fully adequate?

The chronic pain of unhealed memories, inadequate bonding with others, long-term unfulfillment, can become like part of the natural landscape. Suffering is no less real because we have learned to take it for granted—and this suffering often does more harm than any other when unencountered and unhealed.

4. What is my body telling me about my feelings? Do I have unusual bodily symptoms or lowered vitality for which there seems to be no medical cause?

Our bodies—given to us as our lifelong companions, guides, and truth tellers—are often the first to signal to us that we are carrying unfaced burdens of pain either from our personal lives or our communities. Learning to listen to our bodies is an essential spiritual discipline and an intrinsic part of healing prayer.

5. Are my dreams telling me anything? Am I dreaming more than usual or less than usual? Has there been a significant change in the type of dream or the way I feel about them?

As with our bodily symptoms, dreams are often truth tellers about unexpected stress, grief, anger, and burdens that we carry either for ourselves or for others.

SUGGESTED MEDITATIONS FOR THE ENCOUNTER WITH OUR PAIN

THE FOLLOWING HEALING meditations are only suggestions. If they feel threatening or unhelpful in any way or if you do not feel ready for the full experience, turn away from the suggested form and pray with other forms of imagery and symbolism that are better for you.

HEALING MEDITATION FOR THE THORN, THE HUNGER, THE CATAPULT

Now thus says the LORD, he who created you . . . he who formed you . . . "Fear not, for I have redeemed you; I have called you by name, you are mine. When you pass through the waters I will be with you; and through the rivers, they shall not overwhelm you; when you walk through the fire you shall not be burned, and the flame shall not consume you. . . . You are precious in my eyes, and honored, and I love you.

—Isaiah 43:1-2, 4, RSV

Relax your body and take a few deep but gentle breaths. Claim the nearness of God the Healer in whatever way is the most real for you. Inwardly lean on this loving strength, breathing slowly the light and love that surrounds you.

When you are ready, turn your attention to your body and let your attention move gently through your bodily self. Is there unusual muscular tension anywhere? Are there areas of nonfeeling? painful stress? Is your body telling you of some special burden, grief, anger, fear, or loneliness? Picture or sense the Healer touching those bodily parts with gentle, loving hands. Sense or picture a warm light forming around your body like an embracing cloak. Rest in this warmth and breathe gently. Now sense the warm light flowing inwardly like a gentle river to the bodily centers of emotional or physical suffering. Let those areas feel bathed in the warm waters of light for as long as you need it.

Now visualize your suffering as if it were a little wounded child, animal, or shrub. Picture the Healer lifting it out of you in healing hands and arms and holding it as long as you need it.

If you feel only numbness and defensive walls, do not try to tear down those walls. They were built over a long period of time and may need long healing. Rather, picture the Healer touching, embracing the inner wall or closed door. That apparent wall or door is really the presence of your frozen pain. God can relate to it directly as part of you and heal the pain in whatever form it manifests itself.

Ask for definite guidance for ways to encounter and transform the causes of your pain. If it is illness, ask for guidance in your medical choices and guidance in whatever inner wounds are augmenting your illness. If it is unfilled hopes and needs, ask to be shown ways by which your disappointing life can begin to be transformed.

If it is the catapult of evil or injustice that has battered you, ask for practical guidance in ways to overcome it and release yourself and others.

Prayer is meant to be not only intensely relational but also intensely practical. Expect, with confidence, guidance to be given. Sometimes it comes immediately in inner symbolism, or inner urging at a deep level, or sudden clarity of understanding. Sometimes it will come in the following hours and days through a letter, a phone call, a chance encounter, a book. Some unexpected door opens, and we will know that a way is shown.

Rest again in the embracing light of God, in the healing hands of God. Breathe slowly and gently of this love. When ready, open your eyes and conclude your prayer.

HEALING MEDITATION FOR THE DISCERNMENT AND BEARING OF THE CROSS

Blessed be the God and Father of our Lord Jesus Christ, the Father of mercies and God of all comfort, who comforts us in all our affliction, so that we may be able to comfort those who are in any affliction. . . . For as we share abundantly in Christ's sufferings, so through Christ we share abundantly in comfort too.
—2 Corinthians 1:3-5, RSV

Relax your body and breathe gently and slowly. In whatever way and symbolism is best for you, claim the nearness of Jesus Christ. Rest in that strong presence.

In that presence, ask if there is a sense of strong calling, urgency, longing for an involvement with and commitment to the pain and problem of another person or a community. Ask if you are truly led into this commitment by Christ. Does your choice seem to be a free one, or do you feel compelled against your will by inner or outer pressure? Is there a sense of joy and authenticity? What is your body telling you as you reflect on this commitment? Are there feelings of heaviness and dullness, or do you feel a surge of vital energy?

If you accept a cross of loving involvement with others, visualize the living Jesus Christ going before you into the situation, filling and blessing the task before you get there. Visualize the Christ embracing the other whose pain you share, covering the other with healing, transforming light.

Picture yourself abiding in the strength and life of the living

Christ each day, as a fruitful branch is connected with the life-giving tree. Breathe deeply and calmly of this in-flowing life and energy. Return to this nurturing, reenergizing prayer each day.

When you are ready, conclude your prayer, knowing that the living Christ goes ahead of you and also walks beside you carrying your cross with you.

HEALING MEDITATION FOR INNER REBIRTH

For all who are led by the Spirit of God are children of God. For you did not receive a spirit of slavery to fall back into fear, but you have received a spirit of adoption. When we cry, "Abba! Father!" it is that very Spirit bearing witness with our spirit that we are children of God . . . and joint heirs with Christ—if, in fact, we suffer with him so that we may also be glorified with him. I consider that the sufferings of this present time are not worth comparing with the glory about to be revealed to us.

—Romans 8:14-18, NRSV

Awake, O sleeper, and arise from the dead, and Christ shall give you light.

—Ephesians 5:14, RSV

Relax your body, breathe slowly and gently, and claim the presence of the Holy Spirit of Christ. Let your attention move through your bodily self. Are there signs of something's changing, stirring, and gathering strength? Have your dreams recently been more vivid with much strong symbolism? Is there a new restlessness and longing?

Ask the Holy Spirit of Christ if something is awakening within you, something deep within you coming into new birth. Ask whether some deep sleeping unawareness or wound is ready now to wake and come forward. Is there some destructive pattern of life from which you are beginning to repent, to turn around? some power or gift beginning to stretch its wings? some new moral choice, a new assertiveness, a new exploration of a different way of life?

If you feel something deep is wakening but do not yet know what it is, ask for a symbolic image to be given you. Visualize this new deep life as a running, joyous child or a bird ready to fly or a vigorous flower or shrub pushing up through the ground or a child about to be born or in some other way suggested to you.

Picture the Christ, the birth-giver, receiving your child, your bird, your shrub with joy and delight and release. Do not overlook any anxiety or pain you feel in this newness, this stretching. When your newborn self feels fear or suffering or grieving over what is left behind, let that inner child be held and comforted and nurtured, even as a mother holds and feeds the crying newborn baby. Remember the Holy Spirit is also called "the Comforter."

When you are ready, rest in God's strength, breathing gently, and conclude your prayer.

We are told in the twentieth chapter of the Gospel of John that after his resurrection, Jesus came among his disciples in his risen body of light and showed them his wounds in his hands and side.

Why would the marks of suffering still be visible in his triumphant, resurrected body? Was it only to identify himself to them? Surely it was more. Are we not also receiving the witness that our wounds are never wasted? Even after we are fully healed and released from suffering, whether in this life or the next, the signs of our wounds—the scars of our deep, committed living—will not be swallowed up in glory. Rather, they will shine forth from within us, no longer as sources of suffering but as sources of radiant light and richer loving.

Waging Spiritual Warfare *with the* Powers

by Walter Wink

NOT LONG AGO, there were people who were social justice advocates and others who were contemplatives. Some acted, others prayed. Today these two activities tend to take place in the same body. With increasing frequency, people are accepting, as the central theological task of our epoch, the integration of action and contemplation. But that integrative task will remain stuck in mere oscillation between the inner and the outer unless we grow beyond an individualistic view of prayer and recognize the major role played by the principalities and powers in *preventing* God from answering our prayers.

Most of us have been taught that unanswered prayer is a result either of our failure or God's refusal. Either we lacked faith (or were too sinful and impure), or God said no out of some inscrutable higher purpose.

Perhaps there are times when our faith is weak. But Jesus explicitly states that it is not how much faith we have that counts, but whether we simply do our duty and exercise whatever faith we do have; and an infinitesimal amount, he says, is enough (Luke 17:5-6). The issue, after all, is not whether we are spiritual giants but whether God really is able to do anything. Faith is not a feeling or a capacity we conjure up but trusting that God can act decisively in the world. So if we have faith like a grain of mustard seed—that is, if we have any faith at all—we should not blame ourselves when our prayers go unanswered.

Nor should we be too swift to ascribe our lack of success in praying to our sins and inadequacies. Morton Kelsey tells how the first really dramatic healing he was ever involved in took place despite his resentment at having to go to the hospital at an inconvenient time and minister to people he scarcely knew. God apparently ignored his attitude and healed the person anyway. Many of us were infected at an early age with the notion that God hears our prayers in direct proportion to the degree of purity of heart or sinlessness we bring to our prayers. We are now able to identify such ideas as bad theology. No one is "good enough" to pray, once we accept those terms. The God revealed by Jesus graciously listens to all who pray, perhaps even *especially* to sinners. It was the corrupt publican, after all, not the impeccable Pharisee, who went home justified (Luke 18:9-14).

Nor is it adequate in certain cases to blame God's nonresponse to our prayers on a higher will for us that, for now, requires a no. No doubt what sometimes appears to us as evil is the very explosion necessary to blast us awake to the destructiveness of our habits. Sickness and tragedy are, unfortunately, at times the indispensable messengers that recall us to our life's purpose. We sometimes do pray for the wrong thing or fail to recognize God's answer because we are looking for something else. But there are situations where God's will seems so transparently evident in the situation that to assert that God says no then is to portray God as a cosmic thug. I still cannot see, after twenty-five years, how the death by leukemia of a six-year-old boy in our parish was in any sense an act of God. And don't even try to tell me that the death of approximately 40,000 children a day (over 14,000,000 a year) is the will of God!

POWERS AND PRINCIPALITIES

THE PROBLEM is that we have left out the principalities and powers. Prayer is not just a two-way transaction. It also involves the great socio-spiritual forces that control so much of reality. I am speaking of the massive institutions and social structures and systems that dominate our world today and of the spirituality at their center. The "Powers" are not demonic beings floating in the sky; they are rather the corporations, the nation-states, the economic systems and religious hierarchies that organize and, to a great extent, dictate the life of human societies. But these Powers are more than their outer physical manifestations. They also have an inner spirit, a corporate personality, a driving interior dynamism that is incarnated in the outer forms. It is this interiority or withinness of institutions that the Bible calls the "angel of a nation," or the "angel of a church" (Daniel 10; Revelation 2–3). It is not simply a personification but a genuine, palpable yet invisible spiritual force that maintains an institution's ethos despite continuous changes of personnel.

Popular expressions hint at this dimension of social reality; we speak of team spirit, corporate cultures, office morale, patriotic sentiment, and even of "The Powers That Be." But we have scarcely begun to appreciate the profundity and range that these expressions faintly indicate.

If we wish to recover a sense of the importance of these Powers in prayer, we can scarcely do better than to consult the Book of Daniel. Daniel marks the moment when the role of the Powers in blocking answers to prayer was, for the first time, revealed to humanity.

"Daniel" is a symbol of Israel's struggling against all efforts to destroy its fidelity to Yahweh. Daniel is depicted as a Jew who had risen to high position in the Persian bureaucracy in Babylon. Three years before, Cyrus had freed the Jews from captivity and offered to rebuild their temple at royal expense. Yet few Jews had responded by returning home. When the story opens, Daniel is in such deep mourning for his people that he cannot eat. In the light of Romans 8:26-27 we might say that the Holy Spirit wanted to prepare him to receive a vision and so released in him a flood of anguish which Daniel wisely chose to face and not repress. So he entered upon a major fast. After twenty-one days an angel came. "Daniel, don't be afraid," the angel said. "God has heard your prayers ever since the first day you decided to humble yourself in order to gain understanding. I have come in answer to your prayer" (Daniel 10:12, TEV).

Why then was the angel twenty-one days in arriving, if the prayer was heard on the very first day that Daniel prayed? Because, the angel continues, "The angel prince of the kingdom of Persia opposed me for twenty-one days." He could not even have managed to get through to Daniel at all, except that "Michael, one of the chief angels, came to help me, because I had been left there alone" to contend with the angel of Persia. Now, while Michael occupies the angel of Persia, the messenger angel has slipped through and is able to deliver the vision of the future for Daniel's exiled people. That mission completed, "Now I have to go back and fight the guardian angel of Persia. After that the guardian angel of Greece will appear. There is no one to help me except Michael, Israel's guardian angel. He is responsible for helping and defending me" (Daniel 10:20–11:1, TEV).

The angel of Persia is able to block God's messenger from answering Daniel's prayer! This is the strangest, most disturbing element in Daniel's narrative. Daniel is praying and fasting and has been heard from the very first day. Yet for twenty-one days Daniel contends with unseen spiritual powers. Perhaps he too had to slough off internalized elements of Babylonian spirituality; he apparently bore as his own a name compounded from the name of a Babylonian god (Belteshazzar). But whatever the changes that may have taken place in him, the real struggle is between two nations. The angel of Persia does not want the nation he guards to lose such a talented subject people. The angel of Persia actively attempts to frustrate God's will and for twenty-one days succeeds. The principalities and powers are able to hold Yahweh at bay!

Daniel continues praying and fasting; God's angel continues to wrestle to get past the angel of Persia, yet nothing is apparently happening. God *seems* not to have answered the prayer. Despite this apparent indifference, however, there is a fierce war being waged in heaven between contending powers. Finally Michael, Israel's own guardian angel, intervenes and the angel gets through.

DEEP MYSTERIES

THIS IS A PERFECTLY ACCURATE depiction, in mythological terms, of the actual experience we have in prayer. We have been praying for decades now for the superpowers to reduce their arsenals; for most of that time it seemed an exercise in abject futility. The "angel of the United States" and the "angel of the Soviet Union" have been locked in a death-struggle in which neither seemed prepared to relax its grip. Then, in the irony of God, the most vociferously anti-Communist president in American history negotiated a nuclear weapons reduction treaty with a Soviet leader whose new course of openness was not predicted by a single American Sovietologist. Whatever their motives were, we can at least assert that none of this would have happened without the decades-long demonstrations and prayers of the peace movements in the United States, Europe, and the Soviet Union. God found an aperture and was able to bring about a miraculous change of direction.

The Cold War has now been widely declared over, perhaps prematurely since the Bush administration has thus far shown little recognition of the immensity of the opportunity handed it. We could still squander this unprecedented opening. We need to fast and pray now as never before that the moment not be lost, and with it, the world.

Notice that the Bible makes no attempt to justify the delay in God's response. It is simply a fact of experience. We do not know why God can't do "better," or why, for example, Michael is not dispatched sooner to help the angel get through. It is a deep mystery. But we are not appealing to mystery in order to paper over an intellectual problem; the Sovietologists are faced with mysteries as well. We just do not know why some things happen and others do not.

What does this say then about the omnipotence of God? about God's ability to redeem? about God's sovereignty over history? The principalities and powers are able to assert their will against the will of God, *and, for a time, prevail!* The wonder, then, is not that our prayers are sometimes unanswered but that any are answered at all! We have long accepted that God is limited by our freedom. The new insight in Daniel is that God is limited by the freedom of institutions and systems as well. We have normally spoken of this limitation as a free choice of God. One may well ask whether God has any choice. In any case, whether by choice or not, God's ability to intervene, uninvited, is extremely circumscribed.

In short, the equation in prayer is not God plus people, but God plus people plus the Powers. What God is able to do in the world is hindered, to a considerable extent, by the rebelliousness, resistance, and self-interest of the Powers.

God *is* powerful to heal; but if the Powers flush PCBs and dioxin into the water we drink or release radioactive gas into the atmosphere or insist on spraying our fruit with known carcinogens, God's healing power is sharply reduced. The situation is no different in kind than normal bodily healing; a clean cut will almost always, wondrously, mend; but if we rub dirt into it, or infectious germs, God's capacity to heal is hindered or even rendered void.

God does want people to be free to become everything God created them to be. I have not the slightest hesitation in declaring such fulfillment to be the will of God. But when one race enslaves another to labor in its fields or dig its mines, or when children's lives are stunted by sexual abuse or physical brutality, or when whole nations are forced to submit to the exploitation of other states more powerful, then what is God to do? We may pray for justice and liberation, as indeed we must, and *God hears us on the very first day.* But God's ability to intervene against the freedom of these rebellious creatures is sometimes tragically restricted in ways we cannot pretend to understand. It takes considerable spiritual maturity to live in the tension between these two facts: God *has* heard our prayer, and the Powers are blocking God's response.

97

PRAYER AS SOCIAL ACTION

If the Powers can thwart God so effectively, can we even speak of divine providence in the world? If our prayers are answered so sporadically, or with such great delays, can we really trust in God? Can God be relied on? Is a limited God really God at all? We have to face these questions, because our capacity to pray depends on some kind of working idea of God's providential care for us.

In the Nazi death camps, for example, where the intercessors stormed heaven with their supplications for deliverance, why did God not succeed in saving more Jews? Etty Hillesum, a Dutch Jew anticipating her deportation to a "work camp" that proved to be a death chamber, prayed:

> *I shall try to help You, God, to stop my strength ebbing away, though I cannot vouch for it in advance. But one thing is becoming increasingly clear to me: that You cannot help us, that we must help You to help ourselves. And that is all we can manage these days and also all that really matters: that we safeguard that little piece of You, God, in ourselves. And perhaps in others as well. Alas, there doesn't seem to be much You Yourself can do about our circumstances, about our lives. Neither do I hold You responsible. You cannot help us but we must help You and defend Your dwelling place inside us to the last.*[1]

One need not vouch for the theology in this statement to honor the experience it addresses. The Powers were holding God at bay. God appeared to be doing nothing. Meanwhile, unseen, there was war in heaven. When people not only submit to evil but actively affirm it, malignant powers are unleashed for which everyday life offers no preparation. The angel of Germany was worshiped as an idol and was acclaimed the supreme being. God, elbowed out of heaven, was out prowling every street at all hours and could find few to help.

In such a time, God may appear to be impotent. Perhaps God is. Yet Hitler's thousand-year Reich was brought down in only twelve years. God may be unable to intervene directly but nevertheless showers the world with "coincidences" that require only a human response to become effective. God is not mocked. The wheels of justice may turn slowly, but they are inexorable. Take

---

[1] *An Interrupted Life* (New York: Pocket Books, 1983), pp. 186–87.

Daniel again. After fifty years of captivity, God had at last raised up Cyrus to deliver the Jews from Babylon, and God's people chose rather to remain in exile. Daniel, fasting and praying, creates a fresh opening for God. Into that breach God pours the vision of a new life in a restored Holy Land, as an enticement and lure to coax Judah home.

Prayer is not magic; it does not always "work." But it is one task we alone can do. Human freedom, responsibly exercised, enables God's initiatives for liberation to become efficacious. The sobering news that the Powers can temporarily thwart God is more than matched by the knowledge that our intercessions will ultimately prevail. Whether we have to wait twenty-one days or twenty-one years or twenty-one centuries changes nothing for faith. It knows how massive and intractable the Powers are. We cannot stop praying for what is right because our prayers are seemingly unanswered. We know they are heard the very first day that we pray.

Daniel had to wait twenty-one days to receive his vision of the restitution of the Jews to Palestine; it would be two centuries before any sizable number returned. Modern-day Jews had to wait nineteen centuries for a Jewish state in Palestine. Gandhi struggled with the angel of the British Empire for twenty-six years; the Aquino revolution in the Philippines unseated Marcos in only a matter of days. Whether the water rises drop by drop or through a flash flood, eventually the pressure bursts the dam of oppression and the Powers fall. They are but mortal creatures, and they are all the more vicious when they know their time is short (Revelation 12:12). Many innocent people may die while the Powers appear to gain in invincibility with every death, but that is only an illusion. Their very brutality and desperation is evidence that their legitimacy is fast eroding. Their appeal to force is itself an admission that they can no longer command voluntary consent. Whenever sufficient numbers of people withdraw their consent, the Powers inevitably fall.

Prayer that ignores the Powers ends by blaming God for evils committed by the Powers. But prayer that acknowledges the Powers becomes a form of social action. Indeed, no justice struggle is complete that has not first discerned not only the outer, political manifestations of the Powers but also their inner spirituality and has lifted the Powers, inner and outer, to God for transformation. Otherwise we change only the shell and leave the spirit intact.

Prayer in the face of the Powers is no rosy "My God and I" proposition. It is a spiritual war of attrition. God's hands are effectively tied when we fail to pray. That is the dignity and urgency of our praying. History belongs to the intercessors, who believe a new world into being. Ched Myers says,

> *To pray is to learn to believe in a transformation of self and world, which seems, empirically, impossible.... What is unbelief but the despair, dictated by the dominant powers, that nothing can really change, a despair that renders revolutionary vision and practice impotent.... Faith entails political imagination, the ability to envision a world that is not dominated by the powers.*[2]

In a field of such titanic forces, it makes no sense to cling to small hopes. We are emboldened to ask for something bigger. The same faith that looks clear-eyed at the immensity of the forces arrayed against God is the faith that affirms God's miracle-working power. Trust in miracles is, in fact, the only rational stance in a world that is infinitely permeable to God's incessant lures. We are commissioned to pray for miracles because nothing less is sufficient. We pray to God not because we understand these mysteries but because we have learned from our tradition and from experience that God, indeed, *is* sufficient for us, whatever the Powers may do.

---

[2] Ched Myers, *Binding the Strong Man* (Maryknoll, NY: Orbis Press, 1988), pp. 225, 305.

For a fuller treatment of Daniel 10, see *Unmasking the Powers* (Philadelphia: Fortress Press, 1986), Chapter Four, "The Angels of the Nations."

How Long, O Lord?

by Elizabeth J. Canham

How long will it take us to get there?" asked my six-year-old nephew as we drove out for supper one evening. "About two Tom and Jerrys," replied his father, who knew that thirty minutes was an impossible concept for Christopher, but the length of a TV cartoon would make some sense. As I listened to the conversation I realized that the question was often mine too. How long will it take to overcome this fear, to know the next step on my journey, to see that friend healed, to deal with a broken relationship? I ask "How long, O Lord?" but God doesn't tell me how many Tom and Jerrys it will take. Mostly the question seems to be met with silence, and we must simply wait *for* the Lord's reply; sometimes the question is greeted with an invitation to wait *on* the Lord in patience and trust.

WAITING FOR AND WAITING ON

Waiting is one of the most difficult, and most God-like, parts of our experience. It is often difficult because it reminds us that we have not arrived, that we are unfinished, and that the present moment is one in which to live the "not yet" of faith. And waiting is frequently made more difficult by our fear of what may be, or our doubt that waiting will result in joy. But it is also God-like. Scripture bears witness to the God who waits again and again for the right moment to act in the life of a community or an individual, and that waiting is especially poignant as God takes flesh in the body of a young woman and becomes subject to the nine months of pregnancy. God's waiting affects us, and frequently we interpret it as inaction on the part of the Creator to whom we cry out. Dealing with the feelings generated by the sense that nothing is happening is an essential part of our growth in prayer and faith.

The psalms are full of allusions to waiting and offer us a way to pray the distress ("waiting for") as well as the trust ("waiting on") that we feel as we live in the between times of unfulfilled hope. When life is consumed with problems or our bodies are pain-racked, we may want to pray in the words of Psalm 77:9, "Has God forgotten to be gracious? Has he in anger shut up his compassion?"[1] for we really do entertain thoughts of abandonment. That sense of being forgotten is even more acute in Psalm 22:1-2: "My God, my God, why have you forsaken me? Why are you so far from helping me, from the words of my groaning? O my God, I cry by day but you do not answer; and by night, but find no rest." These are real prayers uttered by those who are overwhelmed by the badness of life and the nonanswers of a silent God.

Alongside these expressions of despair there are prayers of hope and of thanksgiving as the psalmists learn to wait patiently, trusting that God still cares. "For God alone my soul waits in silence; from him comes my salvation" (Psalm 62:1). This verse expresses the confidence of one who, still aware of oppressive enemies all around, has learned to be still and quiet in the presence of the Creator who alone can save. The writer of Psalm 130, after crying to God from the depths says: "I wait for the LORD, my soul waits, and in his word I hope; my soul waits for the LORD more than those who watch for the morning" (vv. 5-6). Here there is an alert anticipation, a waiting on God in hopeful trust by one who has consented to be present in the waiting instead of consumed by the tentative quality of life.

I find myself praying in both of these forms, sometimes asking God why there seems to be no end to the waiting, no answer to my questions, no relief from my fears. But I also pray as one who has experienced the compassion of God in the past and who finds in those earlier times of renewal a reason for trusting the future. Often the prayer of confidence and trust follows the cry of anguish, for in the expression of pain I consent to be honest with God, confessing the limitations of my faith and finding, like Thomas, that the One I thought was gone now stands before me. Two psalms, 74 and 40, deal with the issue of waiting and our varied response to the experience of incompleteness. They offer a way to connect our waiting times with those of God's people in many ages and circumstances.

---

[1] All scripture quotations are from the *New Revised Standard Version of the Bible.*

WAITING FOR GOD

IN PSALM 73 the question "Why do the innocent suffer?" is posed, and Psalm 74 then takes one of the most painful examples of such suffering, that of exile. According to Hebrew tradition Asaph, the author of Psalm 74, is one of only four prophets who dares to challenge God in such direct terms. He asks whether the Almighty has abandoned the covenant people forever and makes it clear that not only is the chosen nation endangered by exile, but God's stature in the world is in question. The psalm opens with a question: "O God, why do you cast us off forever? Why does your anger smoke against the sheep of your pasture?" The image of God as Shepherd of Israel (Psalm 80:1) seems incompatible with the current experience of exile, especially since God appears to *remain* angry with the sheep, unlike the human shepherd who, though he may strike the sheep to keep it on a safe path, does not continue to administer blows.

The Hebrew scriptures frequently call upon the covenant people to remember God's mercy and compassion and to celebrate the many saving events in their past history. Now the psalmist calls upon God to remember, to take notice of the suffering, and to see the enemy's devastation of the holy places in the land. He beseeches God, "direct your steps to the perpetual ruins," which may not only be an invitation to come and look at the destruction of the place where God and Israel convene, but also a request that God trample and crush the enemy who now gloats over this aggression. In past times prophets have been raised up and have offered signs of hope to God's people in times of oppression, but now Asaph can see no signs, and no prophets bring encouragement to a displaced people. He cries out in anguish: "How long, O God, is the foe to scoff? Is the enemy to revile your name forever?" and he longs for God to take out the hand, symbol of initiative and power, from its hiding place. In the first eleven verses of this psalm there is depression, despair, impotence, and a sense that life is a meaningless series of disasters over which the nation has no control.

The experience of exile is excruciatingly painful. To be cut off from one's roots, bereft of home and heritage, and compelled to exist in a hostile environment is a dreadfully lonely experience. All the familiar patterns that sustain life are gone. So are the comfortable people, the regular rituals both personal and communal, and all that gives shape to existence and provides a rhythm for living. Exile means disorientation and a loss of the equilibrium for which we all long. It compels us to ask the most fundamental questions about who we are—questions that are easy to avoid if we cling to the familiar. To be in exile is to be in question and to have no certainty that there will ever again be a place we can call home. Few of us experience exile in such a dramatic way as the people of Judah, who were torn from Jerusalem and transplanted in Babylon after watching their northern neighbors in Israel suffer a similar fate. Yet we all have to deal with losses, with changes that leave us feeling rootless, and with seasons of our lives in which God seems no longer to be listening when we cry out for help. It is in those times that the psalms can help us give voice to the anguish and lostness.

In 1981 I left my native England and asked the Episcopal Church in the United States to test my vocation to the priesthood since the Church of England does not yet ordain women. My self-imposed exile began with much sadness at the loss of home, but it was also filled with hopeful anticipation as the fulfillment of my call drew near. In the first months I was busy planning the ordination, adjusting to full-time parish ministry, meeting new friends, and enjoying the novelty of living in a new country. When my first temporary appointment came to an end, I moved to New York City to complete further graduate studies and look for a new position. It was then, more than a year after I left England, that I began to really experience a painful sense of loss, and to feel that I did not really belong in that teeming, vibrant, exciting, and tough city. With meager financial resources, no permanent parish appointment, and now distant from the new friends I had made in New Jersey, I felt lonely and dislocated. Who was I? Had the move to the U.S. been a mistake? Would I ever be able to integrate with this culture and would people want what I had to offer, or would I join the ranks of unemployed clergy? Where was God?

Like Asaph, I began to record my fear and disappointment, not in the form of a psalm, but in daily journal entries in which I now see overwhelming fear and bits of paranoia. I remembered the clarity with which I had chosen to move to the United States and, occasionally I remembered God's grace in past times of loss. One of God's gifts to me at this time was a series of very vivid dreams that I recorded and in which I found much wisdom as I reflected on their meaning. I would probably not have been able to receive the message, "wait patiently for God," but I could begin to see more clearly that the feeling of oppression and abandonment might not last forever. Some of my fear was based on reality and the present situation was one to be lived through, not avoided by some mind-numbing escape or denied through pious platitudes. As I cried out, "How long, O God?" somehow the waiting for answers became more tolerable, and I learned to make little acts of trust that took a great deal more effort than the big decision to cross the Atlantic.

One of the dreams helped with the "Who am I?" question. I dreamed that I was producing a play, but the actors had not learned their lines. I would gather one group and find that they had left their scripts behind, and those who wanted to begin had parts that came much later in the play. Then a small goat walked onstage, and someone pointed to it and said: "You know, you should give her a much bigger part, she's very talented." I realized that there was a child inside the goatskin, but I dismissed the remark because I was preoccupied with getting the play started. The same chaos continued; I was again told to pay attention to the "goat"; and then I woke. It is little wonder that dreams have been described as "God's forgotten language."[2] With clarity and playfulness God "spoke" to me, for the dream accurately reflected the chaotic feelings of disorder I was experiencing and the sense that I "could not get my act together." Remembering that we are participants as well as observers of our dreams, I thought about the various characters. I was certainly like those who had not yet learned the lines; I had not really adjusted to life in New York City and was not yet sure how to speak my part. At the same time I resembled those anxious to get the play started; my impatience because nothing seemed to be happening made the feelings of exile more acute. But the dream told me it was not yet time for the big scene. Instead, it was necessary to wait out the muddle. And that meant that the whole thing was "getting my goat"!

But perhaps the most important issue was the invitation to notice the little "kid," the child within who, though talented, was now doubting her ability to be of use. I had to hear that message twice before I took it in. Through that dream I was learning to be in exile. Over the next few months I learned to connect with the stories of other exiles, God's people in Babylon hanging their harps upon the willows by the water, learning to sing the Lord's song on alien soil (Psalm 137); Jacob, fleeing from home and family, finding God through the dream given him as he journeyed and preparing him for the return many years later; Esther, a Hebrew woman exiled in the harem of the Persian king, confronting her fear, stepping outside cultural gender expectations and saving her people from extinc-

---

[2] John A. Sanford, *Dreams: God's Forgotten Language* (New York: Crossroad, 1982).

tion. The experience of exile, painful though it was, became the crucible in which faith was refined in them and the faithfulness of God was made known to future generations.

REMEMBERING GOD

IN THE SECOND HALF of Psalm 74, Asaph continues to speak to God. But now he remembers the powerful acts of salvation in the past and begins to hope again. "Yet God my King is from of old, working salvation in the earth" (v. 12) seems to suggest that, though there is not much evidence of God's omnipotence in the present situation, change is possible. The Creator who divided the Red Sea in two, crushing Pharaoh (Leviathan) and his hosts and leading out of bondage an oppressed people, is surely able to act once more on behalf of the covenant community now in exile. Water was sacred in Egypt, and when the rivers were turned to blood, their god was defiled; when the pursuing Egyptians were drowned, they were being destroyed by that which they worshiped. In contrast God led the chosen people to fresh water in the desert, demonstrated sovereignty over the seasons and luminaries, and was made known as the supreme Creator. As the psalmist recalls these events, the puny image of God who is powerless and forgetful is replaced by a sense of wonder. The psalm ends with a further request that God pay attention to the covenant, so that the petitioner does not turn back empty-handed. The cause for which he pleads is not simply that of Israel, but of the God with whom the nation is inextricably bound up and whose honor is at stake.

There is great wisdom in some of the old gospel hymns. "Count your blessings, name them one by one," advises the song, and it goes on to say that we will be surprised by what the Lord has done. How true that is. One of the most positive ways to end the day—even the worst of days—is to pause and consider where thanksgiving is appropriate in our lives. We may begin by being grateful for such basic things as breath, adequate food, shelter, the capacity for thought and gradually become aware of little, unnoticed events that were causes of joy during a day that may have seemed very routine. The smile by the woman at the checkout counter; the first crocus in bud, evidence of approaching spring; the scripture verse that came to mind; the memory of some act of kindness on the part of a neighbor; all these, as they are recalled, begin to change our perspective of life and of God. Remembering makes the waiting time more bearable, for it fills the present emptiness with hope and allows God to be bigger than the present moment might suggest.

Another old gospel song says, "Tell me the old, old story of unseen things above" and suggests the importance of the role of the community in keeping alive an awareness of God's action in human history. The psalms, whether written by an individual dealing with some intensely personal experience, or for corporate, liturgical use, have become an integral part of worship in the Hebrew and Christian tradition. They represent a vibrant and compelling call to remember and to celebrate the involvement of God in sacred history by telling the stories over and over again. This is essential because, as the song says, we forget so soon, "the early dew of morning has passed away at noon." Remembering is prayer. Often the existing psalms become a vehicle for that recalling and sharing of God's action in our lives. Sometimes we may feel compelled to write our own prayer-psalm in order to invite God to participate in the anguish or joy that we experience. Not long ago, feeling very impotent in the presence of a much loved person with Alzheimer's disease, I wrote this prayer based on Psalm 64:

Hear my voice, O God, when I groan
because I feel so helpless.
Why should one you created suffer so deeply
the disorientation and lostness of a mind
confused?
We know how to make bombs well enough
to blast our planet into oblivion,
why do you not give us the ability
to prevent degenerative disease?
Fragmented, brittle hours of lostness
enshroud her day.
Seventy-eight, a flickering candle
burning at twilight.
Yet, I remember, there were the good days.
Lark singing overhead and wild spring
flowers in the hedge.
"A pearl," she said, "this day is a pearl,
strung on my necklace of translucent
memories."
When she saw mountains for the first time,
"I can't believe it," she cried, face
radiant with gratitude.
We hiked summers away through mist and rain

and walked in winter snow.
It's hard to reach her now as she struggles
in the dark, seeping swamps of confusion.
Like timeless Job I hurl into emptiness
the unanswerable "WHY?"
and in the waiting I remember—
there were the good days.

WAITING ON GOD

THE PSALMS also put us in touch with an attitude of waiting on God in childlike trust even in adverse circumstances. Psalm 40, attributed to David, is an expression of thanksgiving following deliverance after a painful illness. "I waited patiently for the LORD; he inclined to me and heard my cry. He drew me up from the desolate pit, out of the miry bog, and set my feet upon a rock" (vv. 1-2). David saw his illness as a watery grave that threatened to swallow him alive as the Red Sea had swallowed the Egyptians. He felt that he was sinking in the clay, the very substance with which the oppressed Israelites were compelled to manufacture bricks. Now God had "firmed" his steps, enabled him to stand securely on a rock. So he sings of deliverance. One Jewish commentator suggests that it is incumbent upon us to create an original hymn of praise to God following every miracle the Creator works on our behalf! David extends this song beyond his personal experience of healing to a communal celebration that causes many others to see, fear, and put their trust in the Lord who is *our* God.

It becomes clear later in the psalm that trouble is not over for David. There are those who wish him dead and who scorn him (v. 14). He is still asking God for protection and vindication, but something has happened that enables him to trust and to wait patiently on God. The reason for this attitude of quiet trust is indicated in v. 6, "You have given me an open ear" or, translated literally from the Hebrew, "You have dug receptive ears for me." David has received from God the capacity to hear, through the cacophony of fearful sounds, the gentle voice of the Creator that brings reassurance and hope. He has learned to listen as he waits and to catch the love song of the Compassionate One who cradles David in safety even while battle rages around him.

Waiting patiently on God becomes possible as we are tuned in to the Word of God that addresses us in our need. A few mornings ago I was pondering a verse from Psalm 46: "The LORD of Hosts is with us; the God of Jacob is our refuge." I needed to enter into a place of confidence and to receive strength for the day in which I anticipated some difficult decisions and meetings. I experienced this verse as a gift from God, repeated it thankfully, allowed it to become part of my prayer. Then, as I sat in silence, I became aware of another persistent voice repeating old discouraging messages in the background. It was a familiar sound that told me life is fragile, the present moment insecure, and the future unpredictable. As the voice spoke, anxiety grew and fear began to replace confidence in God my Refuge. Then God gave me an open ear. With clarity I knew that I had a choice to make between the two voices; I didn't have to pay attention to the discordant sounds that invoked fear, for now they were removed from the realm of the unconscious and their shrill emptiness exposed for what it truly was.

What happened for David, and what I experienced last week, was a return to the awareness of God's loving omnipotence and of our call to love and serve the divine purpose. David can say, "I love to do your will"; his true natural inclination and most genuine desire was to freely serve his Creator. His will was so inextricably bound up with God's Torah, deep within him, that there was no need to search through a scroll of parchment to discover what God wanted. He had only to scrutinize his own innermost parts, his heart and his conscience, to know the truth so that God's will might control his tastes and appetites, his likes and dislikes. As he tuned out the voice of fear, he heard again the truth about God and himself. In this knowledge, no external circumstances could shake his confidence or shatter his faith, for nothing could rob him of the reality of God's truth within. It became possible to wait.

Daring to journey within and to discover the law of God engraved deeply in our hearts means life. Another voice may try persistently to tell us that God's will means loss, a denial of our greatest longings, and an existence of stoic endurance. These lies keep us from fullness of life and the joy that comes from discovering that in the deepest part of ourselves we are at one with the Creator in what we truly desire. To wait with and on such a God is to find oneself in harmony with the cosmos, which is ever waiting, ever coming to fullness. It means a refusal of the myth that to wait is to be diminished. It announces to the world that the God who waits is Creator of all times and seasons and gives meaning to the waiting times of our experience.

The Booty of
the Dove

by Mary Rose O'Reilley

Home is the riddle of the wise
The booty of the dove.
　　　　　—Emily Dickinson

January: I have come to St. Francis Center[1]—a "living room,"
as they call it, for the homeless, chronically alcoholic, and mentally ill—to teach writing. I came, at first, with the romantic
fantasy that there would be a lot of creativity on the street. I came
because I believe that finding voice as a writer means gaining a small
space of freedom and self-determination. I wanted to give away sanity and wholeness instead of a payroll deduction and tins of pump-
kin pie filling. As I said, it was a fantasy.

Most of my students at St. Francis have turned out to be docile
and imitative writers. Their work rings predictable changes on plots
that spill from TV, for TV runs incessantly in every shelter, hospital, asylum, and rehab center. These writers are obsessed, moreover,
with correctness; they complain when the pencils I bring in don't
have erasers.

I have come because I believe that a writing group—the kind
we work with nowadays in high school and college and professional
life—can be a challenging and cherishing community. But I have
never before sat in a writing group where the students carry
weapons. Docile, I have called Steve, Lucas, and Mark: "M'am,"
they say, and open doors for me. But Mark is dour and growls when
any writing buddy sits too close, Lucas is fresh from prison (he
proudly tells me), and yesterday's knife fight at St. Francis Center
was over a stolen bingo card.

This day, I have brought a writing project that I developed, during a stint of grade school teaching, from the work of Sylvia Ash-

---

[1] The names of the center and the clients have been changed to protect the privacy
of the clients.

ton-Warner. Ashton-Warner, a New Zealander, taught Maori children to read by finding out what words they needed to control. She made a primer out of the words that linked them to fear or ecstasy, witchcraft or the passions of love.

My version of this exercise asks students to write down words they like on small slips of paper. Then they paste their words on a piece of construction paper, adding connectives or drawings, as they like. For inspiration, I have brought some poems that combine words and images. It's an exercise that is easy to do with young children, but sophisticated enough for serious writers.

But where, today, is my class? Mark and Lucas are in detox; Steve is playing chess with himself in the corner. "You can tell the guys who've been in jail," Lucas has told me, "by how they play chess."

"Andy? Do you want to work with me? Write, or draw?" Andy is about twenty. He wears filthy dreadlocks, and his skin is a grey veil of dirt. He winces if you talk to him. As always, he slides away from my question, then slips in from behind: "What kind of writing?" But when I look he is gone, like the angels that appear from time to time in your peripheral vision.

In the end, I have only one taker, a man sitting in the corner of the room, named Paul, who responds to my invitation as though I had offered him a present. "Oh, YES, thank you. I'd like to very much." Paul is slight, about thirty-five, and dirty hair sticks out on his forehead like the bill of a cap. His polyester shirt is too small for him, and the buttons strain across his chest. What's most disconcerting is his right eye, unfocused and buried in swollen tissue. It drools puss, which he keeps trying to wipe away.

Paul writes the following words: *one, two, stop, go, digitalis, Paulie, now, hart, faiful*. I sit and work beside him. From my own hoard of words, he borrows *prairie*.

As he works, Paul tells me about his life as an engineer on the man-made island of Britannia, near the tip of Japan. Of his battles with the headhunters and cannibals there. Worse, he tells me that the headhunters are now invading the Minneapolis suburbs, arriving in business suits, with concealed blowguns. He is always having to go and fight them hand-to-hand. You can tell a headhunter, no matter how cleverly disguised, by making him spit on a tissue. If it disappears—the spit? the tissue?—I hesitate to ask—that's the *sign*.

By now he is drawing elaborate crystalline structures in many colors on his construction paper, imprisoning or enshrining the words inside. I don't usually ask people about their words when I do this exercise, afraid of getting too nosy and therapeutic. But I want to know about the word *faiful,* which, upside down, I read as *falafel.* Has Paul been hanging out behind a Lebanese deli?

"*Faiful,*" Paul reads obediently, like a good child asked to spell a word and use it in a sentence. "I would like to have a *faiful* friend."

When we are done, he hangs his words and his crystals on the St. Francis Center bulletin board.

"What's your favorite word, Paul?"

"NOW," he says. "Now now now."

Clara, the social worker from Client Services, takes me aside to check up on Paul. "He seldom talks to anyone. How is he doing?"

"He's OK," I say, noncommittally. Sitting daily in this living room, I have picked up the evasive shrug and loyalties that shut out cop and social worker. "Maybe we should get a doctor to look at his eye." I don't really want to talk to her about Paul's words or his business. That's as "faiful" as I can be.

"We're trying to get him committed," Clara says apologetically. Involuntary commitment is an embarrassing subject at St. Francis Center. "Just to get him *started.* Most of the time we can't get him to sleep inside, even. He sleeps in the Selby tunnel."

When I walk to my bus stop in stinging snow, I will pass the tunnel mouth, unlighted, seemingly abandoned, but full of eyes.

February: There is no question of teaching writing any more. There are not enough erasers in the world. So we paint and color—very popular activities—talk, play bingo.

"Why do you come here?" one of the guys asks me. He is a Hispanic man who draws intricate and beautiful scenes of palm trees and parrots, which he always tears up at the end of the day.

"Juan, I don't know. It's a good way to be with people." I'm ashamed of all the reasons that brought me at first: to teach, to give, to understand, to spy, to feel better. Now I come out of dumb instinct. I like Juan and Paul and Lucas and Andy, who is a year or so older than my son; my life is linked with theirs in some obscure way. For the record, I don't like murderous Mark and I'm relatively indifferent to Clara, the social worker. I'm devoted to Stew, a Mennonite volunteer, and to Seth, probably the nuttiest human being in the city, who spends his days cutting newspaper into tiny elfish paper dolls, who dresses in shreds of motley, and who has the air of someone famous in disguise. Why do I come here? This has become my community, my un-writing group. "Juan, I don't know."

I'm a single parent, alone a lot. I don't like parties—they make me feel unreal. I like being with people though, and I like making art out of old candy wrappers and trash. "Are you lonely?" Juan pursues.

Since I'm afraid he'll ask me for a date, I dodge that one. "Not at the moment." By temperament, fate, or possibly vocation, I'm a solitary. But I don't feel like explaining all that to Juan.

*M*arch: Today I sit for a long time talking to Becky. I don't usually just sit with people. I'd rather keep my hands busy with the watercolor paints. But Becky has lured me with the bait of wanting help with a job application, and so we begin to talk about her life.

The conversation is giving me flashbacks. When I was ten or twelve, there was a school field—once prairie—near my house, where a killdeer nested. If my sister and I approached the nest, the killdeer would pretend to have a broken wing and stagger along the ground, trying to lure us away from her eggs.

People seem to do the same dance. I guess I do it myself, and maybe that's why I get so annoyed when someone drags me into it down at St. Francis Center, where the Killdeer Dance often headlines the floor show. Not wanting to confess the real pain, we wallow in phony pain. (It's *we* now. I've gone over, like Damian to the side of the so-called lepers.)

"I think I'm pregnant," Becky confides. "I hope I am; it would give me something to pass my days."

She has been sitting for an hour, slack-jawed, staring. Her face is small and attractive, though vacuous, her hair peroxided to bronze with a few inches of dark root. Looking at her body crumpled in the chair, I can't tell if she is pregnant, heavy, or simply sliding back to earth, the way some women seem to do. She smells stale and greasy. So do I, of course, by now.

"I miscarried three times. I had a baby who lived only three days. . . ."

Why do I think this is not true? A killdeer crying nowhere near the nest?

". . . I took a beating. I took twelve blows to my head with a baseball bat. I've had plastic surgery all over my face."

Does she catch me searching her face for scars?

"I've got bumps on my head. You could feel them. I can feel

them, anyhow. The baby's legs were broken, her back was broken. She only lived a few days."

"Are you getting some prenatal care now?" I ask.

"I don't want to bother with WIC. It's too much hassle."

"The man you're with, is he OK about the baby?"

She begins a confusing story. "I was afraid to tell him. He thinks I was sleeping with this other guy. I did sleep in the guy's bed, but we had a board between us"—like Tristan and Isolde, I think—"he's so fat. He's three times as big as me. He makes my skin crawl."

"But the man you're with?"

"Oh, he wants the baby very badly. He makes me eat calves' liver."

"Better you than me."

"I hope I'm pregnant. It will give me something to pass my days."

She tells me about the temporary work she does, making sandwiches for a take-out lunch place. Becky is the sort of person the welfare reformers might point a finger at. She *could* hold down a full-time job, they would say.

But should she? Could she? Would she make friends at work? Who would listen to her monologues, her killdeer cry? As we talk through the job application, I see her in my mind's eye at the luncheonette, with rubber gloves on her hands, packing sandwiches, the other women avoiding her as the kids must have avoided her on the playground. I see her going home to bundle with her fat man.

There is a new young worker in Client Services. He is worried about Becky. "Did you get your food? Do you need more?"

"No, she's pregnant, though," I tell him. "She needs nice vegetables."

"How am I going to get this food home?" Becky whines when the new young worker hands her the bag. I know that in a few minutes she will have gotten him to drive her. He's given her a lot of nice frozen shrimp and the best canned goods.

"Can you come around the back?" I hear him say. "I'll pick you up in my car."

April: Somebody has started a fad of opening wallets, showing off pictures of lost children, Christmas trees, proms, anniversaries: the booty of the dove. Seth is cutting out his intricate paper dolls. The living room is pretty quiet.

A few weeks ago, as I rode the bus downtown to rehearse the *St. Matthew Passion* with a choral group I belong to, Seth got on.

My first impulse was to spring up and greet him; my second was to bury my face in the Bach score. I was riding with my friend, Caroline, a county judge. Would she think I was crazy? Would Seth? Would I be showing off my friendship with a street person? Would Seth deny me? By the time I processed all these subtle questions and buried my face in the score, Seth had gotten off the bus. Becky has found shelter in a Catholic Worker community. Lucas is dead, crushed by a garbage truck. Andy, with the dreadlocks, is also missing. One frigid night in February, all the shelter directors got on the phone to one another and agreed to shut Andy out on the street: that way, the police would be obliged to put him in the hospital. It's a quick way to get an involuntary commitment. I saw it in the paper with a photo of the police patting him down. My son adjusted his glasses and peered into the mystery of the news; he, too, works at the center: "Is that *our* Andy? He hates to be touched."

He is our Andy, and I suspect that we are his. We are time-warped together like some partners in a dance who infinitely miss each other.

Today my youngest daughter has come to paint with us. She collaborates for a while with Seth on paper dolls. "I like him, but you won't bring him home, will you?" she asks behind her hand.

I pretend not to hear, not to know. I haven't even got the courage to talk to Seth on the bus. Cozy in the St. Francis living room, we watch the people passing on the street, looking in, looking away.

"Why do you come here?" one of the Native American women asks.

"Marie, I don't know. It's a good place to be with people."

Holy Time,
Holy Timing

by Jean M. Blomquist

A FEW YEARS AGO my husband and I headed off for the Grand Canyon during our Easter break. After a two-day drive from our home in California, we scanned the flat Arizona horizon, dotted with scrubby evergreens, for signs of the canyon. The earth gave no clues as to what lay ahead. Then, shortly after passing through the park entrance on the afternoon of Holy Saturday, we pulled into the first scenic overlook and, as one person put it, the canyon was "very immediately there." Photographs, movies, and stories did not prepare me for this awesome sight. I stood in silence, trying to take in its eternal immensity and breathtaking beauty—the spectrum of oranges, reds, and russets; the massive walls and "temples" of layered red, creamy gold, tan, and gray; the turquoise sky that stretched across the horizon.

We camped on the South Rim, where temperatures dipped so low that water froze in our tent. We rose early on Easter morning and made our way through the bone-chilling darkness to the windy canyon rim. Along with several hundred other people, we celebrated the holy miracle of Easter as the sun rose above the canyon.

On Monday morning, we began a three-day backpack trip into the canyon. The climate of the upper rim is similar to that of southern Canada; at the bottom of the canyon, along the Colorado River, the climate is like the Sonoran Desert of northern Mexico. I was happy to leave the cold rim and venture into the warmer climes below. But entering the canyon took me far beyond different climate zones. I confronted time itself: *chronos*, measurable, clocklike time; and *kairos*, time that can't be measured.[1] In the canyon, time is both terrible and wonder-full. Rock walls, looming thousands of feet high and immense, sweeping spaces memorialize what time has taken

---

[1] In English we have only one word for time. In Greek there are at least two: *chronos*, which means measurable, clocklike, or calendar time; and *kairos*, which has a variety of meanings including the opportune or favorable time. It is often used in the New Testament to name a time of, or determined by, God. I use *kairos* here as time in its fullness, time made spacious and gracious by the presence of God.

away, as well as what time has left behind. Chronological time, the aeons represented in the layers of rock that create the canyon walls, stretches into timelessness, into time so vast that it is incomprehensible.

We began our hike at the South Kaibab trailhead (elev. 7,260 feet), where the rock, Kaibab Limestone, is geologically young—a mere 250 million years old. As the trail switchbacked downward, we passed through many strata of rock, including one that had once been the bottom of a sea. After hiking several knee-wrenching hours, we reached the bottom of the canyon (elev. 2,480 feet) and ran our grimy hands in wonder along the Vishnu schist, rock that is nearly two *billion* years old and that once was part of a mountain range higher than the Himalayas.

God existed before all this and was present in the earth's labored heaving and settling, the painstaking building up and the patient wearing down. And God, the Ancient of Days, very clearly was present now. I felt the Holy Presence keenly. My joy grew in this silent sacred place as I found myself within the very heart of God—the place where *chronos* and *kairos*, time and timelessness, meet. In the stillness of a moment, I found an eternity.

I carried much more than my 45-pound backpack and a lot of red dust out of the canyon. I carried that holy encounter of *chronos* and *kairos* with me. My experience in the canyon was the epitome of God's holy timing: the bringing of each *chronos* moment into a fullness so that it becomes *kairos*. In this fullness of time, moments brim with vibrancy, vitality, grace, and peace, so that they become time-less. All need to count and to measure drops away, and we become "as a little child"; we become one with God and with all that is. Is it possible, I wondered, for each moment of my life to become a *kairos* moment?

TAMING OUR TIME

OUR CULTURE is obsessed with *chronos* time. We value punctuality or "being on time." We strive to keep things "on schedule." On vacation, we want "to make the most of the time" we have, so we often pack so many activities in that we return exhausted. And we often lament that we just don't "have enough time." Powerful cultural mores (and in some cases, laws) establish timetables for our lives: when to start and finish school, establish a career, marry, buy a house, have children, retire, and so on. The feeling is often that once we are "on track"—if we ever get there in the first place—it is almost impossible, not to mention risky or reckless, to get "off track," regardless of whether society's timing is right for us personally or not. I have wrestled with this concept of timing for many years, especially around the issues of career and family. How do I, in the midst of such strong societal pressures, remain open to God's timing, to *kairos*, to holy timing? And what does that mean each day as I try to balance the personal, professional, and spiritual aspects of my life?

I've discovered at least two things—neither of which I yet fully comprehend. First, there is a holy timing that deals with the larger order and rhythm of our life events. For example, I did not meet the man to whom I am now happily married until I had healed sufficiently from a painful divorce years before. Second, each moment, regardless of what we are doing, can be a *kairos* moment. The long stretch of holy timing and the immediate *chronos* moment link our lives with God. The challenge that continually confronts us as people of faith is to incorporate God's holy timing into our lives. We seek to discover the meeting place of *chronos* and *kairos* and to open our hearts to the holy within each *chronos* minute.

To discover holy timing, we must strive for a continuous, centered interaction with the Spirit, who gently and reliably—though often excruciatingly slowly for impatient people like me—reveals when it is time to plant or to reap, to wait or to act, to reckon or to ripen. This holy timing grows past personal and societal "shoulds" and "oughts." It delves into and grows out of our fullness of "heart," in the Hebraic sense of one's whole being: body, intellect, feeling, will, intuition, imagination, action.

The familiar cadence of Ecclesiastes 3, "a time to be born, and a time to die; a time to plant, and a time to pluck up what is planted" (v. 2, RSV), reveals the tension of holy timing, the rhythmic pulse of living the seeming dichotomies, the contradictions, the counterpoints of day-to-day existence. But why and how does timing matter in the life of faith? Is there any relation between our work time and our leisure time? Can leisure be an important part of our spiritual journey, a crucial component of our spiritual plowing and planting?

HOLY RESTING

The rhythm of working and resting is God's pattern (Genesis 2:2-3). God blesses and hallows—makes holy—the seventh day, the day of rest. God later affirms again the sacredness of rest. At their lengthy téte-á-téte on Mt. Sinai, God says to Moses, "Therefore the people of Israel shall keep the sabbath, observing the sabbath throughout their generations, as a perpetual covenant. It is a sign for ever between me and the people of Israel that in six days the LORD made heaven and earth, and on the seventh day [God] rested, and was refreshed" (Exodus 31:16-17, RSV). So this sabbath day, this resting, enfleshes the covenant God has with us and we have with God. The sabbath was created *for* us, as Jesus said (Mark 2:27). The day of rest, each moment of rest, is a "sign" of God's covenant with us.

The purpose of our resting is to refresh ourselves. It is a time for us once again to be made new, to become "fresh"—pure, strong, vivid; and as Webster put it, to have our "original qualities unimpaired: as full of or renewed in vigor or readiness for action." In short, rest helps us become clearer, keener keepers of the covenant. Leisure can be a necessary fallow time that readies us for the next planting time. Rest fills us with vigor or readiness for action, for living out who we are as God's covenant people in our daily lives. This interval in the busy rhythm of our lives not only is good for us but also benefits others. Renewed for action and interaction, we are better able to listen and respond to the calling of the Spirit and the needs of those around us.

Our resting allows us to quiet ourselves so we can hear the Word—or words—of God. As our bodies and minds relax, our spirits quiet so we can hear God's still, small voice. When we rest, we are not only more receptive to God but to ourselves and others as well. We begin to know ourselves in a new way—untired, unhurried, unstressed, unmasked. Often when we are rested we deal more gently with ourselves and with others who are a part of our lives. We discover, and live, what really matters in life. Our minds, so carefully controlled and occupied most of the time, can wander freely and wonder at the marvels of the ordinary and the extraordinary: the deep orange and black of a Monarch butterfly, floating in an azure autumn sky; the welcome release of taut muscles in our shoulders and necks; the exquisite beauty of our love for those dear to us. Our resting can expand our imagination and spawn new creative possibilities for living, working, and being in the world. Our resting reminds us of the continual benevolence of God, the wonder of life, and the magnitude of joy that is possible when our lives are in rhythm with God's holy timing.

RESISTING OUR REST

B UT IF ALL THIS IS TRUE, why is it that we often fear or resist leisure? Why do we feel guilty when we are not working? Or, bringing the question uncomfortably close, why do *I* feel guilty when I am not working? Is it because I feel I am of value only when I am working? Is only my "doing," not my "being," worthwhile? Must I always be "productive"? Our drive to "produce" and to be "successful" may reveal our secret fears that we are inadequate, that we must "earn our keep" by "doing." Our rest time, our time of simply "being," reminds us of God's love for us: "You are precious in my eyes, and honored, and I love you" (Isaiah 43:4*a*, RSV).

The holy time of leisure confronts us with the uncomfortable possibility, even the unsettling reality, that we are loved for who we are—not for what we do. As we confront the reality of our value as human *beings* rather than as "human doings" (to use counselor-lecturer John Bradshaw's apt term), we are stretched beyond ourselves to knowing this is true of others as well. We are all precious; we are all loved for who we are. We are loved *because* we are.

So leisure, contrary to what we usually think, is not always comfortable. It is not always "easy living," but it is authentic living. It can be a prickly reminder that there is—as there always seems to be—one more thing to give over into the hands of God.

I remember a long-anticipated getaway with my husband that was quite a different experience than our time in the Grand Canyon. We ditched all the stress and obligations at work and home and drove north through the beautiful vineyards of Napa Valley to Calistoga, a little town nestled against the hills at the northern end of the valley. Calistoga is known for its mud and mineral baths. We splurged on "the works"—a mud bath followed by a whirlpool mineral bath, a cooling-down "blanket wrap" (where you are wrapped in a woolen blanket and left in a quiet, dim room with relaxing music while your body begins to cool down from the baths), and then a full-hour massage. It was wonderful! At the end, we were so relaxed we nearly had to be rolled back to our room, where we took a long, luxurious nap.

What we didn't anticipate, however, was the welling up of difficult feelings, fears, and issues that our normally tense and busy bodies held captive below the surface of consciousness. Why, we wondered, were we depressed when we were supposed to be having a good time? The relaxing of our bodies and the unburdening of our minds allowed us to hear the Spirit speaking to us. The leisure weekend became a spiritual retreat. I don't remember now the particular issues and challenges that confronted each of us, but our leisure time became prayer time. We had wanted to "escape" that weekend. Naively, we may have thought that we could avoid the tensions and stresses by leaving them behind—although this had rarely worked before. Instead we were offered a chance to move through them to a new place of understanding and insight; we were given an opportunity for deep peace instead of escape. Here, in quite a different way, *chronos* met—and became—*kairos*.

Kairos moments do not come only at "peak" times in our lives—the times of awe and wonder such as we experienced so powerfully in the Grand Canyon. Our Calistoga outing reminded us that even in our fear, blindness, ignorance, and times of feeling we don't "belong," God is present with us. Even the moments that feel devoid of God can be *kairos* moments that hold the seeds of courage, vision, and wisdom. In opening ourselves to the *kairos* of desolate, empty, lonely, or confusing times, we embrace the possibility of hope and new life rising within us, just as the welcome warmth of the morning sun spreads across the dark abyss of the Grand Canyon. The times we least expect are often fertile soil for the growth of the Spirit within us.

LEISURE'S INVITATION

OUR LEISURE invites us into the wholeness of life—into the joys and the sorrows, the delightful and the difficult. By stilling our minds, relaxing our bodies, and quieting our spirits, we can perhaps hear the words of God or the rustling of the Spirit in a new way. It is in this deep listening—taking into account our intellect, imagination, and all the qualities of the Hebrew "heart"—that we begin to hear the quiet, persistent cadence of our own holy timing.

Leisure sharpens our ability to tune into God's movement in every moment of our lives. When we listen without distractions, we become more aware of the Spirit's movement and our responses to it: a sense of well-being when a right decision has been made, a tight stomach that signals "Wait a minute" or "Be careful," or that scared but excited feeling when a new possibility opens up that we should pursue. This awareness and whole-being knowledge can be carried into our everyday lives, where we are often dulled by routine, frazzled by commitments, overwhelmed by stress. Listening to

God in leisure can help us to recognize God in the complexity of the rest of our lives. It may also help us when the cadence of our lives as a whole shifts, when we face new personal and spiritual challenges and opportunities such as a new job, significant changes in our personal lives, or retirement.

Our resting is not passive. It is an active covenanting with God where life may be lived fully, where each *chronos* moment is a potential *kairos*. At each stage of our lives, we face the challenge of living our covenant with God in all that we are and in all that we do. Some of the specific challenges may vary as we move through the years of childhood and adolescence, of work and family building, of retirement. But some challenges remain consistent through time: to know that we are loved for who we *are*; that God is present always; that each and every moment is both *chronos* and *kairos*; that all we encounter through the years—the winding trails and circuitous routes, the canyons and the high plateaus—is part of God's holy timing.

A little trail wisdom may help us all: Don't try to do it all at once. Take breaks. Build leisure into your journey. Carry plenty of water and drink even when you don't think you are thirsty, because, if neglected, the springs of life within us can dry up without our even knowing it. Eat some of your food now; you need the nourishment, and besides, your pack won't be as heavy at journey's end. Watch your step, but more important, stop often and enjoy the view. God is here. *Kairos* meets *chronos* now. Each moment is holy. All time is God's.

The Wild Geese

by Wendell Berry

Horseback on Sunday morning,
harvest over, we taste persimmon
and wild grape, sharp sweet
of summer's end. In time's maze
over the fall fields, we name names
that went west from here, names
that rest on graves. We open
a persimmon seed to find the tree
that stands in promise,
pale, in the seed's marrow.
Geese appear high over us,
pass, and the sky closes. Abandon,
as in love or sleep, holds
them to their way, clear,
in the ancient faith: what we need
is here. And we pray, not
for new earth or heaven, but to be
quiet in heart, and in eye
clear. What we need is here.

Discerning

The Extraordinary in the Ordinary

by Esther de Waal

A WOMAN KNEELS on the hard earth floor in her small hut in the Outer Hebrides, those harsh and inhospitable islands lying off the west coast of Scotland. She has already washed by splashing her face with three palmfuls of water (for this is in the nineteenth century), and as she did so she involved the name of the Trinity.

The palmful of the God of Life
The palmful of the Christ of Love
The palmful of the Spirit of Peace
Triune
Of grace.

Now at daybreak, and before the rest of her family is awake, she starts to do what is her daily chore: to stir into life the fire banked down the night before. Nothing could be more mundane, more prosaic, than this essential household obligation, performed day by day and year by year. Yet by her gestures and her words she transforms it and brings to the action a deeper meaning. As she works, she says aloud in a quiet crooning to herself:

I will kindle my fire this morning
In the presence of the holy
angels of heaven.

And as the embers burst into flame that fire becomes symbolic of the flame of love that we should keep burning for the whole family of humankind.

God, kindle thou in my heart within
A flame of love to my neighbor,
To my foe, to my friend,

to my kindred all,
To the brave, to the knave, to the thrall,
O Son of the loveliest Mary,
From the lowliest thing that liveth
To the name that is highest of all.

She has made the mundane the edge of glory. She has allowed the extraordinary to break in on the ordinary.

As "lifting" the peats had been the first duty of the day, so smothering, or "smooring," them is the last. This too becomes a symbolic action, one performed with a sense of a world beyond that with which she is dealing, so that as she handles the peats she is touching something that has its significance at a far deeper level. She divides the peats into three sections, one for each member of the Trinity. Then she lays down the first in the name of the God of Life, the second in the name of the God of Peace, and the third in the name of the God of Grace. She next covers the circle of peat with ashes, enough to subdue but not extinguish the fire, in the name of the Three of Light. The slightly raised heap in the center becomes the Hearth of the Three. When this is finished, she closes her eyes, stretches out her hand, and softly intones one of the many smooring prayers.

The Sacred Three
To save
To shield
To surround
The hearth
The house
The household
This eve
This night
And every night
Each single night.
Amen.

In doing all this, the woman has been following the Celtic practice handed down from generation to generation (and known to us because it was orally collected at the end of the last century). It was a practice in which ordinary people in their daily lives took the tasks that lay to hand but treated them sacramentally, as pointing to a greater reality that lay beyond them. It is an approach to life that we have been in danger of losing, this sense of allowing the extraordinary to break in on the ordinary. Perhaps it is something that we can rediscover, something which Celtic spirituality can give to us if we would let it renew our vision by teaching our eyes to see again, our ears to hear, our hands to handle. Then, like the disciples on the way to Emmaus who trudged along feeling so disconsolate and let down, we shall discover that Christ was in fact alongside us all the time. The fault lay with us, for we had simply failed to notice.

Celtic spirituality remains like some hidden spring, a source of life and renewal for us if we choose to turn to it and learn from it. Neglected, almost forgotten, driven to the edges of the church, it tells us of an approach to God wrought out of harsh lives, often lived in conditions of extreme poverty, discomfort, and relentless hard work (albeit in scenes of the greatest natural beauty) on the frontiers of Britain, in Wales and Scotland and Ireland. Whatever the place or the age, this spirituality has its underlying continuity. Whether the prayers or poems come from an eighth-century Irish hermit or from a nineteenth-century Scottish farmer, they are all rooted in the simple belief that in all the unspectacular immediacy of daily living—both in the natural world and in daily work—God is close at hand.

An eighth-century hermit in Ireland rejoices in the presence of God as he experiences it in his solitude, and as, in that solitude and silence, the birds and the wild creatures speak to him of his Creator.

I have a hut in a wood: only my Lord knows it. An ash tree closes it on one side and a hazel like a great tree on the other.

A tree of apples of great bounty like a mansion sout: a pretty bush, thick as a fist, of small hazel nuts, branching and green.

The sound of the wind against a branching wood, grey cloud, riverfalls, the cry of the swan, delightful music!

Beautiful are the pines which make music for me unhindered: through Christ I am no worse off at any time than you.

*Though you relish that which you enjoy exceeding all
wealth, I am content with that which is given me by
my gentle Christ.*

Equally, a woman milking her cow or a man driving his flocks
to the pastures knows that God, Mary, and the saints are there close
beside in whatever they are doing. For as well as this sense of God's
immanence in creation, God's presence is even more keenly felt in
the daily round of human tasks and at the most important junctures
of life. Thus, getting up, washing, making the fire, milking and
weaving, fishing and farming, going to bed, as well as birth and
death, become occasions for recognizing the proximity of God. All
these things can be seen at two levels—as practical occasions to be
dealt with, but simultaneously as signs of the all-encompassing mystery of God. As he set out for his day's work, a man would sing or
intone a song (which was also a prayer, the distinction would seem
absurd and irrelevant) that assumed that God was there walking
beside him.

*My walk this day with God
My walk this day with Christ
My walk this day with Spirit
The Threefold all-kindly
Ho! Ho! Ho! the Threefold all-kindly.*

*My shielding this day from ill,
My shielding this night from harm,
Ho! Ho! Both my soul and my body,
Be by Father, by Son, by Holy Spirit,
By Father, by Son, by Holy Spirit.*

*Be the Father shielding me,
Be the Son shielding me,
Be the Spirit shielding me,
As Three and as One:
Ho! Ho! Ho! As Three and as One.*

The sense of walking with God is so vivid and so immediate
and carries such a feeling of security and happiness that he is actually laughing to himself as he goes along.

This strong sense of companionship sometimes seems to mean
that God is actively involved in the work itself. This was particu-

larly true, of course, for the herdsman who knew that the King of
Shepherds would watch over both shepherds and sheep as God had
always done. So when talking to the animals they would remind
them of this:

> Be the herding of God the Son
> about your feet,
> Safe and whole may ye home return.

Time and again we find examples like this in which the barriers between past and present, between humans and animals, and
above all between God and the world of God's creating, are crossed
so totally that our twentieth-century rational minds are left bewil-
dered. For a man will remind his cows of that terrible day when
Christ was lost in the temple, Christ the Herdsman, and how all
the cows had suffered then throughout that long night until he was
found again.

> The night the Herdsman was out
> No shackle went on a cow
> Lowing ceased not from the mouth of calf
> Wailing the Herdsman of the flock
> Wailing the Herdsman of the flock.

For in this Celtic world the barriers that we know (and perhaps that we have built up for ourselves and still quite unconsciously
continue to keep in good repair) simply do not exist. There seems
to be no distinction between time and eternity, between heaven
and earth, between the secular and the sacred, between the people
now on earth and the saints in heaven—between the ordinary and
the extraordinary.

Thus a woman will find it entirely natural to turn to the saints
to ask them to help her in her milking by holding the cow for her.

> Come, Mary, and milk my cow,
> Come, Bride, and encompass her,
> Come, Columba, the benign,
> And twine thine arms around my cow.

> Come, Mary Virgin, to my cow,
> Come, great Bride, the beauteous,
> Come, thou milkmaid of Jesus Christ,
> And place thine arms beneath my cow.

When the time comes for her to start to make the butter, she counts on this same partnership as she churns the milk, and she has an added sense of urgency about the work since she is aware of Jesus and some of the disciples outside impatiently waiting for some of her baking spread with fresh butter.

> *Come, thou Brigit, handmaid calm*
> *Hasten the butter on the cream;*
> *Seest thou impatient Peter yonder*
> *Waiting the buttered bannock white and*
> *yellow.*

> *Come, thou Mary Mother mild,*
> *Hasten the butter on the cream;*
> *Seest thou Paul and John and Jesus*
> *Waiting the gracious butter yonder.*

At the end of the day, when at last the time comes to go to bed, it is entirely natural that this sense of companionship should continue through the hours of sleeping.

> *With God will I lie down this night*
> *And God will be lying down with me.*
> *With Christ will I lie down this night*
> *And Christ will be lying down with me.*

> *With Spirit I lie down this night*
> *The Spirit will lie down with me;*
> *God, Christ, and Spirit Three*
> *Be they all down-lying with me.*

Nothing could be more tender, secure, and totally unself-conscious than these bed-blessings. Another addressed to the Trinity concludes:

> *I will lie down this night with*
> *the Three of my love,*
> *And the Three of my love will lie down*
> *with me.*

As we read these words we can glimpse that experience of the presence of God that has been the reality of these people's lives ever since the start of the day. It is a gift that they have and that they bring to us, of taking this moment, this place, this happening as the time and place for an encounter with God. So God meets us where we are, at home, at work, in the daily, in the ordinary.

The Celtic approach to God opens up a world in which nothing is too common to be exalted and nothing is so exalted that it cannot be made common. Heaven lies "a foot and a half above the height of a man" says an old Kerry-woman in the southwest of Ireland today, and for her this poem, which originated in the tenth or eleventh century, still expresses her own feelings about how good it would be to see "the men of Heaven" enjoying a cheerful drinking session in her own home.

I would like to have the men of Heaven
In my own house;
With vats of good cheer
Laid out for them.

I would like to have the three Marys,
Their fame is so great.
I would like people
From every corner of Heaven.

I would like them to be cheerful
In their drinking.
I would like to have Jesus too
Here amongst them.

I would like a great lake of beer
For the King of Kings.
I would like to be watching
Heaven's family
Drinking it through all eternity.

As we watch these people and listen to them, it is tempting to put the blame for our own lack of everyday piety on a society in which time has been conquered and technology determines the way we run our lives. But the loss ultimately lies within ourselves. Ironically, when travel and the media have blown all horizons wide open, our own inner horizons seem to have become narrower and our vision contracted. How can we find again the seeing eye and the feeling touch? Essentially this is a spirituality that asks of us a return to a greater awareness (and here, of course, it has much in common with the approach to God of many other peoples). Thomas Merton taught us much about perception washed clear by contemplative prayer. But for most of us, his base in the hermitage at Gethsemane is a far cry from the lives that we are actually leading. What the Celtic understanding brings us is the chance to break down the barrier between the active and the contemplative life and instead to make the busy, boring, relentless daily life tasks the basis for continuous praying and for finding the presence of God. What a waste it is to be surrounded by heaven, by a sky "made white by angels' wings," and to be unaware of it. Perhaps the first step is that we really should want to unearth God in our midst. For letting heaven break through will not happen automatically. It lies to hand, but it needs a determination on our part to find it. Yet, if we can rediscover this vision, then we too may be able to transform what lies to hand, let the mundane become the edge of glory, and find the extraordinary in the ordinary.

The Boundaries of Our Habitation

by John W. Vannorsdall

*And [God] made from one every nation of [humankind] to live
on all the face of the earth, having determined allotted periods and
the boundaries of their habitation, that they should seek God, in
the hope that they might feel after him and find him. Yet he is not
far from each one of us.*

—Acts 17:26-27, RSV

A FEW MONTHS AGO my wife and I received a letter from
an old friend who then headed the Boston City Mission.
She said that it was the hardest job she had ever had, "an evil
time for reminding people about their stewardship toward their sisters and brothers who are poor. Those who once contributed are
hunkered down, as their own lives become more uncertain. In the
meantime, the problems of the poor continue to mount in dramatic
proportions, creating quiet desperation."

And then, as though recalling that not all desperation was quiet,
she described an incident in which a woman came to see a member of the staff, seeking help—a woman obviously disturbed.
Halfway through the conversation, the woman paused, reached into
her purse, and took out a whistle, and, to quote our friend, "she just
blew the hell out of it."

"This is a paradigm for my life," she wrote. "Whistle blowing
everywhere—staff, clients, suburban folks wide-eyed about city
challenges, pastors clinging white-knuckled to ministry." And then
these concluding words. "So far, I still get up in the morning, surrounded by some incredible confidence of God with me."

Underlying this letter is one of the reversals that is central to
the gospel, the jarring shift from what we expect to what God pro-
poses. A youngster sees the world differently when hanging by the
knees from the limb of a tree, and Christians see the world differently through the eyes of Christ. In this perspective, a graveyard

135

becomes a place of celebration, and we don't think it strange that the last become first or the meek inherit the earth. So what underlies the letter from Boston is another of these changed perspectives, one that I don't fully understand, but that has something to do with God in the midst of blowing whistles. It is a reversal at least implied in the sermon that Paul gave in Athens.

Said Paul to those who gathered around him, "[God] made from one every nation of [humankind] to live on all the face of the earth, having determined allotted periods and the boundaries of their habitation." In part, Paul, is quoting from Psalm 74 which reads, "Thou hast fixed all the bounds of the earth; thou hast made summer and winter" (v. 17, RSV). The seasons of our lives, the boundaries of our habitation.

And the reversal which the text suggests, and to that I invite your curiosity, is to understand the limitations of seasons and the boundaries of our habitation as gifts of God, rather than the judgment of God. To see the passage of time—the boundaries of locality and the constant blowing of whistles—as the geography within which God is to be sought, within which God, in search of us, chose to be.

What does this mean? It means that as much as we may wish to be ubiquitous, everywhere proclaiming the gospel and healing the wounds of the world, most of us will instead be limited, at least for the present, to Caribou, Maine, or Wehauken, New Jersey, or wherever our particular community is located. It means that our ministry will be incarnate in time, where one by one, face by face, word by word, the people of God will take flesh and become our neighbors.

Here, within the boundaries of our habitation, we will experience summer's drought and the winter of our discontent. This is where the clocks do their work: thin our hair, wrinkle our face, waste our muscles, mock our best laid plans, laugh at our good intentions, and torment us with anniversaries. The God-appointed seasons of our lives, the boundaries of our habitation. To the world, these are the enemies of human life and freedom. But to us, who live by the reversals of God, time and geography are the God-furnished setting within which God comes in search of us.

Each of us has an invisible whistle that we take out from time to time and "just blow the hell out of." We have limitations that drive us to desperation. Our minds are not quick enough, so we are defeated in conversations. We grew up reticent, and so now visitation is painful. We are too tall, too short. We are such dreamers that we can't change a tire. We are so methodical that we see no visions.

Besides all this, we are called to minister in a world so filled with potholes that the front end is always out of line. A world where too many are shot, too many are in prison, too many babies die, and too many jokes are sick.

But this is the room and we are the people that God has furnished for ministry, and it should be marvelous in our eyes. If we are not baptized into this boundaried death, we are not baptized into Christ. If this is not the place where The Table is spread, then our eating and drinking is just another meal on our way to nowhere. If we can't hear the whistles blowing, we have no ears for God's calling Adam.

In this reversed way of seeing the world, the thief who breaks in and steals from us is not only a thief but also a challenge to our material attachments. In this reversed way of seeing, the shortness of time not only threatens but also gives focus, demanding that we decide what really matters. In this reversed way of seeing, the person who says no to our dreams not only drains the day of pleasure but is also critic to our agenda and caution to our ambitions. The tiredness of our body, the shortcomings of our frame or personality, are not only a nail in our shoe but also the invitation to sit down, to be quiet, and to hear the praise and promise of God.

The racism in and around us, the anger in and around us, the desperation in and around us, all are despised boundaries of our habitation, but they are also the garden within which our Lord walks in the cool of the day, the bed where we sleep and rise. This is the only place where the great words—*joy, peace, freedom, salvation*—make any sense. Only in a blowing-whistles cemetery does resurrection have any meaning.

A few weeks ago I received a letter from a man I've never met. He shared his story—a church home, growing away from church, college and medical school and then to Vietnam as a battalion surgeon, a place where he grew in cynicism.

What he wanted to report was that literally in the midst of the rice paddies, under the most inhuman circumstances, the sounds and smells of war, he heard on his small portable radio what he called the one sane voice, the words of a radio preacher.

This one voice was not enough to stand against the blood, but what he had heard in the rice paddies, he heard again at the baptism of his daughter, and he was drawn into the hearing of the Word and the life of the congregation. He will never be the same, never without the scars of Vietnam. Nevertheless, he wrote, "It is as if I have been swept up by, and become captive to, the wonderful message of God's grace."

Of all the surprising reversals in the New Testament, the hardest for many of us is to see the seasons of our lives and the boundaries of our habitation themselves as God's gift of locality, to understand that the stuff and nonsense of everyday is the medium within which Christ lived, died, and was raised. It is within the sound of blowing whistles that we still get up in the morning, surrounded by some incredible confidence that God is with us. It is within the rice paddies of the dying that the wind-borne grace of God, gently blowing through the seasons of our lives and the boundaries of our habitation, becomes our salvation.

Hints, Signs, *and* Showings

THE COMPASSION OF GOD

by Wendy M. Wright

To presume to speak of the nature of God, even of a
quality of God's nature such as compassion, is a bold under-
taking. To presume to know something of ultimate mystery, one must also be aware of all that one does not know.

Yet there are hints. There are signs and showings. We have our
own experience; we have the witness and reflection of our faith
communities; we have the words of scripture and the lives of the
holy men and women of our tradition. We have the hints, the signs,
and the showings.

GREATER THAN YOUR OWN ACCUSING HEART

It is fall of 1974. I am sitting curled up in an overstuffed
armchair in the guest room of a comfortable, vintage-1920s
retreat house in the isolated foothills of Southern California.
The generous windows frame an olive green and burnt sienna landscape flecked with the grays of the thick, dry underbrush, the euca-
lyptus and scrub oak. The bright gold of the sun is turning to purple in the crevices of the hills. From a portable tape recorder on
the bed to my left, the voice of a local Franciscan priest is com-
menting on the first letter of John (3:20).

It has been a tiresome pilgrimage to this remote and quiet
moment. Divorce, relocation, returning to school, depression, bouts
of meaninglessness, painful self-examination have gutted me empty.
I identify with the voiceless, purposeless presence of the trees outside. The priest's voice suddenly comes into the center of consciousness. "God is greater than your own accusing heart," he
quotes. Then he elaborates on this phrase, returning to it again.
"God is greater than your own accusing heart."

In the gutted center of my consciousness the phrase takes root. I see—no, I experience—the truth that my pain, my confusion, my sense of failure is surrounded and embraced by a compassionate presence *greater* than myself. It is *my* heart, not God's that continues to offer accusation, that mercilessly judges. God steps forth as loving arms; as the patient, longing heart of a mother aching to gather her children in and hold them, to speak wordlessly with the tender pressure of hand and breast of their beauty, dignity, and belovedness.

I begin to know the compassion of God. Greater and more generous than our own knowing, our own evaluations, our own tidy and fearful categorizations, it pursues and overtakes us like a fretful mother or a concerned father. It follows us and finds us wherever we are.

I love the biblical narrative of Jonah because it tells the story of such a God, a God who so loved the people of Nineveh that a would-not-be prophet was hounded down to warn them of the disastrous consequences of their present attitudes. This was a God who ached to have them come back home, so tried to speak to them through Jonah. However, Jonah was reluctant and tried to run away. But God ran after Jonah. God followed Jonah to the bottom of the sea, into the belly of a sea creature, the seemingly most remote of spots, and took Jonah, as it were by the ear, and sent him off on God's errand of mercy. Having heard God's message, the Ninevites responded to God's desire. They turned their hearts homeward and were joyously welcomed back.

I love the story because God's compassion was greater than both the ignorance of the Ninevites and the arrogance of Jonah. Jonah, righteous man that he was, was as skeptical and as judgmental as most of us are prone to be. He resented God's forgiveness of the prodigal Ninevites, resented that they, who were so unworthy, should be spared. Yet God's compassion was greater than Jonah's accusing heart. It stretched wider and deeper than he or we can conceive. Divine compassion follows us into the hidden valley of our arrogance and into the ignorance of our faithless, fragmented lives. It follows and finds us.

DESIRING OUR DESIRE

I T I S A T Y P I C A L D A Y in mid-February or March in Santa Barbara sometime in the last half of the seventies. It is a scene that has repeated itself over and over again. I am in the parking lot of the university where I am attending graduate school, saying goodbye for the day to my major professor, who is also my friend and a fellow traveler on the journey home to God. We rehearse the same old joke, "Let's get away from this place. Let's skip out and drive up the coast to Buellton for pea soup." (Buellton is a community noted solely for being the home of a soup manufacturing company that decorates its labels with two funny Abbott and Costello type chefs named "Hap-pea" and "Split-pea.") Then we laugh and say that when we finally get around to doing that, the eschaton will have arrived. And we head to our respective homes and families.

The two of us have been repeating this same ritual for years. Somehow, in its own peculiar way, it expresses the shared love, the religious longings, the playful humor that characterize our friendship. It is hard to part. While other persons may know each of us more intimately (his wife and my husband especially), there is a special kind of knowing that we share. Somehow we recognize in each other the deep, inarticulate longing of the heart, the desire for God.

Who is this man to me? He is mentor, coworker, colleague. But more than that he is someone whose ardent searching for God matches my own. He is someone who intuits what my life wants to become and who prepares the environment, through his own caring enthusiasm, for that becoming to occur. He is there when I—the unchurched one—stand, awestruck and perplexed, in front of the old mission church saying, "I belong here." And he knows what I mean. He is there, understanding, when I venture into the cloister of the monastic community of the Poor Clares and breathe in the silence as though it were the first air I have ever breathed. He is there at the Trappistine monastery, making arrangements for a student of his (me) to take an extended retreat. He sends me a note saying that on the altar that day there was one red rose because he knows of my devotion to Mary whose symbol is the rose. He is there, gently challenging me when I seem to be straying from the path home. He enables me to trust my passion for God. And I, in my own very different way, do the same for him.

God's life grows in us through the tender nurturance of other people. Our passion for God is fired by that same passion met in the hearts of our fellow travelers and friends. We learn our longing for God through our longing for each other. But always our mutual longing must be aware of our shared and greater passion for God. It must always remember not to close in on itself but remain empty-handed, expectant, not clinging.

Douglas Steere, the wonderful Quaker writer, in an essay entitled "On Listening to Another" suggests something of the passionate equality of the exchange between friends.

141

> *Have you ever sat with a friend when in the course of an easy and pleasant conversation the talk took a new turn and you both listened avidly to the other and to something that was emerging in your visit? You found yourselves saying things that astonished you and finally you stopped talking and there was an immense naturalness about the long silent pause that followed. In the silent interval you were possessed by what you had discovered together. If that has happened to you, you know that when you came up out of such an experience, there is a memory of rapture and a feeling in the heart of having touched holy ground.*[1]

I echo his insight and add that the capacity for the "feeling in the heart" elicited in the passionate interchange between friends is given to us by our passionate God. Through our passion for one another we are transformed into the image and likeness of our passionate, compassionate God. God desires our mutual desire. Through it we find our way home.

SUFFERING WITH US

IT IS LATE SUMMER OF 1983. I am standing over the changing table, removing a damp diaper from our newborn daughter's bottom. The cheerful clown mobile suspended above our heads is circling to what has become, to my ears, a melancholy tune. For weeks now I have wakened between three and four in the morning to the sound of weeping. Not to my infant or preschool daughter's cries but to what I can only describe as the weeping of the world. Sometimes it is distant and eerie, a vaguely troubling presence that can, with a minimum of effort, be explained away. Other times it is fully audible, the cacophony of crying separating itself into distinct voices, each one carrying with it a full emotional burden. The terror and suffering that lies behind each voice slaps me like a wave and drags at my heart with the vigor of its undertow. There is nowhere I can go. Even in the sunlight of these simple child-tending times, the crying surfaces. The dark experience of the night impinges on my days. I feel like I'm going mad. I look down at the sweet face of my baby and see it mutate into the disfigured face of a napalmed child.

For months I wander around in this waking nightmare. No, it

---

[1] Douglas V. Steere, *Gleanings: A Random Harvest* (Nashville, TN: Upper Room, 1986), p. 73.

is not simply my imagination. These are, I know, truly the voices of my sisters and brothers. How do I respond? What can I do? What is the weeping asking of me? My life goes on as usual: walk our kindergartner to school in the morning, put the baby down for a nap midmorning and spend the brief time reading, pick up our kindergartner at noon, do lunch, go grocery shopping or to the laundromat. So goes the busy, domestic cycle. But underneath, the weeping continues, clouding the calm surface of my life. As my birthday approaches, I learn that a notable retreat director is to give a day of reflection at a nearby parish church. It is not my usual circle, but I jump at the chance to spend my special day in a contemplative mode.

I cannot say that I remember what that Jesuit priest spoke about. But I do remember sitting quietly in the pews of an ornate Spanish colonial-style church in the midst of well-heeled, well-dressed matrons, trying to fight off the urge to clap my hands over my ears and scream aloud, "Stop it! Stop it! I can't stand it anymore!" Waves of fear and anguish in the wake of the weeping washed relentlessly over my consciousness.

And then suddenly it all became very still and very clear. And I saw him. I saw the face of the crucified God. And I knew that he was with the weeping. I knew that the weeping was his weeping and that the weeping ones were he. And that there was no separation between our suffering and God's suffering. The wonderful phrase from Julian of Norwich's *Showings*, "Betwixt God and ourselves there is no between," took on a luminous quality.

I knew that I had seen the face of God. It was an appearance of the face that I had seen depicted countless times outside of myself. But it was not an appearance I had loved nor known in an intimate way. The faces of God I had loved were the gentle healer, the tender shepherd, and the generous, forgiving mother. Here was the same face, but now it was contorted with suffering. Creased in its pain-wracked folds were all the unspeakable and unbearable experiences of humankind.

I am not sure what happened there in that ornate Spanish church among those poised and scented matrons, but I know that I experienced a deep outflowing of love, a love so powerful that the terror and the weeping were enveloped in its path. God is *with* us. God suffers *with* us. God is *with* our passion. Our passion, our suffering, is God's own.

GIVING NEW BIRTH

IT IS THE MIDDLE OF THE NIGHT, JUNE 28, 1985. I am standing awkwardly leaning over the side of a hospital bed in the labor room at Brigham and Women's Hospital in Boston. My husband is sitting in an armchair across the room looking at me questioningly. I have been in and out of labor for a couple of days now, and they have just told us to go back home. It could be a long time before this third baby decides to arrive on the scene. But I am in considerable pain. Something feels wrong to me even though I am not at all dilated.

With two previous cesarean sections, one preceded by a long, debilitating labor, I have a hope that we might have this child by a normal delivery. But I have misgivings as well. I am assured by the medical personnel at this high tech institution that the newest studies indicate no increased chance of uterine rupture after repeated cesareans (especially if the incision is lateral, as is mine). I don't like the thought of major surgery again. The recovery is too hard, and there are risks in any surgical procedure. But everything is so slow. And there is so much curiously situated pain. I try to compare it to the early labor of the other two times. A sense of foreboding, of something not right, fills me. I try to chase it away.

I bide my time. I am afraid to go home. But I certainly do not want to hang around this place racking up costs for another few days. I am aware once more of the terrible, unretractable quality of childbirth. There is no way to postpone, no way to opt out, no way to change your mind now. Right through the middle. That's the only direction to go. It is the most heightened sense of reality I know.

Several hours go by while I wait to see if the contractions become productive. They certainly are draining my energy, pulling me into a pit of pain that continues to trouble me. A cheery young obstetrician pops in to see me and encourages us to go home. "What if there is a rupture?" I inquire. "Rupture? Oh, that happens only once in a hundred cases." He looks at me with a knowing smile, "That won't happen to you."

I am torn about going. Something tells me this is it, whatever *it* is. Then the contractions really do pick up, although they continue to be only mildly productive. The personnel agree I probably should stay here although it looks like it's going to be a long hard wait. Hours inch by. Then, what is it that tells me? I don't know. I tell my husband I am opting for another cesarean. It is not working. Something is wrong. "But you're doing so well," he says. "Remember how awful the surgery was before. You wanted to avoid that this time." "I know," I say, "but I'm completely exhausted already. And I don't know why, but I have this terrible feeling." The doctor is summoned, and it is agreed that another section should be performed.

As I wait to be prepared for surgery a nurse rushes in. I am told that there will be a delay because another woman who seemed to be having a normal delivery was suddenly in distress. The entire night surgical team was tied up, as was the operating room. More hours creep by. By this time I am in great distress and the peculiar sense of foreboding has increased. It is made more surreal by the nearby drama of survival. Stray attendants periodically stick their heads in to check on me and report on the gravity of the struggle going on down the hall: every available surgeon, anesthesiologist, and nurse seems to be involved trying to save the unknown woman's life. Several times it is reported that her condition has stabilized and then she begins hemorrhaging again.

The hours drag by. The unproductive, relentless contractions have sucked up whatever energy I still have left. I'm not sure at this point that I can face major surgery. But there seems to be nowhere else to go. The pain is so omnipresent that it engulfs all other awareness. Finally, the other woman's dark night has turned to dawn, and I am told they are preparing the room. I dread the impending intrusion on my body but dread some other unknown even more. Where will I anchor myself interiorly for this passage? Because I insist on being awake for the delivery (as I was with my other two children), I need somehow to find a firm psychic footing.

On my back, being rolled down a corridor, my physical energy is so deeply eroded I cannot lift my head or raise an arm to help the attendants lift me. Then I call them forth, one by one, the names of the persons whose love has given me life: parents, husband, children, friends, mentors, students. One by one their presences follow the calling of their names. Like a swiftly gathering circle of dancers that surround me, the unique dynamics of each love envelops me as it joins the circle: the entire history of each relationship collapsed into one felt presence. They hover over me, the love we have shared burning in all its intensity, holding me, cradling me, carrying me through the narrow passage I am entering.

Time blurs, is both infinite and of no duration. The bright lights of the operating room. The hovering presences. The worried eyes of my husband to my left that try to smile down at me above the surgical mask he has donned. At one point I am sickened by the anesthesia and vomit helplessly onto my face and hair. The surgeon who has been called in to do the surgery, a younger woman with caring, maternal eyes, looks at me over the cloth that shields me from the sight of the instruments slicing through my flesh. "You made the right decision," she says somewhat shakily. "The uterine scar is pulled paper thin. It's barely hanging together. You wouldn't have had much time left."

Then they bring forth my son, a gasping, beautiful new life, and hold him close for me to touch. The best I can do is slightly turn my head so they run his tender naked body against my cheek, and I speak his name for the first time. My husband's shaken voice reaches out to me. "Thank you for my son. I know how much this has cost."

Later, in my hospital room, the slender body of my new baby swaddled close in bed with me, I begin to realize what has happened. A vital, life-giving part of myself, in fact *the* life-giving organ, has been used up, given away in giving new life. I begin to mourn. Tears well up, first at the sense of loss, then at the sense of the "rightness" of the loss. The knowledge that we are here to give life to one another and that the giving comes from the very substance of our own being becomes real to me in a new way. The narrow passageway through dying, in this case the proximity of probable physical death and the reality of the exhaustion of the most intimate generative part of myself, heightens the meaning of the newness lying next to me.

I call up my spiritual director and weep into the phone, words about giving away and being used up and being spent and in all that bringing forth newness, my dying becoming new birth. He listens and comments simply, "I feel like I am in the presence of the paschal mystery." Yes. I know.

Something of God's compassion became real to me in this experience. For I now can never move through the cycle of Holy Week and Easter without reflecting on the process of birthing, which is a self-gift so that new life might come into its own. For God so loved the world that God labored and gave of Herself, that through the blood and the waters of her birthing, we would be given new life. The cross is the compassionate self-gift of God, our Mother, whose own body became the crucible through which all humankind and creation itself receives the gasping, vibrant energy of new life.

Closely linked to this loving mystery of death and dying is the loving mystery of the circle of hovering presences that surrounded me in my passage through death to life. Each of those loves, those relationships, participates in the same mystery: the reciprocal giving and receiving, the shared dance of small dyings that become another's rising, and another's dyings that become one's own rising. We are at one and the same time one another's mothers and one another's midwives, welcoming the vital, creative newness that our loving creates.

THE FULLNESS OF ALL THINGS

IT IS A CHILLY MONDAY AFTERNOON IN WINTER, 1990. I am sitting, a Bible opened on my lap, in my living room in Omaha with two other women whose names are Sheila and, today, Sarah (other Mondays Sheila has brought different companions whose names I cannot recall). They are Jehovah's Witnesses, and they have been coming here to do "Bible study," as they call it, for several weeks. My family has looked askance at this. "Jenny's mother just shuts the door on these people," my elder daughter reports. "What are they going to say in the theology department when you start coming into class and teaching that Armageddon is near?" my husband teases. My two youngest just resent the intrusion and run into the room breaking into our discussion periodically with doleful tales about so-and-so's taking someone else's toy.

I must admit that my fascination with these women and their aggressive missionary faith perplexes me as well. In part it is explainable by the fact that I find all religious traditions fascinating and that whenever I have had the chance I have visited and been energized by Sikh ashrams, Vedanta temples, Tibetan Buddhist meditation sessions, Greek Orthodox Easter vigils, and Pentecostal meetings.

But another part of my fascination with Sheila and her cohorts is with the imagery that animates their religiosity. They hand me little pamphlets at the end of our sessions that depict, in graphic fashion, the eschatological visions of Isaiah. People of different races, dressed in different ethnic costumes, embrace joyfully. Men, women, and children are shown playing together in an earthly garden of great beauty. Fountains flow with pure water. Fruits and flowers spring up from green meadows. Animals roam unhindered and unharming through waving fields of grain. Pictured there is the Witnesses' version of the terrestrial kingdom of God promised by the prophets. The pamphlets invite the reader to consider the apocalyptic signs of the times that point to the proximity of the advent of this kingdom and to become one of the small remnant of true followers of Jehovah who are alerting all humankind to the coming end of all governments as we know them and with that the end of war, famine, disease, and death.

There is nothing insipid or bizarre about these pictures. In fact, they tug at the deepest springs of the human heart, inviting our participation, fueling our most powerful longings. It is these images, which the rest of the Christian world shares but which are, for the most part, only on the margins of religious consciousness, that arrest my attention. That these images so completely capture the loyalty and imagination of the Witnesses challenges me. These women's every waking moment is energized by a passion for the fullness of things. They live the eschatological hope with joyful self-abandon. This must be rather like what the early Christians must have experienced, traipsing around, tugging at the sleeves of a preoccupied populace: "Look, look! Look at the hope to which we are called! Look at the fullness of things promised by our God!"

It is true that there is a theological gulf between myself and my visitors that is hard to cross. But I love the way in which their hearts are open to radical hope. It seems to me even more astonishing than the vigorous hope for a world renewed that fires Christian advocates of social justice because it points beyond human hope to the hope of God. For the Witnesses it is not we, through our own efforts, who bring about or help God bring about the fullness of things. It is God who does it.

While I would hesitate on moral grounds, simply to "leave all that up to God," the Witnesses have brought God's compassion into focus for me. The eschatological fervor that they bring to my doorway does jog me out of complacency. Look, look! Look at the hope to which we are called! Look at the fullness of things promised by our God! Like a bowstring pulled taut and held ready to propel the arrow to its mark, this passion of theirs for the fullness of things propels my attention to our compassionate God whose beneficence is imaged in the sensual, fragrant language of the scriptures.

Through the words of our holy books we are imaginatively invited into a reality that confounds our realism and our cynicism. The fullness of all things. The fruition of our most earnest dreaming. Our hearts are created to enjoy these, our minds to comprehend such dreams. Joy unbounded. Love so wide and generous it becomes rapture. Abundance so overflowing it splits like a ripe fig and gushes forth like a geyser. Justice so sure, all creatures join hand

and paw to dance its sweetness. God's compassion is imaged for us in the lush, greening prophecies of Isaiah and in Jesus' impassioned preaching of the kingdom.

Who or what is this God whose compassion offers and invites us to such a hope that it takes our breath away? We have hints, signs, and showings. May we take them to heart.

The Peace *that* Is Not *of* This World

by Henri J. M. Nouwen

Peace I bequeath to you, my own peace I give you, a peace the world cannot give, this is my gift to you.

—John 14:27, JB

URING THE PAST TWO YEARS I moved from Harvard to Daybreak; that is, from an institution for the best and the brightest to a community for mentally handicapped people. Daybreak, close to Toronto, is part of an international federation of communities called l'Arche—the Ark—where mentally handicapped men and women and their assistants try to live together in the spirit of the Beatitudes. I live in a house with six handicapped people and four assistants. None of the assistants is specially trained to work with people with mental handicaps, but we receive all the help we need from doctors, psychiatrists, behavioral management people, social workers, and physiotherapists in town. When there are no special crises we live together as a family, gradually forgetting who is handicapped and who is not. We are simply John, Bill, Trevor, Raymond, Adam, Rose, Steve, Jane, Naomi, and Henri. All have our gifts, our struggles, our strengths and weaknesses. We eat together, play together, pray together, and go out together. We all have our own preferences in terms of work, food, and movies; and we all have our problems in getting along with someone in the house, whether handicapped or not. We laugh a lot. We cry a lot too. Sometimes both at the same time. Every morning when I say, "Good morning, Raymond," he says, "I am not awake yet. Saying good morning to everyone each day is unreal." Christmas Eve Trevor wrapped marshmallows in silver paper as peace gifts for everyone, and at the Christmas dinner he climbed on a chair, lifted his glass, and said, "Ladies and gentlemen, this is not a celebration, this is Christmas." When one of the men speaking on the phone with someone was bothered by the cigarette smoke of an assistant, he yelled angrily, "Stop smoking; I can't hear." And every guest who comes for dinner is received by Bill with the question, "Hey, tell me, what is a turkey in suspense?" When the newcomer confesses ignorance, Bill, with a big grin on his face, says, "I will tell you tomorrow." And then he starts laughing so loud that the visitor has to laugh with him whether he finds the joke funny or not so funny.

That is l'Arche; that is Daybreak; that is the family of ten I am living with day in and day out. What can life in this family of a few poor people reveal about the peace of Christ for which we are searching? Let me tell you the story of Adam, one of the ten people in our home, and let him become the silent spokesman for the peace that is not of this world.

Never having worked with handicapped people, I was not only apprehensive but even afraid to enter this unfamiliar world. This fear did not lessen when I was invited to work directly with Adam. Adam is the weakest person of our family. He is a twenty-five-year-old man who cannot speak, cannot dress or undress himself, cannot walk alone or eat without much help. He does not cry, or laugh, and only occasionally makes eye contact. His back is distorted and his arm and leg movements are very twisted. He suffers from severe epilepsy and, notwithstanding heavy medication, there are few days without grand-mal seizures. Sometimes, as he grows suddenly rigid, he utters a howling groan, and on a few occasions I saw a big tear coming down his cheek. It takes me about an hour and a half to wake Adam up, give him his medication, undress him, carry him into his bath, wash him, shave him, clean his teeth, dress him, walk him to the kitchen, give him his breakfast, put him in his wheelchair, and bring him to the place where he spends most of the day with different therapeutic exercises. When a grand-mal seizure occurs during this sequence of activities, much more time is needed, and often he has to return to sleep to regain some of the energy spent during such a seizure.

I tell you all of this not to give you a nursing report but to share with you something quite intimate. After a month of working this way with Adam, something started to happen to me that never happened to me before. This deeply handicapped young man, who by many outsiders is considered a vegetable, a distortion of humanity, a useless animal-like creature who should not have been allowed to be born, started to become my dearest companion. As my fears gradually decreased, a love started to emerge in me so full of tenderness and affection that most of my other tasks seemed boring and superficial compared with the hours spent with Adam. Out of this broken body and broken mind emerged a most beautiful human being offering me a greater gift than I would ever be able to offer him.

It is hard to me to find adequate words for this experience, but somehow Adam revealed to me who he was and who I was and how we can love each other. As I carried his naked body into the water, made big waves to let the water run fast around his chest and neck, rubbed noses with him, and told him all sorts of stories about him and me, I knew that two friends were communicating far beyond the realm of thought or emotion. Deep speaks to deep, spirit speaks to spirit, heart speaks to heart. I started to realize that there was a mutuality of love not based on shared knowledge or shared feelings but on a shared humanity. The longer I stayed with Adam, the more clearly I started to see him as my gentle teacher, teaching me what no book, school, or professor ever could have taught me.

Am I romanticizing, making something beautiful out of something ugly, projecting my hidden need to be a father on this deeply retarded man, spiritualizing what in essence is a shameful human condition that needs to be prevented at all costs? I am enough of a psychologically trained intellectual to raise these questions. Recently, as I was writing this article, Adam's parents came for a visit. I asked them, "Tell me, during all the years you had Adam in your home, what did he give you?" His father smiled and said without a moment of hesitation, "He brought us peace...he is our peacemaker...our son of peace."

Let me, then, tell you about Adam's peace, a peace which the world cannot give. I am moved by the simple fact that probably the most important task I have is to give words to the peace of one who has no words. The gift of peace hidden in Adam's utter weakness is a gift not of the world but certainly a gift *for* the world. For this gift to become known, someone has to lift it up and hand it on. That maybe is the deepest meaning of being an assistant to handicapped people. It is helping them to share their gifts.

Adam's peace is first of all a peace rooted in *being*. How simple a truth but how hard to live! Being is more important than doing. Adam can do nothing. He is completely dependent on others every moment of his life. His gift is his pure *being with us*. Every time in the evening when I run home to "do" Adam—that means help him with his supper and put him to bed—I realize that the best thing I can do for Adam is to be with him. If Adam wants anything, it is that you are with him. And indeed that is the great joy: paying total attention to his breathing, his eating, his careful steps; looking at how he tries to lift a spoon to his mouth, or offers his left arm a little to make it easier for you to take off his shirt; always wondering about possible pains that he cannot express but that still ask for relief.

Most of my past life has been built around the idea that my value depends on what I do. I made it through grade school, high school, and university. I earned my degrees and awards, and I made my career. Yes, with many others, I fought my way up to the lonely top of a little success, a little popularity, and a little power. But as I sit beside the slow and heavy-breathing Adam, I start seeing how violent that journey was. So filled with desires to be better than others, so marked by rivalry and competition, so pervaded with compulsions and obsessions, and so spotted with moments of suspicion, jealousy, resentment, and revenge. Oh sure, most of what I did was called ministry, the ministry of justice and peace, the ministry of forgiveness and reconciliation, the ministry of healing and wholeness. But when those who want peace are as interested in success, popularity, and power as those who want war, what then *is* the real difference between war and peace? When the peace is as much of this world as the war is, what other choice is there but the choice between a war which we euphemistically call pacification and a peace in which the peacemakers violate each others' deepest values?

A DAM SAYS TO ME, "Peace is first of all the art of being." I know he is right because after four months of being with Adam I am discovering in myself an inner at-homeness that I did not know before. I am even feeling the unusual desire to do a lot less and be a lot more, preferably with Adam.

As I cover him with his sheets and blankets and turn out the lights, I pray with Adam. He is always very quiet as if he knows that my praying voice sounds a little different from my speaking voice. I whisper in his ear, "May all the angels protect you," and often he looks up to me from his pillow and seems to know what I am talking about. Since I began to pray with Adam, I have come to know better than before that praying is being with Jesus and simply wasting time with Him. Adam keeps teaching me that.

Adam's peace is not only a peace rooted in being but also a peace rooted in the heart. That true peace belongs to the heart is such a radical statement that only people as handicapped as Adam seem to be able to get it across! Somehow during the centuries we have come to believe that what makes us human is our mind. Many people who do not know any Latin still seem to know the definition of a human being as a reasoning animal: *rationale animal est homo*

(Seneca). But Adam keeps telling me over and over again that what makes us human is not our mind but our heart, not our ability to think but our ability to love. Whoever speaks about Adam as a vegetable or an animal-like creature misses the sacred mystery that Adam is fully capable of receiving and giving love. He is fully human, not a little bit human, not half human, not nearly human, but fully, completely human because he is all heart. And it is our heart that is made in the image and likeness of God. If this were not the case, how could I ever say to you that Adam and I love each other? How could I ever experience new life from simply being with him? How could I ever believe that moving away from teaching many men and women to being taught by Adam is a real step forward? I am speaking here about something very, very real. It is the primacy of the heart.

Let me quickly say here that by heart I do not mean the seat of human emotions in contrast to the mind as the seat of human thought. No, by heart I mean the center of our being where God has hidden the divine gifts of trust, hope, and love. The mind tries to understand, grasp problems, discern different aspects of reality, and probe the mysteries of life. The heart allows us to enter into relationships and become sons and daughters of God and brothers and sisters of one another. Long before our mind is able to exercise its power, our heart is already able to develop a trusting human relationship. I am convinced that this trusting human relationship even precedes the moment of our birth.

Here we are touching the origin of the spiritual life. Often people think that the spiritual life is the latest in coming and follows the development of the biological, emotional, and intellectual life. But living with Adam and reflecting on my experience with him makes me realize that God's loving Spirit has touched us long before we can walk, feel, or talk. The spiritual life is given to us from the moment of our conception. It is the divine gift of love that makes the human person able to reveal a presence much greater than him or herself. When I say that I believe deeply that Adam can give and receive love and that there is a true mutuality between us, I do not make a naive psychological statement overlooking his severe handicaps. I am speaking about a love between us that transcends all thoughts and feelings, precisely because it is rooted in God's love, a love that precedes all human loves. The mystery of Adam is that in his deep mental and emotional brokenness he has become so empty of all human pride that he has become the preferable mediator of that first love. Maybe this will help you see why Adam is giving me a whole new understanding of God's love for the poor and the oppressed. He has offered me a new perspective on the well-known "preferential option" for the poor.

The peace that flows from Adam's broken heart is not of this world. It is not the result of political analysis, round table debates, discernment of the signs of the times, or well-thought-out strategies. All these activities of the mind have their role to play in the complex process of peacemaking. But they all will become easily perverted to a new way of warmaking if they are not put into the service of the divine peace that flows from the broken heart of those who are called the poor in spirit.

The third and most tangible quality of Adam's peace is that, while rooted more in being than in doing and more in the heart than the mind, it is a peace that always calls forth community. The most impressive aspect of my life at l'Arche is that the handicapped people hold us together as a family and that the most handicapped people are the true center of gravity of our togetherness. Adam in his total vulnerability calls us together as a family. And in fact, from the perspective of community formation, he turns everything upside down. The weakest members are the assistants. We come from different countries—Brazil, the United States, Canada, and Holland— and our commitments are ambiguous at best. Some stay longer than others, but most move on after one or two years. Closer to the center are Raymond, Bill, John, and Trevor, who are relatively independent, but still need much help and attention. They are permanent members of the family. They are with us for life, and they keep us honest. Because of them, conflicts never last very long, tensions are talked out, and disagreements resolved. But in the heart of our community are Rose and Adam, both deeply handicapped. And the weaker of the two is Adam.

Adam is the most broken of us all, but without any doubt the strongest bond among us all. Because of Adam there is always someone home, because of Adam there is a quiet rhythm in the house, because of Adam there are moments of silence and quiet, because of Adam there are always words of affection, gentleness, and tenderness, because of Adam there is patience and endurance, because of Adam there are smiles and tears visible to all, because of Adam there is always space for mutual forgiveness and healing . . . yes, because of Adam there is peace among us. How otherwise could people from such different nationalities and cultures, people with such different characters and with such an odd variety of handicaps, whether mental or not, live together in peace? Adam truly calls us together around him and molds this motley group of strangers into a family. Adam, the weakest among us, is our true peacemaker. How mysterious are God's ways: "God chose those who by human standards are fools, to shame the wise; he chose those who by human standards are weak to shame the strong; those who by human standards are common and contemptible—indeed who count for nothing—to reduce to nothing all those who do count for something, so that no human being might feel boastful before God" (1 Corinthians 1:27-30, *my paraphrase*). Adam gives flesh to these words of Paul. He teaches me the true mystery of community.

Most of my adult life I have tried to show the world that I could do it on my own, that I needed others only to get me back on my lonely road. Those who helped me have helped me to become a strong, independent, self-motivated, creative man who would be able to survive in the long search for individual freedom. With many others, I wanted to become a self-sufficient star. And most of my fellow intellectuals joined me in that desire. But all of us highly trained individuals are facing today a world on the brink of total destruction. And now we start to wonder how we might join forces to make peace! What kind of peace can this possibly be? Who can paint a portrait of people who all want to take the center seat? Who can build a beautiful church with people who are only interested in erecting the tower? Who can bake a birthday cake with people who only want to put the candles on? You all know the problem. When all want the honor of being the final peacemaker, there never will be peace.

Adam needs many people and nobody can boast about anything. Adam will never be better. His constant seizures even make it likely, that medically, things will only get worse. There are no successes to claim, and everyone who works with him only does a little bit. My part in his life is very, very small. Some cook for him, others do his laundry, some give him massages, others play him music, take him for a walk, a swim, or a ride. Some look after his blood pressure and regulate his medicine, others look after his teeth. But though with all this assistance Adam does not change and often seems to slip away in a state of total exhaustion, a community of peace has emerged around him. It is a community that certainly does not want to put its light under a basket, because the peace community that Adam has called forth is not there just for Adam, but for all who belong to Adam's race. It is a community that proclaims that God has chosen to descend among us in complete weakness and vulnerability and thus to reveal to us the glory of God.

Thus, as you see, Adam is gradually teaching me something about the peace that is not of this world. It is a peace not constructed by tough competition, hard thinking, and individual stardom, but rooted in simply being present to one another, a peace that speaks about the first love of God by which we are all held and a peace that keeps calling us to community, a fellowship of the weak. Adam has never said a word to me. He will never do so. But every night as I put him to bed I say "thank you" to him. How much closer can one come to the Word that became flesh and dwells among us?

I have told you about Adam and about Adam's peace. But you are not part of l'Arche; you do not live at Daybreak; you are not a member of Adam's family. Like me, however, you search for peace and want to find peace in your heart, your family, and your world. But looking around us in the world we see concentration camps and refugee camps; we see overcrowded prisons; we see the burning of villages, genocidal actions, kidnappings, torture, and murder; we see starving children, neglected elderly, and countless men and women without food, shelter, or a job. We see people sleeping in the city streets, young boys and girls selling themselves for others' pleasure; we see violence and rape and the desperation of millions of fearful and lonely people. Seeing all this, we realize that there is no peace in our world. And still . . . that is what our hearts desire most. You and I may have tried giving money, demonstrating, overseas projects, and many other things, but as we grow older we are faced with the fact that the peace we waited for still has not come. Something in us is in danger of growing cold, bitter, and resentful, and we are tempted to withdraw from it all and limit ourselves to the easier task of personal survival. But that is a demonic temptation.

I have told you about Adam and his peace to offer you a quiet guide with a gentle heart who gives you a little light to walk with through this dark world. Adam does not solve anything. Even with all the support he receives, he cannot change his own utter poverty. As he grows older, he grows poorer and poorer and poorer. A little infection, an unhappy fall, an accidental swallowing of his own tongue during a seizure, and any one of many other small incidents may take him suddenly away from us. When he dies, nobody will be able to boast about anything. And still, what a light he brings! In Adam's name I therefore say to you, "Do not give up working for peace. But always remember that the peace you are working for is not of this world. Do not let yourself be distracted by the great noises of war, the dramatic descriptions of misery, and the sensational exploitations of human cruelty. The newspapers, movies, and war novels may make you numb, but they do not create in you a true desire for peace. They tend to create feelings of shame, guilt, and powerlessness and these feelings are the worst motives for peace work."

Keep your eyes on the Prince of Peace. He is the one who does not cling to his divine power; the one who refuses to turn stones into bread, jump from great heights, and rule with great power; the one who says, "Blessed are the poor, the gentle, those who mourn, and those who hunger and thirst for righteousness; blessed are the merciful, the pure in heart, the peacemakers and those who are persecuted in the cause of uprightness" (see Matthew 5:3-11, my paraphrase); the one who touches the lame, the cripple and the blind; the one who speaks words of forgiveness and encouragement; the one who dies alone, rejected and despised. Keep your eyes on him who becomes poor with the poor, weak with the weak; and who is rejected with the rejected. He is the source of all peace.

Where is this peace to be found? The answer is clear. In weakness. First of all, in our own weakness, in those places of our heart where we feel most broken, most insecure, most in agony, most afraid. Why there? Because there our familiar ways of controlling our world are being stripped away; there we are called to let go of doing much, thinking much, and relying on our self-sufficiency. Right where we are weakest, the peace which is not of this world is hidden.

In Adam's name I say to you, "Claim that peace that remains unknown to so many and make it your own. Because with that peace in your heart you will have new eyes to see and new ears to hear and gradually recognize that same peace in places you would have least expected." Not long ago I was in Honduras. It was my first time in Central America since I had come to Daybreak and become friends with Adam. I suddenly realized that I was a little less consumed by anger about the political manipulations, a little less distracted by the blatant injustices, and a little less paralyzed by the realization that the future of Honduras looks very dark. Visiting the severely handicapped Raphael in the l'Arche community near Tegucigalpa, I saw the same peace I had seen in Adam, and hearing many stories about the gifts of joy offered by the poorest of the poor to the oh-so-serious assistants who came from France, Belgium, the United States, and Canada, I knew that peace is the gift of God often hidden from the wise and wealthy and revealed to the inarticulate and poor.

I am not saying that the questions about peace in Central America, Afghanistan, Northern Ireland, South Africa, Iran, and Iraq are no longer important. Far from that. I am only saying that the seeds of national and international peace are already sown on the soil of our own suffering and the suffering of the poor, and that we truly can trust that these seeds, like the mustard seeds of the gospel, will produce large shrubs in which many birds can find a place to rest. As long as we think and live as if there is no peace yet and that it all is going to depend on ourselves to make it come about, we are on the road of self-destruction. But when we trust that the God of love has already given the peace we are searching for, we will see this peace breaking through the broken soil of our human condition and we will be able to let it grow fast and even heal the economic and political maladies of our time. With this trust in our hearts, we will be able to hear the words: "Blessed are the peacemakers, for they shall inherit the earth." It fills me with a special joy that all the Adams of this world will be the first to receive this inheritance.

Many people live in the night; a few live in the day. We all know about night and day, darkness and light. We know about it in our hearts; we know about it in our families and communities; we know about it in our world. The peace that the world does not give is the light that dispels the darkness. Every bit of that peace makes the day come!

Let me conclude with an old Hasidic tale that summarizes much of what I have tried to say.

> *A Rabbi asked his students: "How can we determine the hour of dawn, when the night ends and the day begins?"*
>
> *One of his students suggested, "When from a distance you can distinguish between a dog and a sheep?"*
>
> *"No," was the answer from the Rabbi.*
>
> *"Is it when one man can distinguish between a fig tree and a grape vine?" asked a second student.*
>
> *"No," the Rabbi said.*
>
> *"Please tell us the answer, then," said the students.*
>
> *"It is, then," said the wise teacher, "when you can look into the face of human beings and you have enough light (in you) to recognize them as your brothers and sisters. Up until then it is night, and darkness is still with us."*

Let us pray for that light. It is the peace the world cannot give.

Silent Story

by Maureen Noworyta

Rattling, a racket,
a rattling I heard
and spun to pale kitchen curtains
tearing back their thin veneer.

My stare, blue bleary, locked her eyes,
brown, clear as a child's
while metal gates slammed down my mind,
barring heart's admission.

Hunger's incessant jab
tattooed the crosshatched face,
street-wise, no pillow for her head;
hands a wreck exposed,
were given stone instead of bread.

Plowing through the alley,
her rusted cart scrapes by my door:
bags of scant stuff bunched in brutal openness.

She clatters across broken cobbles
while I, in kitchen cozy,
smooth close the veil between our worlds,
but can't shut out my sister's secret:
she shelters Christ the Crone.

This Ground *Is* Holy Ground

by Judith E. Smith

FOR MANY YEARS the metaphor of life as a spiritual journey has been powerful for me. It has helped me hear God's call to move out from the safe places and travel new roads. And I have looked for road maps in the words of others who have traveled along the road seeking God. Day by day I have attempted to find my way along the road that they were describing and to reach the same destination. Most of the road maps I have used to guide me were drawn by celibate men who lived solitary, monastic lives. I thought that these voices of authority had all the answers. They were holy voices, and the place where they stood was holy ground. If only I could find my way along the same road they had traveled until I could stand on that same piece of holy ground.

But in recent years their voices have been more difficult for me to understand. The road they describe and the ground on which they stand looks and feels strange and somewhat alien. Their experience often does not fit mine. I thought I knew the questions and was looking for the answers. Somewhere the journey was clearly defined, and my task was to find the right authorities, follow their guidance, and make the same journey that they had made. But I am not so sure of that any more. In fact, I am coming to believe that what I seek is not the right answers at all but the right questions. It is the discovery of new questions that is giving new definition to my journey.

WHAT IS OUR DESTINATION?

IF WE ARE ON A JOURNEY, then the logical first question is, What is our destination? Where is this holy ground? For years I thought I knew the answer to that question. I was seeking God and was convinced that the way to God was through discipline and order. I knew I would never live a perfectly ordered life, but I thought I ought to be moving toward that destination. My natural tendency is to live a bit chaotically (a masterful understatement, according to some of my friends), and I was sure that if I could adequately discipline my life, the chaos would come into some order. And so I proceeded on a determined course to bring everything in my life under control. I thought that if I worked hard enough, I could be a successful professional, a perfect mother, a loving wife, a thoughtful and caring friend to everyone, and in my spare time be well read and committed to social justice activities. After years of obsessive attempts I realized I could not be all of that. And so I entered a time of major reevaluation of my life and my priorities. Finding balance in my life became more important than doing it all. I took a year off from work at significant financial cost and learned to live differently and much less obsessively.

But the change was just beginning. Even deeper than my need to control my life was my need to perform well. All I had done by taking that year off was to alter the rules a bit. Performing no longer meant doing it all. Now it meant keeping my life in perfect balance. Even the radical change I made in leaving my job became another way in which I performed well. Like an actor on a stage, I carefully moved through the next scene. When you are in a play you rehearse it carefully, and its success depends on how well you accomplish what you set out to do. In leaving my job I had made a major change in the script. But my attention was still focused on my precision in following that script. The need always to be in control was a block to my ability to be attentive to the life-giving Spirit within me. I needed more than a script change. Instead, I needed to move from believing that I am defined by and valued for my performance to believing that I am defined by and valued for who I am in my deepest being. It is so simple and yet so difficult to believe that God loves and accepts us—and perhaps even celebrates us!—exactly as we are.

I have not come to this awareness comfortably or through rational reflection on my life. I have come to it by having a head-on collision with my own failure in the relationships that matter most to me. What I discovered in the midst of the devastation was that the God whom I was seeking, the God whom I had glimpsed along the way, became even more real in my experience of failure than in my successful performance. I had moved even further from discipline and order, the destination I had in mind, and was floundering in chaos. And yet I knew in ways I had not known before that God is indeed the source of my very being. Perhaps I had been wrong about the destination. Perhaps the holy ground I was seeking was not a perfectly disciplined and ordered life. But then what was it? After a long struggle to answer that question, I have decided that it is the question that is wrong, not the answer. Perhaps the journey itself is more important than the destination. Perhaps I will never see a clear destination but instead will learn to live with Mystery. Wandering might, in fact, be more appropriate than constantly assessing how far I have come since yesterday.

WHAT IS THE ROAD?

IF THE JOURNEY is more important than the destination, then the logical next question, Which road is the *right* road? is no longer appropriate. If the destination is all-important, then the roads you take must lead you there and their value is determined by the directness with which they reach the final point. But if the journey itself is more important, then it is the nature of the road that matters most.

For most of my life I have focused on accomplishment. Since the accomplishments that mattered to me were not such things as a high salary, a large house, or a fancy car, I really believed that I was somehow free—or at least freer than many others—from the need to achieve that pervades our culture. But I have come to see that my own need to constantly measure progress in my spiritual life, to climb one more rung of that ladder toward perfect inner discipline, was just as distorted as the need to accumulate wealth. My destination might be different, but it was still the destination that I valued, not the journey. I realize now that I hardly know how to think about the road apart from the destination. But I am learning to try. And the questions I am asking now are, How do I decide which road to explore next? Who tells me which direction to go? Typically I have looked outside myself for answers to such questions. I have always had big authorities in my life, people whom I admired. Their opinions mattered to me, and surely they would know better than I which road to take.

Because of the nature of our culture and tradition, most of those authorities have been male. Historically, men were educated and women were not, men could write books and women could not, men dominated the church and the world and God was viewed as male. And so, with a few notable exceptions, the authorities in the Christian tradition are male. I have always wanted my experience to match theirs, thinking that would give it validity and integrity. Thus I have discounted important aspects of my own experience of

God. I have failed to pay attention to the wisdom and experience of many around me who may not carry the weight of the tradition but who speak with authenticity and authority.

Recently I have begun to look around and listen to some of those closest to me, many of whom are women. Often they do not have credentials that are externally validated by the institution of the church, but their wisdom and the depth of their experience touch me deeply. It has been a conscious shift for me to value the stories told in kitchens and basements and bedrooms in the same way I value what is written in books. Stories about family are often seen as just anecdotes, but they carry wisdom and depth and direction for our lives. There is a way of knowing that comes out of the daily lives of women, who usually carry primary responsibility for maintaining personal and family relationships: the mending and cleaning and cooking, the holidays and the relatives and the shopping. In my search to match my experience with that of traditional authorities, I discounted the authority and wisdom growing out of the daily, ordinary experience of community.

For the first time I am learning to pay attention to the deep calling of my own spirit and the Spirit within me. I am learning to listen in new ways to my mothers and sisters and daughters in the faith. Attempting to mold my spiritual life to those traditional voices often has not led me to new depths. I took a major step when I recognized that perhaps that was not due to some shortcoming on my part but simply a reflection that my journey was leading me down different roads. A friend recently taught a preaching course. She told me about a middle-aged woman in the class who preached a sermon that grew out of a personal story of hers. The sermon was very powerful and not only moved my friend but also gave her a deep new insight into the passage of scripture the woman had used. After she finished preaching, the woman apologized for the quality of her sermon, saying "I just don't know how to think theologically." It takes courage for us to claim that there are other ways to "think theologically." It took courage for me to claim that the life of the Spirit in me was no less present because my road was different from that of some of the authorities I had looked to for so long.

Learning to trust that our own inner authority is valid is often difficult for women, especially women who are as other-directed as I have been for much of my life. I have found deep joy in learning to value my own experience, to trust the Spirit of God in me, and to pay attention to the connections between myself and other women. Sometimes those connections are our places of pain. Often that pain is the result of having been told that we are inferior or unworthy because we are women. Images of women in children's books, movies, and television have given us a feeling of being limited. But our shared experiences are also places of power that can call us beyond those limits and enable us to claim our own truth—the truth of the movement of God's grace in the midst of the concrete reality of our daily lives. The voices I listen to are different now. And little by little I listen more to my own voice and love it and value it and trust it.

WHO ARE MY COMPANIONS?

M Y GROWING EXPERIENCE of community has also transformed the third question that shapes my journey. I had long believed that the spiritual journey was primarily a solitary one. You listen to wise voices along the way, but the journey is yours alone, and it is supported by solitude and silence. And so the question for me has been, How do I find the solitude I need? That question has been comfortable for me because I am basically an introvert, and so I have worked to "free" my life of too many demands and too much entanglement.

But when there are little arms around your neck and teenagers wanting to talk and elderly bodies needing your care, when you are trying to juggle job and family, that kind of solitude is virtually impossible. Often life is messy and sometimes genuinely out of control. Myriad demands and entanglements clutter our daily lives. I have always acknowledged their reality and, at the same time, have worked to minimize their pull. But recently I have come to believe that for me some of the deepest experiences of God have come in the midst of community rather than on a lonely road. And so the question has changed. Now I am asking, Who are my companions on this journey? Waiting for the time when I could have more solitude has kept me from paying attention to the ways God was shaping my life in the midst of confusion and chaos. My search for a solitary life as the normative spiritual life has led me to deny my yearning for deep connections with others.

Western culture is so individualistic that it is almost impossible for us to understand truly corporate existence. (Even the word *corporate* has come to mean impersonal corporations rather than deeply connected lives.) But since I have begun to listen to new authorities, the corporate nature of our existence has become a source of life and energy for me. Virginia Woolf wrote a long time ago about the need for "a room of one's own" to provide space and time to nurture one's creativity. I still believe that solitude is an important element in our spiritual life, but I no longer believe that it is a better or more necessary foundation for our creativity. Many people—especially women—have shown again and again how profoundly creative they can be in the midst of a deeply communal existence. I am often amazed at the well of deep and rich and creative spirituality in women who have almost no time to themselves and whose creativity may never result in books or sermons or speeches.

Two images of this creativity come from Alice Walker. She remembers her mother's garden as it was when she was a child and the power it had to nurture them and move them beyond the poverty that depleted their lives:

> *My mother adorned with flowers whatever shabby house we were forced to live in. And not just your typical straggly country strand of zinnias either. She planted ambitious gardens—and still does—with over fifty different varieties of plants that bloom profusely from early March until late November. . . . Because of her creativity with flowers, even my memories of poverty are seen through a screen of blooms—sunflowers, petunias, roses, dahlias, forsythia, spirea, delphiniums, verbena . . . and on and on.*[1]

Walker knows the deep truth that our inner lives are shaped by beauty and nurtured by all of God's creation. Those experiences shape us in ways far more profound than some of the most complex theologies. Walker tells another story that points to the creativity growing out of the hardship of daily life:

> *In the Smithsonian Institution in Washington, D.C., there hangs a quilt unlike any other in the world. In fanciful, inspired, and simple and identifiable figures, it portrays the story of the Crucifixion. It is considered rare, beyond price. Though it follows no known pattern of quiltmaking, and though it is made of bits and pieces of worthless rags, it is obviously the work of a person of powerful imagination and deep spiritual feeling. Below this quilt I saw a note that says it was made by "an anonymous Black woman from Alabama, a hundred years ago."*

---

[1] Alice Walker, *In Search of Our Mothers' Gardens: Womanist Prose* (San Diego: Harcourt, Brace, Jovanovich, 1983), p. 241.

If we would locate this "anonymous" black woman from Alabama,
she would turn out to be one of our grandmothers—an artist who
left her mark in the only materials she could afford, and in the
only medium her position in society allowed her to use.[2]

The creativity of these women did not grow out of solitude and
silence but out of deeply connected and embodied life in community. But the question about companions goes beyond humanity
to connections with all of creation. The ground on which we walk
is indeed holy ground. Out of this ground we live and move and
have our being. We are daily stunned by new evidences of the devastation resulting from our consumptive lifestyle. We are increasingly becoming aware that we may be destroying the earth. But we
seem less aware that at the same time we may well be destroying
our own souls. It is somewhat like thinking that the journey is about
reaching the destination rather than about being on the road. We
have used the earth and its richness for our own ends rather than
living in the earth and discovering that the deep connections
between and among all of creation nourish us and make us whole.

Our companions along the way are very important, but not
simply for the advice they can give or the function they can serve.
They are important because it is our connectedness with other people and with the whole of creation that shapes and forms our lives.
We belong to God, and we are not disconnected from any of God's
creation even when we try to live as though we are. Unfortunately,
I have tried for too long to keep those deep and nourishing connections at arm's length.

WHERE DO WE STOP ALONG THE WAY?

KNOWING MYSELF to be a finite creature, the next important question has been, When I am exhausted, where do I
stop and find renewal so I can start on my way again? I have
assumed that the purpose of the places I stop, when I have to stop
at all, is to prepare me to move on again. After all, the destination
must be reached as quickly and efficiently as possible. But what if
we discover instead that there are places of healing and wholeness
along the way, rich and beautiful places where we can stay and make
camp for a time. Perhaps if we look carefully at what is around us,

---

[2] Walker, *Our Mothers' Gardens*, p. 239.

we will see things that we have not seen before. Perhaps we will find wholeness and healing in the wildflowers and trees, in the running water and the blue sky, in the storm and the rain and the turmoil, which finally end with fresh smells and a sense of newness. Perhaps we will find companions in those places who will provide nourishment for our own spirits. In fact, we may discover that the places we stop are important because they slow down our journey rather than speeding it up and making it more efficient.

For years I have looked ahead, searching for holy places down the road and trying to reach them as soon as possible. Now I believe instead that this ground is sacred, and wherever I stand at this moment is holy. The women who are my companions have opened my eyes to the holy in the ordinary. Deena Metzger wrote: "Each day is a tapestry, threads of broccoli, promotion, couches, children, politics, shopping, building, planting, thinking interweave in intimate connection with insistent cycles of birth, existence, and death."[3] We can become so focused, as I have been, on our accomplishments that we will not even see the holy, sacred, healing grace of God present all around us as we travel. And if we do not stop and look, our woundedness and alienation and fatigue will grow, and we will never be able to hear our own voice. We need to rest and allow our spirits to be healed and made whole along the way, not so that we can do better or travel farther but so that we will make the journey in our own good time. And sometimes we ought to linger, perhaps for a long time, until the beauty of that place has shaped us from the inside.

DO WE EVER ARRIVE?

MY FINAL QUESTION, How will I know when I have reached the destination? brings me full circle, and I face the Mystery again. Perhaps the truth is that we never arrive, not because the journey is too long and too difficult but because we have been there all along. I am coming to believe that there is no final destination except to continue to be on the journey and to know that every place along the way is a holy place because God is present. I believe that God is calling us to stand on our own ground and know that it is holy and let our roots grow deep. And yet at the same time, the journey goes on. It is a para-

---

[3] Deena Metzger, "In Her Own Image," *Heresies I* (May, 1977), p. 7, quoted in Bettina Aptheker, *Tapestries of Life* (Amherst: The University of Massachusetts Press, 1989), p. 39.

dox, I know, but perhaps we are traveling most faithfully when we know ourselves to be most at home.

Perhaps the arrival place, the homecoming, has to do with loving and being at home in our own selves, in our own bodies. We have hidden even from ourselves some of our deepest hopes and dreams and fears. We have paid too little attention to the connectedness of our body with our spirit and our passion with our reason. It is time for us to face our own brokenness, to put aside past expectations and roles, and to discover in our own deepest reality what it means to be fully human. This is not always easy for women who for generations have been led to deny the goodness of their bodies. Perhaps our destination, our homecoming, is to embrace that goodness (even when our bodies do not work perfectly), to cherish our bodies and be unafraid of our feelings, to celebrate who we are, and to live comfortably in our relationship with all creation. Perhaps the homecoming and the journey are not in tension at all but ebb and flow together. As a woman I am beginning to understand this by understanding the rhythms of my own body and my connectedness to the rhythms of nature. I have tried for too long to disconnect myself from that reality. I have tried to "do it better," which meant more rationally and efficiently and objectively. But in truth that may not be what I am to do at all. I have tried to shape my spiritual life by detachment and disconnection, and it has been at best dissatisfying and at worst intolerable. I know myself through attachment and connection, and my call is to community with all of creation, especially with women, whose voices have been lost to me for too long.

Perhaps my experience of separation and disconnection is being healed by my discovery of the inner connections at the core of my being. Perhaps God's call to me is to live deeper, not farther down the road or closer to some destination "out there." Perhaps the journey for me is circular, always moving deeper and deeper into my own life and into the life of the world, finally discovering that in this place, on this holy ground, I am drawn deeper and deeper into God, whom I have been seeking all along.

Unfolded *and* Enfolded *by* Mercy

by Elaine M. Prevallet, S.L.

Beware of the leaven of the Pharisees, which is hypocrisy. Nothing is covered up that will not be revealed, or hidden that will not be known. Therefore whatever you have said in the dark shall be heard in the light, and what you have whispered in private rooms shall be proclaimed upon the housetops.

—Luke 12:1-3, RSV

NOTHING IS HIDDEN

THE QUESTION of congruence, the relation between what is on the inside and what is on the outside, occupies a central place in the middle of Luke's Gospel. Jesus speaks in terms of both wisdom and prophecy: "Something greater than Solomon is here. . . . something greater than Jonah is here" (Luke 11:31-32). He urges us to develop our ability to read and interpret the signs that lie in plain view (Luke 11:29; 12:54-56). We are called to combine a prophet's ability to see through events to their meaning with wisdom's discernment of behaviors appropriate for everyday life. That combination seems especially critical for our times.

In the passage cited above, Jesus warns about hypocrisy, which seems to involve some disparity between those dimensions of our lives that are readily observed and those that we would like to hide or that we think of as hidden. As a society, we are inclined to hide the things that we are collectively unwilling or unable to deal with. We try to cover up our trash in landfills so that we will not have to confront the embarrassment of our wastefulness. We try to hide our nuclear waste so that we will not have to confront the obscenity of our violence and destructiveness. We hide our poor and homeless in ghettos where we will not have to see them or in third world countries distant enough that their suffering does not impinge on our pleasure, so that we do not have to confront our greed and selfishness. We attempt to hide our aging with creams and opera-tions, and we hide our aged in homes and institutions. We hide our death in iron caskets to avoid confronting the reality of our bod-ies' return to the earth, the final insult to our illusions of invinci-bility.

Jesus' words alert us to the fact that there is a relation between what goes on inside us and what is manifest in the external world. The condition of the planet and the society is a manifestation of the condition of our hearts and minds. It is all of a piece. What is on the outside reflects the inner reality, and what is on the inside will inevitably manifest itself outwardly.

It is a bit scary, really, to think that in fact nothing is hidden, that we cannot prevent our inner reality from manifesting itself out-wardly. Perhaps that is the Creator's way of giving us a chance to see a reflection of our own inner condition. But we like to operate on the assumption that we can put a good face on things. We seem willing enough to claim the connection between "the American Dream" and the enterprising, pragmatic kind of people we are, but we disown the connection between the shadow side of our society and the kind of people we are. Each of us tries to hide our inner "trash": our violence, our mortality, the poverty of our inadequacy. If it does sometimes seem easy to fool ourselves in this way, Jesus' words come to us as a fresh caution. The universe is designed for congruence, for simplicity. Our energies will translate themselves into offspring of their own kind. If we are unwilling to deal with them on the inside, we will have to confront them on the outside. We can choose whether to make the connection.

UNFOLDING IMAGES

Your eye is the lamp of your body; when your eye is sound, your whole body is full of light.
—Luke 11:34, RSV

IT IS INTERESTING to set the word *simplicity* alongside other words that have the same root. The root *plex* means "fold." Related words—multiplicity, duplicity, complicity—might sug-gest images of material spread out with many folds, two folds, folded together. Simplicity means spread out without folds. The noun *sim-plicity* is not frequently used in the New Testament, but where it does appear, it refers to a manner of giving: a ready generosity, a liberality of spirit, a free-flowing altruism that is not folded in on itself. This background may shed fresh light on the word and may help us to see it in some new ways. To be simple is to be free-flowing, unimpeded, not caught in folds or pockets, not sidetracked.

In Jesus' saying about the eye as the lamp of the body, the word translated "sound" is often translated "simple" or "single." Jesus connects a simple or single "eye" (our way of seeing) with a translucency of our bodies. We can imagine lights freely flowing, connecting the outer world and the inner world, with the eye as the aperture. There are no folds or pockets trapping the light, no impediments. The channel is clear.

As I read about the "new physics," I try to imagine myself as a configuration of energy. I have to practice this, though, because it means a real change in my image of myself and the world. I have been accustomed to thinking of myself as a "skin-encapsulated ego" (I think the phrase is Alan Watts's). I have taken for granted that my reality is separate from that of others.

But the truth of my being is that I am able to be open to what is going on beyond the confines of my skin. I am permeable; there is a flow of energy between me and the world. Some of what I take in will be joy. Some will be pain. But communion and compassion are capacities that bind me to my earth-companions; they are essential to my being human.

A helpful way for me to think about this is to imagine myself as a concentration of light. Such an image breaks down my sense of separation and reveals that I live in continuity with my environment. It blurs my edges. I imagine that the light is shining most brightly when it is flowing freely and directly from the center of my self. The light becomes dim and darkens around the edges when it gets stuck in my "ego stuff." This image of light brings me into more conscious contact with the world that surrounds me and gives me life. That contact and awareness includes not just human creatures but all earth's creatures. I imagine we are all light, variously configured, variously concentrated, flowing into and around one another.

But besides this deliberate and conscious imaging, I have many other self-images operating automatically. For instance, I have an inner picture of myself as a competent, likable, peaceful person. That is the way I want people to see me, so I try to maintain that image before others. When someone challenges me, ignores me, or does not like me, that self-image is threatened. Then my department of defense, with its stockpile of subtle as well as violent weapons, rushes in to secure the endangered image. Or sometimes that self-image gets sabotaged from within: I blush or hesitate or stammer, and my insecurity is revealed. My body itself has betrayed my self-image. The truth will come out! Again the department of defense rushes in to protect.

Of course this self-image is only illusion, only a fiction that I keep trying to establish as reality. But energy used in these defenses is energy that is not available for the tasks I might want to be about. It is stuck in a fold, deflected from other use, and wasted on internal management. The light becomes dimmer and the edges a little darker.

I also use energy to maintain my self-image before my own selves. Each of us has a certain cast of inner characters who talk and argue with one another. Within me, there are (among others) a critical self that harangues me that nothing I do is ever good enough; a defensive self that keeps explaining why I did what I did; a doubting self that always reminds me that somebody else could do it better. These voices can argue endlessly with one another, each trying to establish its own image of who I am, how I am looking, how I am doing. Again, the energy that gets used in these arguments is energy dissipated, diffused; it is energy caught in a fold and stuck there, working on this illusory task. The light is deflected from its task of relating me to the outer world; it grows dimmer, it darkens around the edges.

We can expand the context of this image-making capacity. We Christians image ourselves in certain significant roles. We see things in our society and culture that we know are wrong, unjust, evil. We want to do our part to unmask their cultural disguise, to reveal evil as it truly is, to change it so that the human family and all creation may live more fully. And we want to take seriously the responsibility to be people of prayer, of deep inner lives. But sometimes our good intentions get tangled up with our own ego needs: our efforts (conscious or unconscious) to earn grace, to justify our existence, to attain a sense of self-worth or value. We search for security in a certain identity—the "committed Christian" (generous, always available), the "messiah" (expert in the art of political Christianity), the "guru" (expert in the art of the spiritual life). Then the leaven of hypocrisy begins to work. Our voices become strident; we divide the world into "we" and "they"; we carry the whole burden of the world and all its evil on our shoulders. Our muscles, our stomachs, and our mouths become taut with frustration at our inability to change people or alter the course of events. Our hearts become hardened, love turns to bitterness and compassion to judgment. The leaven changes from righteousness to self-righteousness. We subtly begin to internalize the characteristics of the oppressors; we name their arrogance only to appropriate it ourselves. We move from reconciling to dividing, from the attitude of a humble servant to the attitude of a general who knows the battle plan and has only to marshall the troops and put the plan into action. We take on the characteristics of our great loves and hates. The process is gradual, subtle, imperceptible.

Ordinarily we discover these inner workings only as we encounter the world outside ourselves. Engaging in works of service, interacting with others, we may well discover that we are power-hungry; we like to be in charge, have the latest information or the deepest insight. We may recognize that we are arrogant and judgmental of those who see things in a different perspective. We may find we are patronizing toward those who are not as "committed" as we are, or catch ourselves involved in petty rivalries or angers or jealousies. We may come up against a block of fear or passivity or resistance and realize how subtly attached we are to something. Perhaps we notice indifference and hard-heartedness toward a concern of some neighbor nearer than the Soviets or the Nicaraguans. And then we have the opportunity. This is a moment of grace. We can hear those voices and see those self-images for what they are: our efforts to establish an identity of our own design. And what then?

ENFOLDING MERCY

There is, deep within, one voice, at once very strong and very gentle, that can calm the storm. It says something extremely simple, like, "It's okay. I love you anyway." It seems to come from beneath all the other voices, and though it is a quiet voice, it speaks with compelling authority. This is the Voice of Mercy. When this Voice speaks, the arguers become silent and say, like Job, "Behold, I am of small account; what shall I answer thee? I lay my hand on my mouth" (Job 40:4, RSV). When I become aware that the voices are arguing, I can quietly turn myself away from them and face toward the Centerplace (I call it Home) where this Other Voice lives. There is an instantaneous change when I hear the reassuring Voice of Mercy. I relax; the anxiety leaves. Often enough the other voices resume and draw me back. Then I have to keep returning Home until finally the voices stop. When I do, I feel a release of the tension of trying to hold my false self-images in place: the "perpetual re-beginning of [one] who is never discouraged because always forgiven,"[1] as the Rule of Taizé has it. When this Voice speaks, the folds dissolve and the energy regroups at the Center. It becomes simple, spreading out freely. And the light grows brighter again.

We cannot attack this unconscious, automatic image-making with our defense department. Aggression is useless; energy would just be co-opted into yet another defense. The solution, uncongenial as it is, lies in the direction of surrender or submission, in their root meanings of "to give over" or "to send back." Gradually and painfully, we learn to let go, let the energy break free of the pocket or fold it is caught in. We let the fold dissolve. Those "passive actions" are the most difficult for us. We do not know how to not do; it is like relaxing—you cannot do it by trying. I suppose the simplest ways are best: breathing in peace and breathing out tension, remembering our God and returning Home in an inner posture of trust. It does not help much, of course, to say the dissolving happens only by being immersed in trust in the Mercy. Obviously the next question is: How do I do that? And the only answer is, you trust. It is like the question, how do I learn to pray? And the answer is, you pray. We are at the bottom line here. Our contribution is only the effort to maintain a kind of inner alertness or willingness to become aware of these inner workings. The rest is God's work.

"We are the unstable, striving agents of a quiet, fathomless Love," writes Evelyn Underhill.[2] This is the inward working of the Holy Spirit: a subtle, continuous pressure within us to come to know ourselves with deeper honesty and integrity. Only as we become conscious of our false images and identities do we allow our deepest identity as the image of God to be revealed not to us, but to be seen in us or through us. That image is not something we can know and possess and control and take advantage of. It is like light reflected through us. Not our business in one way, and yet in another way our only business, the one thing necessary.

And now let me broaden the context one last time. The image of our planet from outer space—small and fragile, with its delicately balanced interdependent systems—has challenged us to a new self-consciousness. When those pictures from space first appeared, we had hardly begun to recognize the limitations of our nationalisms

---

[1] Brother Roger, *The Rule of Taizé* (New York: The Seabury Press, 1968), p. 53.

[2] Evelyn Underhill, *Abba: Meditations Based on the Lord's Prayer* (Cincinnati, OH: Forward Movement Publications, 1982), p. 40.

and barely felt the urge to transcend the boundaries that divide us. We have only recently begun to think of ourselves as one human family. Now, with what seems breathtaking rapidity, we are newly challenged to push the frame open even wider and to accept our identity as one of the members of the earth-family of all living beings. The devastated environment gives us a stunning sign that human insensitivity has reached global proportions. Suddenly we can see ourselves in a way we could not see before. An opportunity for increased unity with God's creation is presenting itself. A fold is dissolving. A deeper simplicity is available to us.

We humans (in the West, at any rate) have defined ourselves as "the apex of creation." Wittingly or not, that self-image has allowed us to assume that we have the right to control and to use anything and everything to suit our slightest whim and fancy. That definition has given free reign to greed, carelessness, and thoughtless rapacity. It has emphasized our separateness from and our superiority over the rest of creation. "We need a revolution toward equality," writes John Hay. "It is a high distinction just to breathe."[3]

"The name the Navajos gave the First [Human] in their creation myth was 'Anlthtahn-nah-olyah,' which means created-from everything."[4] The notion that we were created from nothing, which runs deep in Christian tradition, points up the transcendence of God and the utter contingency of creatures. Like all truth, that is one side of a paradoxical reality. The other side, which our tradition has not emphasized, is that nature has produced us only after millennia of preparation and development. Our horizontal dependence is as essential to our self-definition as is our vertical dependence. Awareness of both forms of dependence engender in us a sense of profound gratitude and reverence—both toward God and toward creation, our P/progenitors. Gratitude and reverence should lead to courtesy. Can we understand ourselves in such a way as to help all creatures feel at home on our planet? What sort of *metanoia*—change of mind and heart—will we need to accomplish so major a change in our self-understanding?

We have said that without our attempts to serve, without our interaction with those around us, we would never see what is within. The reality of the outer world provides us with images of our inner reality: the war, the exploitation, the effects of greed, the addictive lust for control. Ordinarily, we will see some piece of the picture that calls us to change, to right the wrong. That too is the

---

[3] *The Undiscovered Country* (New York: W. W. Norton, 1984), p. 176.
[4] Hay, *Undiscovered Country,* p. 192.

Voice of Mercy. The poverty, the hunger, the homelessness will cry out, and we will hear the Voice. The people of Central America will struggle to claim their rights, and we will hear the Voice. Species will disappear, polluted land and water will begin to poison us, and we will hear the Voice. Only as we respond will the energy that has been trapped in folds of greed and selfishness begin to open up and flow freely. We will feel compelled to loosen our hold, to share more liberally, to give or to give away. This is the process of being simplified.

It is not a question of great deeds or high heroism. It is only a question of sensitivity to what is right before our eyes—inequities of all kinds, injustices, irreverence, a very basic discourtesy toward one another and toward the whole of creation. It is a question of doing simply and courteously what we do in relation to the reality that presents itself to us. It is a question of letting the folds of arrogant self-images or greed-engendering insecurities dissolve in the Mercy. It is a question of letting the energy flow freely, inside and outside. A question of simplicity.

Sometimes I am amazed when I realize how rarely I am where I am. More often than not, my body is in one place and my mind is in several others. That, I know, is energy diffused. But there are times when I can just be where I am and do what I am doing. There are times when I am not engaged in maintaining a self-image—that is, when I am able just to do what needs to be done and to forget myself in the doing; when I am not thinking at all about how I am doing or looking. When my energy is concentrated in the given of the moment, then it simply flows freely from the center, without diversion into folds or side pockets. Then, I think, the light shines brightly. Then there is a kind of pure power in what is done, the power of authoring, authority. This power is not exactly personal power, because I am not there getting in the way of what is being done. It is quite different from the power of control. Control is a much dimmer light, because control means the department of defense is folding up some of the energy in an effort to keep me in charge, to get the situation to turn out the way I want it to. If the energy can go simply and directly from the center to the matter at hand, it will be tailored to the need or person or task—which may or may not be the way I thought it should be. The energy will flow freely, without impediment.

The experience of simplicity is not easy to identify or name. In fact, we usually speak of it in negatives: it is not this or that. It is neither active nor passive, or it is both. It is neither controlling nor yielding, or it is both. I guess we cannot name it because when it happens we are not there to claim it. That in itself is a grace: I, at any rate, would surely want to control it and make it into one more false image of me as the image of God to be admired. When that image is shining through us, when we and our self-images are out of the way, then we are, momentarily at least, simple. Simply the image of God in this particular human form. What we experience is an unimaginably deep freedom. The light is flowing freely. It's all grace.

CONCLUSION

You . . . cleanse the outside of the cup and of the dish, but inside you are full of extortion and wickedness. You fools! Did not [the one] who made the outside make the inside also? But give for alms those things which are within; and behold, everything is clean for you.

Luke 11:39-41, RSV

IN MANY BIBLES, the last sentence of this passage receives the comment, "meaning obscure." *Alms* is a word we do not use much anymore, but it seems to mean a charitable gift to one in need. The literal translation of the sentence might be "of the things that are within give alms." It may be helpful to think about that word *alms* in the singular, where it means mercy or pity. "Give mercies of the things that are within."

Jesus suggests that we might be fooled into thinking that God cares more about the outside world of behaviors and appearances than about the inner world of images, motives, and intentions. The truth, he seems to say, is that God's creative energy is at work in one as well as in the other, and that if "the things that are within" are negatives like extortion and wickedness, nothing good can be expected to happen in the outer world. Or, if "the things that are within" are mercies, then that is what will be dispensed outwardly. Knowing the character of so much that is within, how can I "make mercies" of it all?

That must mean first of all becoming aware of what is within and its relation to what I do. Sometimes awareness will come while I am engaged in ministry: in the midst of some action or service, an insight or a sense of inner emptying will be given. Sometimes a prayer or study group where exchange can take place in an atmosphere of trust will be the vehicle for an opening of awareness. Surely the discipline of attentiveness, of listening and watching, and disciplines of reflecting, journaling, and praying are indispensable helps to seeing the incongruities. Then we may need to carry the burden of the discrepancies between how we are and how we wish we were, what we do and what we wish we did. We should carry the discrepancy, holding it without being depressed or intimidated by it, suffering our own reality freely and humbly. We carry our failures and successes, our strengths and limitations consciously. And in prayer we also consciously cover them with Mercy, make mercies of them, dissolve them in Mercy.

Julian of Norwich gives us a lovely image of the all-encompassing nature of that Mercy when she speaks of having sight of Jesus' "homely loving":

> I saw that he is to us everything that is good and strengthening for our help. He is our clothing that, for love wrappeth us up and windeth us about; embraceth us, all becloseth us and hangeth about us, for tender love; so that he can never leave us.[5]

I cannot heal myself; I cannot clean the inside of my own cup. I can only hold the contents of the cup and let the mercy-ing Light permeate them. As I, with all my voices and self-images and all my behaviors, allow myself to be unfolded and enfolded by Mercy, I find that I am less anxious about how I am doing or looking. I am free simply to do what I do. That means less energy used pretending, maintaining, judging. The energy has been mercied, so to speak, and can flow out not just in good feelings but in responses genuinely tailored to meet persons and needs. The Light spreads out unobstructed, flowing freely and courteously to blend with its environment. Simply free.

---

[5] *The Revelations of Divine Love,* trans. James Walsh (St. Meinrad, Indiana: Abbey Press, 1975), pp. 52–53.

The Whole Earth Meditation

by Joan Sauro, C.S.J.

ONCE UPON A TIME in my life I had two homes. One was in Albany where I lived and worked. The other was in Syracuse where I was born and where my family still lived. The two homes were connected by the Greyhound bus line that I rode on holidays, birthdays, and summer vacations.

Midpoint between the two homes, near Little Falls, there was a stretch of road where steep rocks and cliffs rose high on either side. A hush always came over the people in the bus whenever we passed through those towering hills. There, to the left and right, you could see the land cut away, standing in a cross section with all of its inner layers exposed.

How vast and intricate it was, how infinite the number of nooks and crannies, the ledges, holes, and pockets. Unconsciously, my eye followed the twists and turns, the sculptured folds and faults, and soon I was lost in them. God must transform this terrain, I thought, inch by inch, with fire if need be, until the whole earth is God's.

By this time I was no longer looking at the outer, natural earth. I was looking at my own inner world, similarly cut away in a kind of cross section. And I was asking God to transform me.

Silently and simply I passed from place to place, as if viewing the land for the first time. All the while the bus was going far and wide, I was going deep and deeper. Through brush and briar I went, over rocky ledge, down dark ravine, into the region of fire and ice. It was passage without words, without compass or map. Some of the layers I saw were familiar. Many I did not recognize as my own.

Some I still do not recognize, although I have taken that journey many times since. But I am learning as I go, learning also to love the place where God dwells.

Perhaps because I first saw inner earth from a bus window, along with a group of other people, I believe the experience is a common one. We share not only a vast outer world but also a precious inner one that is its reflection. If you will look to this inner world of yours, gently and without haste, you too will discover widths and depths remarkably like the outer, natural earth.

You will see layer upon layer, laid over and under, thick and thin, even and irregular. Like the earth, you are sturdy in some places, crumbling in others. At rest. And restless.

In some layers you are soaked with water, green with life, and nurturing. In other layers you are hard, like marble, rock, and slabs of slate.

You can stand in large, empty shelves inside yourself and you can stand before places that are unreachable, unknown even to you. In your inner self there are places where even you have never been.

In some layers your earth stretches out to catch the sun, which shows you to be very warm and beautiful there.

In other places you are filled with deep crevices and holes where no sun reaches. Neither does any other person reach you there.

In your inner self there are layers of collapse where violent upheavals have gone on, leaving you weak, unrestored, and vulnerable.

This is your inner earth, its slopes and plateaus, its reds, greens, pinks, deep down browns, and greys. You are jagged and smooth to touch, filled with lights and shadows, life and death. You are vast, complicated, unfinished, and changing.

All of your history is written on the walls inside you—your parents, family, upbringing, and education, the homes you lived in, the places you visited, every book you ever read, every song you ever sang, every person you ever loved and who loved you. They are all present inside you.

So is every person you ever disliked or ignored, and who hated you. Each of them is also present within you.

All of your dreams and longings are here, your talents, like shiny pieces of gold that catch and hold the sunlight.

All of your faults and breaks are here, upheavals of earth, places where you have been hurt and are likely to be hurt again.

The more you walk your inner earth, the more you touch your deepest self, the more you will find that God has been there before you, that God's name is written on every layer. God lives in the wide sweep of your inner geography and in the smallest molecule.

God is in the clear water that rushes over you, soaking every layer and washing. God surprises you in hidden springs that you never even knew were there.

God is also in every dried-up, lifeless place inside you. Just where you do not think to look.

God is in the warm, gentle sunlight, and God is in the scorching, burning fire that cleans.

God is in the fierce wind, the season of struggle, and in bountiful times, when life and goodness overflow within you. In every season of your life, God is with you in every layer.

Most of all, though, God is in the worn, embattled, broken-down layers because God always loved the poor and the weak. This is where to look for God most in yourself—where you are broken and vulnerable. Where you are scarred and need divine healing.

Look for God where your defense is weakest. At the breach in the wall. The crack in the earth. The ground shifting out of control.

Go to the place called barren. Stand in the place called empty. And you will find God there.

The Spirit of God breathes everywhere within you, just as in the beginning, filling light place and dark, green earth and dry.

Thus does God renew the face of the earth. God always breaks through at your weakest point, where you least resist.

God's love grows where you crumble enough to give what God wants most—your earth.

May you rule me from sea to sea,
from one end of the earth to the other.

May you shine as long as the sun does,
as long as the moon, from age to age.

May you be like rain in the meadows,
like soft showers watering the earth.

May your justice flower in the land,
and profound peace

until there is no more sun or moon.

—based on Psalm 72

Grand Canyon

by Parker J. Palmer

They say the layered earth rose up
Ancient rock leviathan
Trailing ages in its wake
Lifting earthmass toward the sun
And coursing water cut the rock away
To leave these many-storied walls
Exposé of ages gone
Around this breathless emptiness
More wondrous far than earth had ever known

My life has risen layered too
Each day, each year in turn has left
Its fossil life and sediments
Evidence of lived and unlived hours
The tedium, the anguish, yes the joy
That some heart-deep vitality
Keeps pressing upward toward the day I die

And Spirit cuts like water through it all
Carving out this emptiness
So inner eye can see
The soaring height of canyon walls within
Walls whose very color, texture, form
Redeem in beauty all my life has been
The darkness and the light, the false, the true
While deep below the living waters run
Cutting deeper through my parts
To resurrect my gravebound heart

Making, always making, all things new

Responding

STEPHEN ALCORN

Participating *in the* New Creation

by Mary Conrow Coelho

A T THE BEGINNING of our journey in the Christian life, many of us were converted and entered a period of profound hope and excitement over the new life opening before us. We felt we were saved, we knew we had changed, and we were profoundly grateful for this gift. We understood what it meant to be in the world but not of it. We had left behind some of the alienating, death-dealing patterns that mar the world, and we lived with a new knowledge of the possibilities of the new creation.

We hoped to be faithful to a new vision of life, but as the years passed, if we were honest, we were forced to admit we had not changed as profoundly as we had once believed. Perhaps we were often fearful; perhaps we were envious or covetous, or were troubled with a persistent, irrational anger; perhaps we recognized patterns of behavior that distanced us from others; perhaps we felt bored or stuck in our lives, or found ourselves too often without hope in the face of personal problems and world instability and violence.

Although we initially blamed others or our circumstances for these behaviors, we eventually acknowledged they were part of our personalities. As we recognized these persistent patterns, we realized that we were still deeply part of the alienated and broken dimensions of the world.

Our transformation had been real but limited in its effects on the personality. These behaviors are imbedded in deeply-rooted, early personality patterns we assumed in relation to our parents and other significant figures and are therefore largely prerational and unconscious.

We realized we must begin a painful encounter with ourselves and look more deeply at who we are. This would be essential if we were truly to come to live deeply in a relation of love to God and neighbor and not out of the alienating, estranged, and often violent ways of much of the world.

How then are we to be in the world but not of it? We will consider four primary intentions or fundamental commitments to life.

They are attitudes toward life that facilitate the essential transformation of the soul as we live into the unfolding grace of baptism. They are basic forms of allegiance and consent to life. They do not earn us transformation and relationship to God, who does not first ask us to develop some goodness before coming to us. They are forms of cooperation with the change and development God seeks.

THE PROCESS OF PREPARATION IS OCCURRING IN US

FIRST, we must know and believe in the depths of our hearts and souls that the necessary transformation and preparation for a closer relationship with God and neighbor is in fact occurring in us. We must trust the integrity of our created lives and God's faithfulness to the process of conversion.

It is often said that we would not be seeking God if we had not already begun to find God. This can be a source of confidence, a place from which to trust that the gradual transformation and finding will continue. We are responsible for the best use of our lives, and we can commit ourselves to trusting that the depth and fullness of transformation can be ours. What we are doing is cooperating with God's preparation of our hearts and souls, a process of rebirthing under the prompting of divine grace. Nicholas de Cusa has God say to humankind: "Be thou thyself and I shall be thine." We have to become the people we were created to be.

The growth involves changes that are gradual, often almost imperceptible. Much of the essential transformation of the soul occurs quietly and secretly, and fundamental changes are often first known consciously only through dreams. After the passage of years, we will become able to be aware of changes and observe them. The changes are slow because we are not concerned with arbitrary acts of will but with deep inner consent at an emotional level. We dare to change at this level only when we have sufficient new experience to be able to believe and trust that we can and then dare to react to life differently.

When we have undertaken the commitment to develop our lives in God to the fullest, we will need to find the necessary support to insure that our intention will not be crowded out by other commitments that often seem more pressing only because they are more immediate.

The process of change is slow and always difficult, and this is compounded by the indifference of the general culture to this process. If we are fortunate, this support may be found in our local church, but we may have to seek beyond it in the larger church. We may be called to reconsider the quantity and quality of church commitments if they have taken on excessive busyness and do not stir and touch the depths of our person. Long-term small groups, such as a prayer group, a group for the study and interpretation of dreams, a personally engaging Bible study group, or a house church are particularly valuable because the personal interaction, including the group affirmation of one another and the frictions and struggles that inevitably arise, can provide the occasion for essential insight into the people we are. Often a spiritual director, a spiritual friend, or some form of counseling may provide the needed support, the needed mirroring to allow us to see both ourselves and the long-term continuity of our journey.

SIMPLICITY AND OUR ATTITUDE TOWARD TIME

THE SECOND COMMITMENT to continued transformation concerns our attitude toward time. As we seek a life imbued with God's spirit, we must seek to discover the timing of the life of the Spirit in our soul. It has its own pace. Once while spending a few days at a monastery, I realized I was often looking at my watch to see if it was time for a meal or a service in the chapel. But, I thought suddenly, it did not matter what my watch said. What mattered in the monastery was the bell that announced the passing of the day's schedule.

Time, clock time, is also not what matters in the life of the Spirit, but the unique timing of the events of the soul that speak of its relationship to God. David Steindl-Rast writes of listening to the soundless bell of "time, not our time" wherever we may be and then doing what needs to be done.[1]

Our culture encourages an attitude toward time that is hurried, sees it as always in short supply, especially because we increasingly feel time has a big price tag on it. It is common for people to feel out of control, distracted, fragmented, tense, incapable of praying or listening, and pulled in many directions.

For most of us it is essential to simplify our lives and provide the leisure to acquaint ourselves with the rhythms of our hearts and souls. Were our lives simpler, we would be more vulnerable to the

---

[1] David Steindl-Rast, "Man of Prayer," in *Thomas Merton, Monk*, Patrick Hart, ed. (Kalamazoo, MI. Cistercian Publications, 1983), p. 81.

subtle workings of the soul and to feelings and signals from the body. It is in our idleness and our dreams that the submerged truth sometimes comes to the surface. With a simpler lifestyle we would no longer maintain a forced march to avoid suffering, to ignore our feelings, to evade issues of sexuality, and to avoid ourselves or our spouse.

We must consciously decide not to falsely fill our lives with activity, even if it means some painful emptiness. That emptiness was there anyway, and we gain nothing by covering it over with busyness. If our lives are too complicated, we will not know the present reality of who we are. We will not be available to the now when we may be shown ourselves and our God. Moments of time come to us with a fullness that we are invited to embrace.

The suggestion to adopt an attitude of leisure is not easily accepted by people in the United States. But it is an honest recognition that personal transformation is a slow process that takes time and attention. Progress in prayer is slow. There is a beautiful line from *The Imitation of Christ*: "Blessed are those who are glad to have time to spare for God."[2] In short, if we are too busy, we will betray our true self, including its relationship to God.

COURAGE TO FACE OUR INNER PAIN

IF WE ARE TRULY to cooperate with the transformation of our soul, we must have courage to face pain and suffering. Honestly seeking God may even require us to pray to be shown what is wrong. We may cry, "Lord, make me what I should be, change me whatever the cost."[3] We must ask why we are absent from God and alienated from our neighbors. This is an indication of courage and strength and willingness to see and face ourselves—an essential step if we are seeking to become open to the Spirit and to a fuller participation in the new creation. We are seeking to overcome the desperate and pervasive escapism that holds us in bondage.

If we can face our inner pain, it means we are willing not to pull away from full involvement in both the pain and joy of life. Often unconsciously, out of the pain of early rejection, early wounding, early isolation from those close to us, we continue the same patterns of separation and alienation in our adult relationships.

God waits for us to be willing to feel and recognize the deep-

[2] Thomas à Kempis, *The Imitation of Christ* (London: Oxford University Press, 1961), p. 49.

[3] Anthony Bloom, *Courage to Pray* (New York: Paulist Press, 1973), p. 17.

seated pain of this alienation. When we are given the gift of seeing it and feeling it, many times in different guises, we can mourn it and admit the havoc it has wrought in our lives. We are at the same time more open to the workings of the Holy Spirit, to our creative energy, to our capacity of love, all grounded in the dynamic trinitarian life of God. We are no longer unconsciously putting limits on the terms in which we will say yes to life. God wants to invade us, including our deep, unrecognized sadness, so that we may be loved in the midst of it. With this love, the hold of the pain on our lives is healed.

We may wonder if it is possible to avoid encounter with the deep-seated pain buried in the hearts of the large majority of lives. The answer is no. We have built up a hard shell of personality that wards off our inner pain for us, but this armor-like personality is not equipped to deal with God, and it is not equipped to love. Encounter with God would make it either inflated or disoriented. So the old must die if the new is to be born. The exterior, false person can be dismantled and changed as the inner reasons for its protective function are healed. The emerging person with less armor-like protection is learning, as William Blake wrote, "to bear the beams of love."[4]

EMBODYING THE LOVE OF GOD

THOMAS MERTON insists that there is no union with God without transformation. Paradoxically, the person who has struggled with personal transformation and become psychologically stronger is the person who can be empty and receptive before God. It is the prepared personality that is less resistant to God's love. This vulnerability is an act of strength, since we no longer need to hold tightly to a false self that protects us from our inner pain and fears. We are free at last. We can surrender to God, who is everywhere and always present, and can actively respond as the occasion requires. We have the ease to rest in God in whom we have been found.

As we live in the crucible of God's transforming grace, it is important to notice and celebrate the occasions of the emergence of new life. We gave a genuine gift, we truly celebrated another's accomplishment, we became aware that others love us and we love them, we gave our child more room to be herself and rejoiced in

---

[4] "Songs of Innocence," in *The Prose and Poetry of William Blake* (Garden City, NY: Doubleday and Co., 1965), p. 9.

her, or we had genuine compassion for someone in need and took steps to help. These changes of heart and simple acts of love seem fragile and transient in the face of major human dislocations, but they are the kind of changes that transform life at the individual, interpersonal level. We will sing more if we sing, or dance more if we dance, and pray more urgently when we pray, and give more abundantly when we give. We can celebrate moments when the Holy Spirit is increasingly present or, better said, when we are not so absent. And we can say with Yahweh, "Behold, it was very good."

As we are faithful to the costly growth of the new person we are becoming, we will find that we are able to take new steps in the freedom of the new fullness of our life in God. We will discover that we can forgive because God's love has revealed rejected parts of ourselves to us and we were able to face and acknowledge them, thus accepting life in its brokenness. A closer, more immediate relationship with God will allow us in trust to give up our fears. We are available for a greater intimacy to our neighbor as the deep healing in God allows us to drop the protective barriers that distance us from one another. We will find we are no longer envious because we know who we uniquely are and can celebrate that. Also, we may give up some false desires and covetousness as we find an abundance in God and in daily life. Gradually our life will become richer and a sense of hope will grow. In short, we will be in the world without being of it.

Walking Humbly Before God

by Keith Beasley-Topliffe

I WOULD LIKE to change the world. But when I look at those who are usually held up as models of Christian social action, I despair. I see great world leaders like Dag Hammarskjöld, founders of movements like Mother Teresa or John Wesley, and prophetic preachers like Martin Luther King, Jr. Inspiring, yes, but not models for me. I am not cut out to be a leader or founder or organizer. Nor do I have the fire of a prophet. Still, there must be something I can do beyond sending off money or joining in marches. But what?

Then, as I continue to survey the saints who have been the conscience of the church, I notice a quiet man in plain, undyed clothing, standing off to the side while his more spectacular sisters and brothers occupy center stage. His name is John Woolman, and he knows all my excuses. He, too, is a shy person, unwilling to speak out unless compelled to do so by the Spirit, hesitant about contradicting his elders and his "betters." Yet he more than any other can claim credit for the elimination of slavery among the Quakers of colonial America. Without holding any public office, without any supporting organization except the Society of Friends, he made a significant difference throughout the British colonies.

John Woolman was born in 1720 in Northampton, New Jersey, one of thirteen children in a Quaker family. His youth was apparently fairly ordinary, with the usual degree of adolescent rebellion. In his case, as with so many other saints, this phase of his life was brought to an abrupt end by a serious illness when he was about twenty. As he considered the possibility that he might die, "that Word which is a Fire and Hammer, broke and dissolved my rebellious Heart, and then my Cries were put up in Contrition." He resolved henceforward to "walk humbly" before God.[1]

---

[1] All quotations are taken from Woolman's *Journal*. I have consulted several editions, including an Everyman's Library edition of 1910, an American edition of 1871 (with introduction by John G. Whittier), and a 1913 commentary upon the *Journal* by W Teignmouth Shore entitled *John Woolman: His Life & Our Times*.

Woolman worked as a shopkeeper for a baker and later for a tailor and cloth merchant in the nearby town of Mount Holly. When the tailor died, Woolman took over the business. From time to time, when success threatened to become a distraction, he cut back, sending his customers to other shops, reducing the variety of goods he sold. In 1756, he decided to give up merchandising altogether and work solely as a tailor. "I had," he writes, "learned to be content with a plain Way of Living; . . . and, on serious Consideration, I believed Truth did not require me to engage in much cumbering Affairs." In the meantime (in 1749) he had married. Only one daughter lived to maturity.

In 1742, Woolman was chosen a minister of the Quaker Meeting in Mount Holly. This was the highest "office" he ever held. He traveled frequently to the Monthly Meetings and Yearly Meetings throughout the colonies, and finally to the Yearly Meeting in London, in 1772. While still in England, he died of smallpox.

Throughout his adult life, John Woolman's great cause was slavery. It was not a concern carefully chosen by someone looking for a fight. Rather, the cause seemed to pursue him until he had to face it. The first important incident for him was when his master (the tailor) sold the one slave he owned and asked Woolman to write out the bill of sale. He felt slavery was wrong and was uneasy about writing the document. On the other hand, "I remembered I was hired by the Year, that it was my Master who directed me to do it, and that it was an elderly Man, a Member of our Society, who bought her." And so he went ahead, though he expressed his misgivings. Sometime later, he was asked to produce a similar document and this time asked to be excused.

Several years later, his writing talents were again requested by a man wishing to make his will, including the disposition of many slaves. On his own now, he feared to offend the man and lose his business. Nevertheless, he refused to draw up the will. Another man was similarly refused when he wanted to leave his slaves to his libertine son. He returned some years later, hoping that his son's reformed life would change Woolman's mind. When Woolman again refused, explaining his reluctance, the man finally gave in and agreed to free his slaves. Woolman gladly wrote his will. Again, when called to write the will of a dying friend, he took down all but the part about the man's one slave. "We then had a serious Conference on the Subject; at length he agreeing to set her free, I finished his will."

Such victories, though, were only a small part of Woolman's fight against slavery. His primary means of witness was by travel-

ing about, speaking in Quaker meetings or directly to slave owners in their homes. In 1746, he journeyed through Pennsylvania,
Maryland, Virginia, and North Carolina with Isaac Andrews as his
companion. One of the results of this trip was his first published
writing, "Some Considerations on the Keeping of Negroes,"
though he delayed printing it until 1754.

In 1757 he felt an "exercise" to make another such trip, although
he says, "the Prospect of so weighty a work brought me very low."
After much prayer, though, "I felt a Deliverance from that Tem-
pest . . . and in Calmness of Mind went forward, . . . trusting that the
Lord Jesus Christ . . . would be a Counsellor to me in all Difficulties." He had been anxious on earlier trips about accepting hospitality from slave owners, knowing that his meal and lodging were
the fruit of slave labor. On this trip, therefore, he took along a quantity of silver coins to offer as payment for food and lodging—paid
directly to the slaves when possible.

Woolman spoke out at the Yearly Meeting in Philadelphia in
1758, but the only resolution that could gain the consent of the
body was to send out visitors to slave owners to ask why they kept
slaves. The next year, the Yearly Meeting received many letters urging Friends "to labour against buying and keeping slaves." Woolman's travels had begun to show results. Now was a time to be
"humbly bowed in Thankfulness" before God.

Woolman continued to travel. In visits in Pennsylvania in 1761,
he spoke with "some noted Friends, who kept Negroes." He writes,

> *And, as I was favoured to keep to the Root, and endeavoured to
> discharge what I believed was required of me, I found inward Peace
> therein, from Time to Time, and Thankfulness of Heart to the
> Lord, who was graciously pleased to be a Guide to me.*

One constant concern on such trips was that he would be able
to tread the fine line between insulting those who welcomed him
into their homes and giving in to a desire to be friendly and polite.

> *If we believe the Truth points towards a Conference on some
> Subjects, in a private Way, it is needful to take heed that their
> Kindness, their Freedom, and Affability, do not hinder us from the
> Lord's Work. I have seen that, in the midst of Kindness and
> smooth Conduct, to speak close and home to them that entertain
> us, on Points that relate to their outward Interest, is hard Labour;
> and sometimes, when I have felt Truth lead toward it, I have*

found myself disqualified by a superficial Friendship . . . To attempt to do the Lord's Work in our own Way, and to speak of that which is the Burthen of the Word in a Way easy to the nat- ural Part, doth not reach the Bottom of the Disorder. To see the Failings of our Friends and think hard of them, without opening that which we ought to open, and still carry a Face of Friendship; this tends to undermine the Foundation of true Unity.

The next year, the Yearly Meeting offered to provide for print- ing a second part of Woolman's "Considerations." He felt, though, that since slave owners had contributed to the general fund, they might complain to see the money so used. He published the book at his own expense and sold it at cost, keeping a few copies to hand out on his visits.

In 1765, Woolman's travels took on a new feature: he began to travel on foot. He explains,

Such was the Nature of this Exercise, that I believed the Lord moved me to travel on Foot amongst them, that, by so travelling, I might have a more lively Feeling of the Condition of the oppressed Slaves, set an Example of Lowliness before the Eyes of their Masters, and be more out of the Way of Temptation to unprofitable Converse.

To Woolman's delight, a friend expressed the same "exercise" without having heard of Woolman's, and the two agreed to travel together. After two years of such travels, he writes, "Though trav- elling on Foot was wearisome to my Body; yet thus travelling was agreeable to the State of my Mind."

When Woolman died, many Friends in America still held slaves. Within a few years, however, the situation had changed. By the early 1780s, Yearly Meetings were not only urging the freeing of slaves but even compensation for the work they had performed. In 1784, the Yearly Meeting directed that those who still refused to free their slaves should be disowned by the Society. In 1790, the Society of Friends presented memorials against slavery to the first Congress of the United States.

What can John Woolman teach us about social action? How can we apply his example to our own times? First of all, we can learn to pay attention when the Spirit of Truth calls our attention to the evils we are personally involved with. It was not until Woolman was called upon to write a bill of sale for a slave that the matter became a "burthen" upon his soul.

Woolman also can teach us to seek beyond our immediate concern to the bigger context. Woolman quickly recognized that slavery was but one way in which the rich exploited the poor in pursuit of ever greater riches. He saw that the reluctance to part with slaves came from "a Resolution to prefer that outward Prospects of Gain to all other Considerations." He urged slaveless Friends in the back-settlements of North Carolina to avoid buying slaves, "so will you be preserved from those Dangers which attend such as are aiming at outward Ease and Greatness." Woolman's concern for slaves became a concern for all the poor. He traveled among the North Americans of central Pennsylvania. On his trip to London he slept in steerage with the common sailors.

But Woolman's most important lesson for us is that the word of truth, spoken with conviction and backed up by a life that exemplifies it, can be every bit as potent as a multitude of petitions, great marches, and power politics. Results may take a long time. Like Woolman, we may not live to see the victory. But John Woolman can give us hope that with simple, forthright, personal witness, offered whenever the opportunity presents itself, we can quietly change the world.

From the Great Cloud *of* Witnesses

TWO STORIES

by George Hunsinger

This sermon was originally written for American Christians for the Abolition of Torture.

And what more shall I say? For time would fail me to tell of Gideon, Barak, Samson, Jephthah, of David and Samuel and the prophets—who through faith conquered kingdoms, enforced justice, received promises, stopped the mouths of lions, quenched raging fire, escaped the edge of the sword, won strength out of weakness, became mighty in war, put foreign armies to flight. Women received their dead by resurrection. Some were tortured, refusing to accept release, that they might rise again to a better life. Others suffered mocking and scourging, and even chains and imprisonment. They were stoned, they were sawn in two, they were killed with the sword; they went about in skins of sheep and goats, destitute, afflicted, ill-treated—of whom the world was not worthy—wandering over deserts and mountains, and in dens and caves of the earth. And all these, though well attested by their faith, did not receive what was promised, since God had foreseen something better for us, that apart from us they should not be made perfect. Therefore, since we are surrounded by so great a cloud of witnesses, let us also lay aside every weight, and sin which clings so closely, and let us run with perseverance the race that is set before us, looking to Jesus the pioneer and perfecter of our faith, who for the joy that was set before him endured the cross, despising the shame, and is seated at the right hand of the throne of God.

—Hebrews 11:32–12:2, RSV

The ancient church used to keep lists of those who had died as martyrs to their faith. By the time of the third century, a list of martyrs—that is, a list of local people who had been put to death in the course of their witness to Jesus Christ—could be found circulating in every region or province where the church existed at all. These lists usually did not relate what each victim had suffered, but only the name, the place, and the date of the martyrdom. Eventually the lists of martyrs became calendars of commemoration in the church's liturgical life; and as calendars from each of the various regions came to be combined into one, the number of martyrs was soon found to be far greater than the number of days in the year. Indeed, in one of the great master lists that has come down to us from the fifth or sixth century—known as the Hieronymian Martyrology—the number of those to be remembered exceeds eight thousand names. It is the story of one person from among these eight thousand that I would like to tell here.

But we must not suppose that martyrdom is simply something confined to the ancient past. Whether in our culture the church's relative freedom from the experience of martyrdom is an unmitigated blessing, I shall not attempt to decide. I simply want to point out that it is not only the ancient church that found itself born and sustained in a crucible of suffering. Today in many corners of the earth the church exists in situations where it must live out its witness under circumstances of harassment, imprisonment, and torture. Indeed, too often it turns out to be the case that the perpetrators of this repression are agents of brutal military regimes supplied, supported, and sometimes even installed by the government of the United States. In Latin America, for example, where the church is currently facing a persecution of historic proportions, although we seldom hear of it on the nightly news, the list of contemporary martyrs is staggering and continues to grow. As Penny Lernoux points out about the situation there, "On many occasions, Catholic bishops and priests, including United States citizens, have been tortured or murdered by organizations funded and trained by the United States Government, sometimes with the direct connivance of United States agencies."[1] Therefore, as a companion piece to my story of martyrdom from the ancient church, I will also tell a story—a remarkably parallel story, as it turns out—from the great list of martyrs in Latin America today.

---

[1] *Cry of the People: The Struggle for Human Rights in Latin America* (New York: Penguin Books, 1982), p. xxiii.

The martyr whom we shall consider from the ancient church was named Telemachus. Of his background we know almost nothing except that he lived by the ascetical disciplines of monastic life. In the year 390 or thereabouts he had come from somewhere in the eastern part of the empire to Rome, where he was to make his ultimate act of witness. Father João Bosco Penido Burnier, our contemporary Latin American martyr, was a Jesuit priest who, after receiving a traditional theological education, went to work as a missionary among the downtrodden and impoverished Indian peoples of interior, rural Brazil, where he was to act under his circumstances as Telemachus had once acted in Rome. In other words, despite the enormous distance in time and space that separated them, these two simple and dedicated Christians had certain things in common. They both faced a situation of cruelty and injustice which, as we know by their actions, weighed heavily upon their consciences. They both reached a point where they could not help but act, even if only in some small way, to oppose the injustice nothing would allow them to forget. And they both by their deaths initiated a small but completely unexpected chain of events that led to changes far beyond anything they could have imagined possible when they undertook their simple actions of protest.

The situation of cruelty that Telemachus could not forget was the spectacle of slaughter and carnage produced regularly in the amphitheaters of Rome and known as the gladiatorial games. In these games human beings were killed for mere sport. Not only slaves and criminals, but sometimes, presumably for the sake of diversion, women and dwarfs were forced to fight one another with assorted weapons to the death. Or else, in a typical variation, they were pitted against wild animals, ferocious and unfed, against whom these hapless people had to fend for their lives. According to one advertisement that has come down to us, two thousand gladiators and about 230 wild animals were billed to die in a single celebration.

If we have trouble understanding how a taste for this bloody pastime could have become not only widespread but even a passion among the spectators of the day, we have only to remember the story Augustine tells us about his young friend, Alypius. Alypius was the Christian youth who vowed that by keeping his eyes shut through the entire spectacle, he would attend the games in body but not in soul. But upon hearing a huge cry from the crowd, he opened his eyes out of curiosity and became so fired with passion at the sight of blood that he not only continued to look on but also began to shout with the crowd and after that to attend the games with enthusiasm again and again. Telemachus surely knew that very many Christians frequented these games and that their imaginations were stirred by them. He may also have known that the Christian emperor, Honorius, had been implored without success to bring these bloody spectacles to an end. It was, we suppose, this entire situation, with its elements of cruelty and practical apostasy, which weighed down upon the conscience of Telemachus.

Father João Bosco also confronted an extreme situation of politically sanctioned cruelty. In 1964 the United States government had backed a military coup in Brazil. This coup brought to power a repressive and murderous regime that engineered an "economic miracle" for the few while at the same time it subdued the vast majority of the population by terror and kept it in grinding poverty. The impact of the 1964 coup was directly felt by the Indian peoples among whom Fr. Bosco had come to work as a missionary. Between 1972 and 1976 more than five hundred Indian families had been deprived of the right to their land—land they themselves had cleared and cultivated—so that wealthy property owners could annex this newly valuable territory to their holdings. A concerted campaign of threats, acts of violence, arbitrary arrests, burning of homes, and torture had intimidated the Indian peasants. The authorities regularly sided with the wealthy, and for the poor it was a time of great suffering. Just as Telemachus had been disturbed by the cruelty of the gladiatorial games, so Fr. Bosco had come to be deeply troubled by the terror inflicted almost daily upon the peasants among whom he had chosen to minister.

What, then, did each of our simple Christians do? How did they respond to these terrible situations? Each of them in his own way simply reached a point where he could no longer tolerate the intolerable. Each reached a point where, regardless of what others might or might not do, he himself simply had to say no. We do not know what the immediate circumstances may have been that finally brought the lone Telemachus to action. We know only that one day he entered a Roman amphitheater where combat was in progress, that he descended into the midst of the arena, and that he brought the proceedings to a halt by trying to separate the gladiators. We know also that the stunned crowd then became so infuriated at this interruption of their sport that they stampeded into the arena and, with sticks and stones, beat the poor monk to death. Thus did Telemachus die in faith, not having received what was promised, but having seen and greeted it from afar, and having acknowledged that he was a stranger and an exile on earth (Hebrews 11:13).

Fr. João Bosco took a similar action and, in 1976, met with a similar fate. A report came to the bishop under whom Fr. Bosco worked that two peasant women had been arrested. Their cries of anguish could be heard outside the local police station where they were being beaten and mercilessly tortured. It was later learned that needles were being driven into their bodies and under their fingernails. The bishop was implored to come to the prison to intercede for the victims, and Fr. Bosco insisted on coming with him.

Outside the police station the bishop and the priest were halted by two sergeants and two soldiers, who were expecting them. The officers, clearly in an aggressive mood, began by insulting the clerics, who for their part tried to talk to them calmly and reasonably. But when the priest mentioned that he personally would report their conduct to their superiors, one of the soldiers smashed him in the face and proceeded to shoot him point blank in the head. Thus did Fr. João Bosco, like Telemachus before him, die as a witness to the word of God, not receiving what was promised, but well attested by his faith (Hebrews 11:38–39).

From the deaths of these two martyrs, Telemachus and Fr. João Bosco, we may learn at least two things. First, we may learn that faithfulness is a higher virtue than effectiveness. Telemachus and Fr. João Bosco are remembered today not because they were effective but because they were faithful. They are remembered because they placed their lives completely in God's hands and proceeded to do God's will. Above all, they are remembered because they entered into solidarity with those pushed to the very margins of human society, because they cried out against injustice, and because they gave their lives for those whom the world considered expendable. Thus they bore faithful and concrete witness to Jesus the Crucified, who comes to us himself in all those who are least, for the crucified Jesus has made their sufferings his own.

The second thing we may learn is this: At times effectiveness is, by the grace of God, the very unexpected and miraculous result of faithful actions undertaken for their own sake. Neither Telemachus nor Fr. João Bosco could have anticipated the eventual impact of their actions. But it was actually the death of Telemachus that led the Emperor Honorius to issue an edict abolishing the gladiatorial games. Here is a case where, because one human being dared to say no, the carnage and the cruelty ceased. After Fr. João Bosco died, a similar event took place. The Indian peasants had celebrated the Eucharist in his memory. They then processed with lighted candles to the exact spot where he had been killed and planted a large cross in the earth, bearing the inscription: "Here on October 11, 1976, Father João was assassinated by the police for defending liberty." When this had been accomplished, the peasants spontaneously turned and descended upon the police station, breaking open the prison, releasing the captives, and finally tearing the entire structure, where so many had been maltreated, to the ground. This event, we are told, was a major contribution to the ending of torture as an instrument of government policy in Brazil.

Do you believe that God's grace is made perfect in weakness? Do you believe that you are called to present your body as a living sacrifice, holy and acceptable to God, which is your spiritual worship? Do you believe that though the whole world should say yes to injustice, God still calls you to say no and to enter into solidarity with all those who are dismissed as least? Then remember that God expects you to be faithful. Remember the faithfulness of Telemachus and Fr. João Bosco, of whom the world was not worthy, slain for the word of God. And remember the words of scripture:

Therefore, since we are surrounded by so great a cloud of witnesses, let us also lay aside every weight, and sin which clings so closely, and let us run with perseverance the race that is set before us, looking to Jesus the pioneer and perfecter of our faith, who for the joy that was set before him endured the cross, despising the shame, and is seated at the right hand of the throne of God.
—Hebrews 12:1-2, RSV.

Compassion *and* Commitment

by Gustavo Gutiérrez

To CHOOSE LIFE is to accept the way of the cross, and sometimes it means to leave our way. I think this becomes clear in a well-known text from the Gospel of Luke. It is the parable we call the "Good Samaritan." The beginning of this parable was the question addressed to Jesus, "Who is my neighbor?" The question seems good to us. It seems like the right question. And yet for Jesus it was the wrong question. "Who is my neighbor?" means this: I am in the center with *my* neighbor. "My" is first person. I am here. Please, I would like to know who *around me* is my neighbor. That was the question. "Who is my neighbor?"

You remember the parable. There were three persons: the first two were "colleagues" of mine—and then there was the third person, a Samaritan. The Samaritan leaves his way, goes to the wounded man, and the question of Jesus after was, "Which of these three men proved himself to be a neighbor to the wounded man?" It seems a little strange because spontaneously we think our neighbor is this wounded man. But the question of Jesus was, "Which of these three persons was the neighbor?" because being a neighbor is the result of our approach. Being a neighbor is a dynamic question.

One thing being a neighbor demands is that we leave our way, our present way. The neighbor is not someone whom I find in my own path but rather someone in whose path I place myself. The neighbor is not the person who is nearby. It is the distant one who is the neighbor. Or rather, the distant one will be my neighbor if I am able to approach this person, because being a neighbor is not a static question. It is the result of my action, of my commitment. We are called to be neighbors, and to be neighbors to other persons. Today I think the poor are the "distant" ones for us. They are "distant" in terms of our categories, our way of being human beings and even Christians.

We need to enter into the world of the poor. It means to leave our way today and to go to the "distant one," our neighbor. And I think to try to leave our way and to make neighbors is one way to choose life. Why? Because the action of the Samaritan was to give life—in this case, health to this poor man.

As Christians we must convert the distant person into a close person through our commitment. It is a way to give life and to choose life.

Excerpted from the Cole Lectures given at Vanderbilt Divinity School, January 30, 1990.

Becoming Bearers *of* Reconciliation

by Roberta C. Bondi

ORGIVENESS STANDS at the heart of the Christian life—God's forgiveness of us and our forgiveness of others, God, and ourselves. We pray Jesus' prayer with the whole of God's church, "Forgive us our sins as we forgive those who sin against us." Often, even for very painful offenses against us, we find forgiveness easy. At other times, however, no matter how we try we cannot forgive. We cannot change our hearts, nor does God's grace seem to have the power to touch them. Sometimes this is because we fear that in the very act of forgiving we would acknowledge the right of the other person to take our selves away and treat them as worthless. At other times, when we are not sure why we cannot forgive or know ourselves to be forgiven, I believe it is because we do not allow ourselves to *have a self* to forgive or be forgiven. If this is true for specific acts of forgiveness, how much more does it apply to reconciliation, that fundamental posture of life Paul associates with the new creation.

In order to receive and offer reconciliation, we need to be able to claim a self whose very identity lies in God, a self that we know can neither be given away nor stolen. Many of us have a hard time claiming our identity in God. We believe that the call to love the neighbor sacrificially means pouring ourselves out for others like water into sand until there is nothing left of us. And yet, where can God's forgiving and reconciling grace touch me if not in my very self? How can I share that grace with others if I cannot acknowledge that I have a self to be transformed by that grace? How can I afford to offer forgiveness and seek reconciliation if I believe that doing so means giving others the power to decide whether I ought to have a self at all?

The founders of monasticism in the fourth and fifth centuries in Egypt offer us good help in puzzling through these problems. Abba Alonius, one of the early monastic teachers, said, "If a [person] does not say in his [or her] heart, in the world there is only myself and God, [that person] will not gain peace."[1] Paradoxically

---

[1] Benedicta Ward, S.L.G. (ed.), *The Sayings of the Desert Fathers* (Kalamazoo, MI: Cistercian Pubns., 1975), Alonius #1, p. 30.

Alonius is teaching that all acts of forgiveness, indeed our ability to be reconcilers, stem from our knowing that our most fundamental identity does not come from others at all but from God.

THERE IS ONLY MYSELF AND GOD

THE ANCIENT MONASTICS knew that there cannot be reconciling love where there is no self to do the loving. Thus they knew they were not free to give away that primary self to another person, dissipate it, sell it into bondage, or neglect it, without the whole enterprise of the Christian life's being lost. That self, which they often refer to as the soul, is given by God. Its identity lies in God and its primary relationship is with God. It is the recognition and care of this self that Alonius is talking about when he says, "If a [person] does not say in his [or her] heart, in the world there is only myself and God, he [or she] will not gain peace."

The modern reader can see an example of a disciple's care of that self in the following story. To understand the story, we need to remember that in the Egyptian desert the obedience and loyalty a disciple was thought to owe an abba or amma was nearly absolute:

> A brother questioned Abba Poemen, saying, "I am losing my soul through living near my abba; should I go on living with him?" The old man knew that he was finding this harmful and he was surprised that he even asked if he should stay there. So he said to him, "Stay if you want to." The brother left him and stayed on there. He came back again and said, "I am losing my soul." But the old man did not tell him to leave. He came a third time and said, "I really cannot stay there any longer." Then Abba Poemen said, "Now you are saving yourself; go away and do not stay with him any longer," and he added, "When someone sees that he [or she] is in danger of losing his [or her] soul, he [or she] does not need to ask advice."[2]

What it was that was putting the disciple's very self in jeopardy is irrelevant to the story. What is relevant is the story's lesson: care for the self takes priority even over obedience to the abba.

It was hard then, and it is hard now, to claim and care for one's self. The monastics understood that their relationships with others were closely linked to their relationship with God. Yet they were

---

[2] Ward, *Sayings*, Poemen #189, p. 162.

terribly vulnerable to the belief that their own worth came from the good or bad opinion of others. A fundamental part of monastic training was aimed at learning that the monastic's identity is neither constituted by other people's approval nor diminished by other people's insults or lack of recognition. Monastics must come to know in their bones that whether others like them and approve of them or not is fundamentally irrelevant to who they are in God.

The ability or inability to lay hold of this identity apart from other people's reaction to us affects us at every point in our lives together. At a public level, the civil rights movement could never have taken place without men and women like Martin Luther King, Jr., who were willing to stand against the very laws of the land and be counted outlaws for their actions. At a more private level, fear of judgment prevents men and women from finding creative resolutions to marriages that are destroying their spouses, themselves, and their children. On a smaller but also devastating scale, many of us suffer anxieties about whether we are pleasing others or are liked by others that keep us continually off balance and unable to live firmly out of our identity in God.

The conclusion of Alonius's saying is that we should be striving to "gain peace." Surely this rugged desert Christian means more by this phrase than "peace of mind," resting tranquilly in God's hands while the anguish of everyday life passes by without leaving any traces. Speaking about monastic life Poemen said, "Even if [we] were to make a new heaven and earth, [we] could not live free from care."[3] Peace does not cut us off from others, nor is it even dependent upon freedom from a certain amount of external chaos. A story about Abba Poemen illustrates the point well:

> *Abba Poemen's brethren said to him, "Let us*
> *leave this place, for the monasteries here*
> *worry us and we are losing our souls; even the*
> *little children who cry do not let us have interior peace."*
> *Abba Poemen said to them,*
> *"Is it because of the voices of angels that you wish*
> *to go away from here?"*[4]

Peace is a deep disposition of heart. It is humility, an ability to let go of the need to be right in our own eyes or the eyes of others, an ability based on the knowledge that our rightness or wrongness in any issue is totally irrelevant to God's love for us or for our

---

[3] Ward, *Sayings,* Poemen #48, p. 146.
[4] Ward, *Sayings,* Poemen #155, p. 159.

neighbor. The peace that comes with claiming our self in God is the foundation of our ability to carry God's reconciling love to others in the most humble places and humble, everyday ways. Again, Poemen's wisdom shows the way:

> A brother going to market asked Abba Poemen,
> "How do you advise me to behave?" The old man
> said to him, "Make friends with anyone who tries
> to bully you and sell your produce in peace."[5]

Peace is God's gift to us, but a gift to be shared for the reconciliation of the world.

UNDERSTANDING WHAT HAS HAPPENED

SAYING "in the world there is only myself and God" is one thing. Living it out in a world of jobs and possessions and people that tell us daily, "You belong to me" is another matter altogether. Is it really possible for people like ourselves to live from the peace that makes reconciliation possible? Abba Poemen once said, "Not understanding what has happened prevents us from going on to something better."[6]

Having fully claimed our identity in God cannot be the starting point of our life in God. It is an ongoing part of our whole life's work. Rather than becoming demoralized at how great the task seems, we need to take up Abba Poemen's advice and strive to understand what prevents us from claiming our identity in God.

Using the language of "the passions," ancient Christian writers utilized the popular psychology of their day to describe the internal human dynamics that keep all human beings from functioning as God intended us to function. The passions, as these teachers spoke of them, afflict all of us as a result of living in a fallen world. The origins of individual sin, they are habits of seeing, feeling, thinking, and acting that characteristically blind us to who we ourselves, our neighbors, and God really are. Thus we are unable to respond appropriately. The passions distort everything.

The monastic teachers are not using the term *passion* as we do today. Restrictively, we use the word *passion* basically to refer to

---

[5] Ward, *Sayings*, Poemen #163, p. 159.
[6] Ward, *Sayings*, Poemen #200, p. 163.

strong emotions, negative or positive. But for the monastics, no state of mind or desire, no matter how strong, qualified as a passion unless it was destructive. It is important to know that they did not identify positive emotions and desires like love, compassion, or courage as passions.[7]

Each person suffers from her or his own peculiar combination of life- and love-destroying passions. The abbas and ammas, however, often speak of three intertwining passions that function in an especially devastating way to keep us from claiming our identity in God. Though the early teachers speak of these passions under other names, we can call them perfectionism, judgmentalism, and despair.

Perfectionism is the secret belief that our value, our true and entire identity, comes not from God but from what we do and how we do it. One manifestation of perfectionism in the desert was the compulsion beginners often felt to go beyond the advice of the abbas or ammas regarding frequency of prayer. Unable to trust that their value to God did not come at least partly from their own efforts to pray, they would wake up several times a night to pray when they ought to have been sleeping. Consequently, they would quickly exhaust themselves and soon leave monastic life altogether.

Perfectionism today comes in many guises. When we secretly believe that if we only did more—prayed more, loved more, worked harder—we would be "better" people, we are suffering from perfectionism. Procrastination, when it reflects an inability to complete projects for fear of failure, is a form of perfectionism. Inability to make changes in our lives unless they are radical and sweeping often comes from a kind of "all or nothing" thinking that is perfectionistic. In one of its most painful and pervasive forms, perfectionism can keep us in a constant state of guilt over our imagined failures. In all its expressions perfectionism causes us to feel that our right to our very life is tied up in whether we succeed or not at whatever is important to us.

Closely related to perfectionism is judgmentalism, an impediment to claiming our true self in God, as well as a symptom of the absence of that self. Here we place the distortions of perfectionism on other people. Continually being critical and complaining of others in small ways was a serious form of judgmentalism against which the monastic teachers wrote. Being so offended by another's fail-

---

[7] The early monastic understanding of the passions is unfamiliar to contemporary readers. Yet it is remarkably compatible with modern psychological theory. For more on the passions and our struggles with them, see my book, *To Love as God Loves* (Philadelphia: Fortress Press, 1987), Chapter 4.

ure that one was prepared to declare him or her unfit for monastic life was another. A third form was more a matter of being distracted from one's own purpose or even embittered by other people's failure to keep all the monastic rules. It was often accompanied by a willingness to set the offending party straight. This kind of judgmentalism particularly put the self in danger, as Poemen taught: "Instructing one's neighbour is for the [person] who is whole and without passions; for what is the use of building the house of another, while destroying one's own?"[8] Judgmentalism in all its forms was destructive to the whole Christian enterprise.

Is this relevant to us who are not monastics? On the surface our situation is different. We live by choice in society. We have to make judgments about better or worse ways of living. We vote in elections; we sit on juries; we choose our friends; we monitor our children's companions. The monastic literature does not expect people like ourselves to live otherwise. It does, however, ask us to consider deeply the tie between judgmentalism and an impoverished sense of our fundamental identity in God. Sniping at the people we live with, dismissing whole groups of people (drug addicts, atheists, the rich, the poor), bitterly resenting others who "get away with" things that are not permitted to us—all such patterns corrode our knowledge of our true identity and so undermine our call to be bearers of reconciliation.

Despair, the third passion that holds us back from growth into our identity in God, can be the culmination of any of the other passions. It is the conviction that however things are now, they will never be any better. I cannot help myself, nor can God. We may even convince ourselves that the hopeless situation is actually the will of God. This is common in the case of women in battering situations. But on a less dramatic level it is also true of many people who remain in destructive jobs or relationships. Hopelessness may also be the fruit of a belief that we have committed sins so terrible that we must give up our right to make claims on the people around us, or even on God. Despair is the ultimate passion. It is a giving up of the self altogether. We cannot hear what Abba Mios told the soldier:

A soldier asked Abba Mios if God accepted repentance. After the old man had taught him many things he said, "Tell me, my dear, if your cloak is torn, do you throw it away?" He replied, "No, I mend it and use it again." The old man said to him, "If you are

---

[8] Ward, *Sayings*, Poemen #127, p. 156.

so careful about your cloak, will not God be equally careful about [God's] creature?"[9]

How can we begin to exchange our passions for our true identity in God? We must begin by praying for ourselves. This is often not easy. Many people are unaccustomed to thinking of themselves as valuable in God's eyes. Others believe that it is selfish to pray for oneself in the face of the needs of the world. But the monastic teachers were firm. Difficult as it may be, we still must pray for ourselves.

> *A brother said to Abba Anthony, "Pray for me."*
> *The old man said to him, "I will have no mercy*
> *upon you, nor will God have any, if you yourself*
> *do not make an effort and if you do not pray to God."*[10]

God does not force the fact of our true identity upon us. We must "make an effort" to seek it and ask for it.

MAKING AN EFFORT

W E "make an effort" in three mutually reinforcing ways. First, we listen to scripture and what it has to say to us at the point of our struggles to claim our identity in God. Second, we learn to be introspective. And third, we learn to act in ways consistent with what we pray for. Together, these ways suggest the full meaning of praying for ourselves.

Abba Poemen, who had great faith in the slow but steady healing power of scripture, once said,

> *The nature of water is soft, that of stone is hard; but if a bottle is hung above the stone, allowing the water to fall drop by drop, it wears away the stone. So it is with the word of God; it is soft and our heart is hard, but the [person] who hears the word of God often opens his [or her] heart to the fear of God.*[11]

The Old Testament and the New are full of stories and teaching about what it means to have a self in God. The stories of creation stand at the beginning of the Bible not just because they are meant to be chronological accounts of what came first in human

---

[9] Ward, *Sayings,* Mios #3, p. 127.
[10] Ward, *Sayings,* Anthony #16, p. 30.
[11] Ward, *Sayings,* Poemen #183, p. 162.

history. They are there to tell every hearer and reader of scripture, "You live in God's creation; you are responsible for it and to it. But before all else, you have a self. It is made in God's image, and it belongs to God."

The necessity of reclaiming this self from the grip of social, religious, and cultural expectations is a fundamental part of Jesus' teaching. Sometimes Jesus calls people literally to leave their old identities, as we see in his selection of his disciples or in his invitation to the rich young ruler to abandon all his property and the social status that went with it. Even to us who do not abandon everything to follow him, Jesus calls through scripture to claim our identity in God. But he warns us: that claim always involves leaving behind an old image of the self that belongs to one's family, a congregation, a boss, or more general social obligations. And forsaking that old image will sometimes hurt so much that it feels like death (Luke 9:23-24).

Most people do not have the time or the opportunity for an exhaustive study of scripture. It is important, however, to spend a little time every day, or at least a few times each week, reading scripture in the expectation that it will speak freeing and illuminating words to us. A good modern commentary is of enormous help to the reader who wishes to understand the origin, background, and original intent of the writer. Many commentaries also discuss the shared interpretation of the church over the centuries.

Even with a commentary, however, we must do the work of reading attentively and listening actively if we are to hear in our hearts as well as our heads what scripture tells us about claiming our identity in God. As we read, and later in the day as we think about what we have read, we must ask persistently, "What does this passage tell me about my identity in God?" Scripture itself offers many metaphors to encourage our persistence. Jacob wrestled with God all night, and through his persistence he received a blessing from God. Luke's Gospel says that Jesus told the story of the widow who argued with the corrupt judge until she finally received justice (Luke 18:1-8) for the very purpose of encouraging his hearers "to pray continually and never lose heart." As we persist in our serious struggle with scripture and with God to claim our identities in God, we know that what we seek we shall indeed find.

Our most earnest encounters with scripture will not help us actually make progress in claiming our identity in God unless we are able to look within ourselves and see how our own passions are thwarting our desire for that identity. How do we find the passions when we look within ourselves for them? Some are easy to spot if we are honest and we really want to find them. In the fourth century, Evagrius Ponticus recommended becoming close enough observers of ourselves to track our states of mind and behavior throughout the day. Part of the very nature of a passion, however, is its capacity to blind us. Where there is a passion there is usually some form of self-deception, what Dorotheos of Gaza calls "lying in our imagination." The alcoholic characteristically explains away her drinking to herself. The people struggling to claim an identity in God are likely to rationalize the ways in which they collude in giving away that identity.

The early monastics had their spiritual fathers and mothers as well as fellow monks to help them see and understand their passions. We all need help too. We can get some of that help by listening to and considering seriously the truth of what even hostile people around us say to us: "You're always working"; "Don't take yourself so seriously"; "You're always blaming me." Even more valuable are Christian friends who know us, share our values, and will speak the truth as they understand it.

Some of the passions that keep us from claiming ourselves in God seem unreachable even with the help of much introspection and the conversation of friends. The roots of these passions are too far back in the past, concealed in events and memories that wound and bind us. In these cases psychologists, pastoral counselors, or psychiatrists can be of amazing help. Their indirect ways of helping us understand ourselves often resemble the methods of spiritual counsel employed by the monastic teachers. These modern counterparts to ancient spiritual guides can help us find the specific places in ourselves that we need to submit to God's healing. At the same time, they also can help us see how we can *act* to aid the healing and claiming of our identity.

Wishing to claim our identity in God is the first step in making the effort about which Anthony speaks. Wishing is the beginning of both hope and action. As an exercise of hope we can begin to ponder actively and imaginatively throughout the day what it would actually mean to have our identities in God. At the same time, we must work at giving up heroic images of instant transformation. Even if we are working toward a major decision about our lives (for example, career, marriage, or parenting) we still prepare for the larger decisions by learning to claim our identity a little at a time on a daily basis.

As part of our daily work we need resolutely to decide that we will not collude internally in the destruction of our own identity in God. We must give up calling ourselves names or otherwise punishing ourselves for our apparent inadequacies. Few of us respond well to bullying. Most of us are only demoralized by it, the exact opposite of what we are asking God for in our prayer.

Much harder and often more painful is the effort to stop collaborating in external ways in the destruction of our identity in God. Praying for courage and steadiness, we can begin to make small decisions for ourselves that support our identity. We can say no when asked to help out at church when we need time to ourselves, even though it makes us feel guilty. We can work at building a discipline of prayer, even though we feel we should be doing something "useful." When we are abused, we can refuse to accept the abuse as something we somehow deserve.

Finally, we can examine our own life histories for occasions when we have made decisions that either flowed from or encouraged the growth of our identity in God. By developing an eye for such holy moments, we strengthen our readiness to work actively with God's continuing grace. In all these ways, we begin to live the wisdom of Moses, the great black abba from the Sudan:

> If a [person's] deeds are not in harmony with his
> [or her] prayer, [that person] labors in vain.
> The brother said, "What is this harmony between
> practice and prayer?" The old man said, "We
> should no longer do those things against which we pray."[12]

CONCLUSION

WHEN WE SEEK our identity in God, we are not finally searching for a healthy, self-confident self, a fully realized self, or even a good character. Paradoxically, what follows from learning to say, "In the world there is only myself and God," is the deep, heart knowledge that the self does not exist for itself alone. According to Irenaeus of Lyons, God created us to be God's friends, to share God's life.[13] From this friendship flows the reconciliation of the world.

---

[12] Ward, *Sayings*, Moses, from seven instructions to Poemen #4, p. 120.

[13] St. Irenaeus, *Proof of the Apostolic Preaching*, trans. Joseph P. Smith, S.J., *Ancient Christian Writers*, No. 16 (Westminster, MD: The Newman Press, 1952), para. 12, p. 55.

Moving *toward* Forgiveness

by Marjorie J. Thompson

Certain of the brethren said to Abba Anthony: We would like you to tell us some word, by which we may be saved. Then the elder said: You have heard the Scriptures, they ought to be enough for you. But they said: We want to hear something also from you, Father. The elder answered them: You have heard the Lord say: If a man strikes you on the left cheek, show him also the other one. They said to him: This we cannot do. He said to them: If you can't turn the other cheek, at least take it patiently on one of them. They replied: We can't do that either. He said: If you cannot even do that, at least do not go striking others more than you would want them to strike you. They said: We cannot do this either. Then the elder said to his disciple: Go cook up some food for these brethren, for they are very weak. Finally he said to them: If you cannot even do this, how can I help you? All I can do is pray.[1]

With telling authenticity and humor, this story from the tradition of desert wisdom reveals how hard forgiveness is for us human creatures. Indeed, we have a great deal of difficulty with forgiveness—difficulty that takes several shapes.

WHAT IS FORGIVENESS?

FIRST, I BELIEVE we sometimes have trouble understanding the precise nature of forgiveness. I would like to begin by suggesting that forgiveness is *not* certain things with which we often confuse it.

Forgiving does not mean denying our hurt. What on the surface appears to be a forgiving attitude may merely reveal that we have succeeded in suppressing our pain. If we bury our hurt or pretend it isn't real, we experience no sense of being wronged that

---

[1] Thomas Merton, *The Wisdom of the Desert* (New York: New Directions, 1960), pp. 75–76.

would require our forgiveness. Forgiveness is a possibility only when we acknowledge the negative impact of a person's actions or attitudes on our lives. This holds true whether or not harm was intended by the offender. Until we are honest about our actual feelings, forgiveness has no meaning.

It is important to underscore that forgiveness bears no resemblance to resigned martyrdom. A person with a weak sense of self may too easily take on blame for the actions of others. A person who finds a unique sense of identity by appearing pitiable can learn to play the martyr with great effectiveness. In either case, resignation to the role of victim will prevent any genuine process of forgiveness. If we feel we deserve to be blamed, degraded, or abused, again we will have disguised the offense that needs forgiveness, not by denial but by taking inappropriate responsibility for the offense.

One spiritual writer has astutely pointed out that forgiveness does not mean "putting the other one on probation." We may think we have forgiven someone only to catch ourselves waiting impatiently for evidence that the person's behavior merits our clemency. If the offender doesn't measure up to our expectations, the "gift" of mercy is withdrawn: "To grant forgiveness at a moment of softening of the heart, in an emotional crisis, is comparatively easy; not to take it back is something that hardly anyone knows how to do."[2] To forgive is not to excuse an unjust behavior. There are evil and destructive behaviors that are inherently inexcusable: fraud, theft, emotional abuse, physical violence, economic exploitation, or any denial of human rights. Who could possibly claim that these are excusable? To excuse such behaviors—at least in the sense of winking and pretending not to notice, or of saying "Oh, that's all right," or even "I'll overlook it this time, just don't do it again"—is to tolerate and condone them. Evil actions are manifestly *not* "all right." They are sins.

Finally, to forgive is not necessarily to forget. Perhaps for small indignities that prick our pride we can simply excuse and forget. But for major assaults that leave us gasping with psychic pain, reeling with the sting of rejection, bowing under the weight of oppressive constraint, or aching with personal loss and grief, we will find ourselves unable either to excuse or to forget. Moreover, there are situations in which it is not desirable to forget. It would be but another expression of arrogance for those of us with European roots to ask Native or African Americans, under the guise of forgive-

---

[2] Anthony Bloom, *Living Prayer* (Springfield, IL: Templegate Publishers, 1966), p. 31.

ness, to forget the way they and their ancestors have been treated by the cultural majority in this country. I understand why our Jewish friends insist that we never forget the horrors of the Holocaust. There are brutalities against body, mind, and spirit that must not be forgotten if we are to avoid replaying them. Blows intentionally rendered to crush the vulnerable cannot, humanly speaking, be forgotten. They can, nonetheless, be forgiven.

If we now have greater clarity concerning what forgiveness is not, what then is it? Let me characterize it this way: To forgive is to make a conscious choice to release the person who has wounded us from the sentence of our judgment, however justified that judgment may be. It represents a choice to leave behind our resentment and desire for retribution, however fair such punishment might seem. It is in this sense that one may speak of "forgetting"; not that the actual wound is ever completely forgotten, but that its power to hold us trapped in continual replay of the event, with all the resentment each remembrance makes fresh, is broken.

Moreover, without in any way mitigating the seriousness of the offense, forgiveness involves excusing persons from the *punitive consequences* they deserve to suffer for their behavior. The behavior remains condemned, but the offender is released from its effects as far as the forgiver is concerned. For the one who releases, such forgiveness is costly both emotionally and spiritually. I believe this reflects in a finite way both the manner in which God forgives us and the costliness of that infinite gift.

Forgiveness constitutes a decision to call forth and rebuild that love which is the only authentic ground of any human relationship. Such love forms the sole secure ground of our relationship with God as well. Indeed, it is only because God continually calls forth and rebuilds this love with us that we are capable of doing so with one another. Thus, to forgive is to participate in the mystery of God's love. Perhaps this is why the old adage rings true: "To err is human; to forgive, divine." Genuine forgiveness draws us right into the heart of divine life.

OUR RESISTANCE TO FORGIVENESS

THIS BRINGS US to the second basic form of our difficulty with forgiveness. We may be quite clear about what is called for but find ourselves unable or unwilling to do it. How do we release a person who has deeply wounded us from the sentence of our condemnation—a judgment that rises spontaneously, unbidden, from feelings of hurt, anger, fear, or resentment?

The experience of being unfairly or inhumanely treated usually leaves us with a desire for revenge. We may be inclined to return the wrong in kind, inverting the Golden Rule: "Do unto others as they have done unto you." We may prefer more sophisticated varieties of punishment that are expressed in oblique ways: withdrawing from the relationship, engaging in "passive aggression," or venting our anger in manipulation and deceit.

If lashing back is not our way of responding to hurt, it is probable that we at least expect restitution. The offender ought to do or say something to mend the hurt, to repay us for the loss of dignity and trust we have experienced. What, then, do we do if the culprit refuses even to acknowledge that a problem exists? How can we forgive if there is no contrition?

Of course it makes forgiving much easier if the offender is willing to admit guilt and ask for pardon. But can we make conscious admission and remorse a condition for the kind of forgiveness that reflects God's love? Jesus' words of forgiveness from the Cross were offered up freely for all who would receive them. Indeed, the reason he gives in that brief prayer for asking God's mercy is precisely that we "know not what we do."

If we don't comprehend the full impact, the true seriousness of our behaviors, how shall we know enough to ask forgiveness? More often than not, those who have hurt us do not comprehend the destructive magnitude of their behavior. We are called to offer unconditional forgiveness, as God in Christ offers it to us. Jesus tells Peter in Matthew 18:22 to forgive "seventy times seven," a hyperbole by which he indicates that those who wish to be his disciples should place no limits on their mercy. Nowhere does Christ exempt us from this call merely because the offending party has not confessed to sin.

This raises an important distinction between forgiveness and reconciliation, two intimately related but distinct spheres. Forgiveness, it seems, can be offered unilaterally, and therefore without conditions. I can forgive a friend who doesn't know she has hurt me; I can forgive a parent or grandparent who is no longer present on this earth; I can forgive persons or groups of persons without their consciously knowing it or having any way to respond.

My one-way forgiveness is a matter of releasing others from judgment in my own heart. Such unilateral forgiveness does more than release me from the corrosive burden of anger and bitterness that eat away my peace of soul, although this is certainly one of the great gifts inherent in forgiveness. It also removes any hidden or overt effects of resentment in my way of relating to the other, person-to-person or with third parties. Moreover, I believe that hidden forgiveness affects the spirit of the person who has been released in ways that go beyond our comprehension or perception.

Reconciliation, on the other hand, is a two-way street. Reconciliation is the promise that lies at the heart of forgiveness; it is the full flower of the seed of forgiveness, even when that seed is hidden from sight. The gift of forgiveness will always feel incomplete if it does not bear fruit in reconciliation. This, I am convinced, holds as true in God's forgiveness of us as it does in our forgiveness of one another. Reconciliation means full restoration of a whole relationship, and as such requires conscious mutuality. No reconciliation can take place unless the offender recognizes the offense, desires to be forgiven, and is willing to receive forgiveness. Thus, the role of acknowledgment and confession of sin belongs to the dynamic of forgiveness in relation to reconciliation, not to forgiveness alone.

THE EFFECTS OF OUR RELUCTANCE

IT IS WORTH EXPLORING further the effects of our frequent, if peculiar, inability to receive forgiveness, as well as our resistance to offering it.

The willingness to receive forgiveness poses a special challenge. Just as we sometimes take back our forgiveness of another person, we frequently take our sins back from God's release of us. Douglas Steere speaks to this perverse dynamic of human pride and control:

> There is . . . a condition for receiving God's gift of forgiveness. [We] must be willing to accept it. Absurd as this may seem, there are few who will believe in and accept the forgiveness of God so completely as to . . . leave their sin with [God] forever. They are always re-opening the vault where they have deposited their sin, . . . forever asking to have it back in order to fondle it, to reconstruct, to query, to worry over it. . . . Thus their sin ties them to the past.[3]

---

[3] *Dimensions of Prayer* (New York: Women's Division of the Board of Global Ministries, United Methodist Church, 1962), pp. 56–57.

Our reluctance to offer forgiveness also ties us to the past and impedes both the present moment and the future potential of life. My lack of forgiveness holds me captive as much as it keeps another person in subjugation to my conscious and unconscious resentment. The Latin word for mercy is very revealing in this regard. *Eleison* literally means "to unbind," as our related English word *liaison* means "bond." When we refuse to forgive, we hold others firmly enmeshed in the bondage of our judgment; when we forgive, we loose others from the attachments of our anger and vengefulness, freeing ourselves in the process.

A most interesting series of meditations on the Syrian Aramaic version of the Lord's Prayer renders this dynamic quite vividly. Here are just a few possible translations of the petition on forgiveness, based on various connotations of the Aramaic words Jesus might have spoken:

> *Loose the cords of mistakes binding us,*
> *as we release the strands we hold of others' guilt.*
>
> *Lighten our load of secret debts*
> *as we relieve others of their need to repay.*
>
> *Forgive our hidden past, the secret shames,*
> *as we consistently forgive what others hide.*

The author of these translations speaks eloquently of forgiveness as a "gift we can give one another, an opportunity to let go of the mistakes that tie ourselves and one another in knots."[4] Indeed, it is this feeling of being "knotted up" with someone that makes forgiveness an experience of liberation for both parties.

This may give us a deeper glimpse into those peculiar words Jesus speaks in Matthew 18:18, "Whatever you bind on earth will be bound in heaven, and whatever you loose on earth will be loosed in heaven." If we insist on remaining bound to someone in resentment, heaven will not force us to change our minds. If we remain unwilling to forgive those who wound us, how can God set us free from the knot of a twisted relationship? God wants more than anything to free us. That is why "the Word became flesh and dwelt among us, full of grace and truth" (John 1:14, RSV)—to give us a way out of our impenetrable morass of sin. But if we refuse to pass the gift of grace along to those in our debt, we prevent the grace

---

[4] Neil Douglas-Klotz, *Prayers of the Cosmos* (San Francisco: Harper & Row, 1990), pp. 30–31.

of God's forgiveness from entering our own lives fully. Then what is bound on earth remains bound in heaven, not by God's design but our own.

From this it seems clear that the one condition set for our receiving God's forgiveness is that we also forgive one another. This condition is implied in the wording of the Lord's Prayer: "Forgive us our sins as we forgive those who sin against us." It would also appear to be the import of the parable of the unforgiving servant in Matthew 18:23-35. Again, it is not that God, in ornery fashion, is bent on punishing our hard hearts. It is simply that an unforgiving heart of itself blocks the mystery of divine grace. It cannot freely receive what God freely gives. Our openness to God and our openness to one another are thus intrinsically linked.

HOW IS FORGIVENESS POSSIBLE?

Now we find ourselves in something of a quandary. We must be willing to forgive others if we desire to receive the gift of God's forgiveness. Yet we cannot force ourselves to forgive. Forced forgiveness is mere grudging acquiescence. Authentic forgiveness flows freely from the heart. But how do we get, or open ourselves to, a change of heart? The cry of the psalmist becomes our own: "Create in me a clean heart, O God!" (51:10, RSV).

Perhaps the starting place is simply to recognize that we do, in fact, need God's presence and grace in order to learn how to relate rightly to one another. The central spiritual fact that we remain helpless to forgive out of our own paltry ego-strength is illustrated in this story from the desert:

> One of the brethren had been insulted by another and he wanted to take revenge. He came to Abba Sisoes and told him what had taken place, saying: I am going to get even, Father. But the elder besought him to leave the affair in the hands of God. No, said the brother, I will not give up until I have made that fellow pay for what he said. Then the elder stood up and began to pray in these terms: O God, Thou art no longer necessary to us, and we no longer need Thee to take care of us since, as this brother says, we both can and will avenge ourselves. At this the brother promised to

---

[5] Merton, *The Wisdom of the Desert*, p. 37.

give up his idea of revenge.[5]

When we recognize our need for God's care, both personally and in our relationships, we may be more prepared to give up our illusion of control. Our deep-seated belief that we ought to be in a position to judge and punish the faults of others is part of our "control agenda" in life. It is a painful but inevitable part of spiritual maturation to discover that vengeance upon the perpetrators of evil is not our responsibility. "'Vengeance is mine,' . . . says the Lord" (Romans 12:19, RSV). Only God has the wisdom to know what consequences are needed in any person's life to heal and restore human sanity and wholeness. As Christians we trust that God's ways of dealing with sin are more merciful than our own inclinations are likely to be.

As we recognize more deeply our dependence on God, we will also come in touch more profoundly with our shortcomings. We may become aware of the beam in our own eye that has prevented us from seeing clearly how small the speck is in our sister's or brother's eye. Discovering the depth of our sin has a way of putting the faults of others in perspective. It is shocking to some when Mother Teresa of Calcutta claims she engages in her ministry of love because she knows there is a Hitler inside her. The great saints are not shocked by any form of degradation in the human heart; they know its potential deep within themselves.

This capacity to identify with human sin to its outer reaches characterizes the humility and lack of judgmentalism present in so many holy ones through the centuries. Mercy for others grows from sorrowful knowledge of the human heart we share. The ability to acknowledge fully one's own sin is thus a powerful path to forgiveness of others. Here is one of my favorite illustrations of this theme from the desert tradition:

> *A brother at Scetis committed a fault. A council was called to which Abba Moses was invited, but he refused to go to it. Then the priest sent someone to say to him, "Come, for everyone is waiting for you." So he got up and went. He took a leaking jug, filled it with water and carried it with him. The others came out to meet him and said to him, "What is this, Father?" The old man said to them, "My sins run out behind me, and I do not see them, and today I am coming to judge the errors of another." When they*

[6] Benedicta Ward, tr., *The Desert Christian: Sayings of the Desert Fathers* (New York: MacMillan Publishing Co., 1975), p. 139.

heard that they said no more to the brother but forgave him.[6]

Here is a compassionate perspective on sin. Compassion literally means "to suffer with." Jesus suffered with and for us from a complete identification with humanity, yet without sin. We can identify with one another not only in the fullness of our humanity, but in our common human sinfulness. How real and vital, then, our compassion should be! If our eyes are fully open, how can we help but suffer with one another, seeing our sin as a form of suffering?

The great Swiss theologian Karl Barth was convinced that God sees even the most despicable human evil as expressions of profound suffering. Can we learn to see with such merciful eyes? I can imagine, given a combination of circumstances, that my reactions of fear or rage might erupt in violence I would either shamefully regret or feel compelled to justify by rationalization. The layering of self-defensive strategies can lead quickly to great injustice against others. My capacity to choose self-interest is a proven fact. How, then, can I remain self-righteous when I manage, by the grace of God, not to fall into the web of rationalization and self-justification that leads to destructive error? If it is by the grace of God that I am prevented from falling, and equally by the grace of God that I am enabled to stand again after falling, how can I refuse the grace of God to a fellow fallen one?

As we learn more about the hidden depths of our heart, our capacity for compassion and mercy grows, and the ability to forgive with it. It is not an impossible task, this divine command to forgive as we have been forgiven. Nor is it unique to Christians. It is simply by the spirit of God, which I believe is made known to us with unique clarity in Christ, that any human being is capable of participating in divine merciful love.

Such grace resided in the Jewish prisoner who wrote these words from a concentration camp in Germany. I can think of no more powerful expression of forgiveness, and the spirit of compassion undergirding it, than these words with which I conclude my own:

Peace to all . . . of evil will! Let there be an end to all vengeance, to all demands for punishment and retribution. . . . Crimes have surpassed all measure, they can no longer be grasped by human understanding. There are too many martyrs. . . . And so, weigh not their sufferings on the scales of thy justice, Lord, and lay not these sufferings to the torturer's charge to exact a terrible reckoning from them. Pay them back in a different way! Put down in favor of the executioners, the informers, the traitors and all . . . of evil will, the courage, the spiritual strength of the others, their humility, their lofty dignity, their constant inner striving and invincible hope, the smile that staunched the tears, their love, their ravaged, broken hearts that remained steadfast and confident in the face of death itself, yes, even at moments of the utmost weakness. . . . Let all this, O Lord, be laid before thee for the forgiveness of sins, as a ransom for the triumph of righteousness, let the good and not the evil be taken into account! And may we remain in our enemies' memory not as their victims, not as a nightmare, not as haunting spectres, but as helpers in their striving to destroy the fury of their criminal passions. There is nothing more that we want of them.[7]

Intercession

CARING FOR SOULS

by Douglas V. Steere

IN THE FRONTISPIECE to Evelyn Underhill's beautiful book *The Golden Sequence*, there is a photograph of one of the carved stone figures high up in an arch of the cathedral of Chartres. I once stretched my neck until I found it. In this stone statue God, the Father, holds Adam ever so tenderly on his lap. Adam, however, is asleep with his chin on his chest and his legs and arms drawn up close to his body, almost like a fetus. God is looking at him with deep caring and compassion, as though he longed for his grace to waken Adam from his drowse and so become aware of the One whose arms upheld him, and of how much he was being loved. Bernard of Clairvaux's words return at the sight of this picture: God "loves both more than you and before you love at all." In intercessory prayer, as in all prayer, the very ground of its efficacy is conditioned by our waking up to the fact that before we ever begin to care for and to pray for another person or a human situation, intercession has already been going on. God holds me and every other son and daughter of Adam in a longing gaze, seeking to wake each of us out of our drowse of preoccupation and self-absorption that we might realize who it is that loves us.

When, in intercession, I hold up some person or situation, I do so knowing full well that I did not begin this concern or begin the intercession. The intercession is already actively operating. I know, falteringly enough to be sure and with only a faint intimation of its cost, what Pascal meant when he said, "Jesus shall be in agony until the end of the world." I know that this costly caring is God's poultice laid over history and over the world, a caring that besieges every soul. And if Teilhard de Chardin is right, this caring extends to every cell in the universe for its healing and its fulfillment. The words of scripture, "He that keepeth Israel shall neither slumber nor sleep" (Psalm 121:4, KJV), give us a hint of this perpetual intercession. Therefore, when I enter the prayer of intercession I do it with an acute realization that I am only adding my caring to the cosmic love of a God who cares. And I also know that together with the prayers of all the departed ones who have joined this siege of love, we are engaged in the costly business of cosmic redemption. I realize, too, that my joining or failing to join the siege of love is of critical importance.

Baron von Hügel wrote to his niece:

> *I wonder whether you realize a deep, great fact? That souls, all human souls, are interconnected . . . . that we can not only pray for each other but suffer for each other. Nothing is more real than this interconnection—this precious power put by God into the very heart of our infirmities.*

Here von Hügel is hinting at the way we are made—the caring love of others is the indispensable means of the operation of God's grace in our intensely interdependent human situation. A friend of mine put it well when he said that God seemed to say to him, "Until you are relieved of pain, use it as a call to prayer."

A METAPHYSIC OF VULNERABLE LOVE

THAT INTERCESSORY PRAYER is anything but superfluous in the whole redemptive process is most plausibly expressed in the Gifford Lectures of Archbishop William Temple, published under the title *Nature, Man, and God.* Here he suggests that while God's ultimate purpose is unchanging, God's strategy is infinitely variable. This may mean that the addition or the withholding of my intercessory prayer in a given situation may have cosmic consequences and may require that God's entire strategy be changed. In other words, I may be a gate opener. If this suggestion has weight, my prayers not only matter, they are of critical importance.

Closely related to this issue of the significance of our intercessory prayer is the whole matter of how our intercessory prayer actually reaches, and how it is able to affect, the person we pray for. No one who dares to attempt to penetrate the mystery of prayer and to go on to suggest a kind of crude metaphysic of intercessory prayer, which I am doing, can begin without confessing that his or her offering is more than the frailest of surmises. But the evidence is deeply impressive that we are not as totally individual or as cut off from each other as on the surface of things may appear to be the case—and as we naively take for granted. Instead, it seems highly plausible that our souls are deeply interconnected in the being of

God. It is as if the souls were wicks dipped into the same cruse of oil, and it is there where we are mingled in the being of God that our prayers are added to the caring siege of love that never ceases its operation.

Any such metaphysic of Christian prayer must, however, at the same time be a metaphysic of vulnerable love, for in all things love invites but refuses to compel. In the perpetual siege and caring for souls that we enter into when we pray for others there is an invitation but never a compulsion to the soul that is prayed for. Simone Weil, the saintly French woman who died in her middle thirties in 1943 in the midst of World War II, went so far in describing God's respect for our freedom in God's perpetual siege of love that hovers over every soul as to speak of God's reticence to infringe upon this freedom. She called it God's act of "decreation." By that she meant that God would seem to have withdrawn ever so slightly from the scene and has permitted semi-autonomy in the original creation. This is in keeping with the nature of God's love to draw out from creation a freely chosen response to that caring love and to prevent our being locked in to some form of spiritual determinism.

My wife and I once visited Deventer in the Netherlands. There is a church in the city that can be reached by climbing up a large, concrete stairway of perhaps one hundred steps. As we stood before the steps, we saw a fascinating drama going on. A little three-year-old boy was well up the steps, climbing them all alone one step at a time. His parents were sitting in a little park at the foot of the steps, watching him make his climb. When he got to the top, he stood up in triumph and waved to them. And they beckoned him to begin to make his descent. He soon began to shout for them to come up and get him, and then to scream for them to come and get him. They sat quietly below and simply beckoned. After what amounted almost to a tantrum of anger for their not coming to rescue him, he finally put one foot on the step below, and then another and another, and he finally worked his way all the way down. When he got to the bottom, he ran, and they received him into their arms.

As I recall this scene, it seemed to give me a clue to the way God has withdrawn in order to give us freedom, even at the risk of our being able to injure ourselves. But God is as deeply involved in this freedom as those wise parents were in their treatment of the child.

If this surmise of Simone Weil and of our Deventer experience is even remotely true, it would seem that our prayers for others might not in any way infringe on the freedom of those we may have prayed for. The effect of our prayers for them would be at most to lower the threshold in the person prayed for and to make the besieging love of God, like the beckoning of the parents, slightly more visible and more inviting. Archbishop Trench suggests that we must not conceive of intercessory prayer as an overcoming of God's reluctance but as a laying hold of God's highest willing. Yet always those being prayed for retain their "freedom to flop," their final freedom of choice to accept or reject the invitation that is being forever offered.

PRAY AS YOU CAN

IF IT IS TRUE that our intercessory prayer may lower the threshold to a person or situation, it may occur to us to ask a further question. How may we be sure that what we pray for is the right thing? You may know the story of the old woman who by mistake had been omitted from the list of invitees to the Vicar's garden party. Hearing from another on the morning of the party that he had forgotten to invite her, the Vicar called her on the telephone, apologized for his omission, and invited her to come anyway, only to get her sharp reply, "It's too late for that. I have already prayed for rain."

Without implying that we might be as far afield as this vigorous old woman was in what she prayed for, the problem is still with us. All of us have had experience of intercession or of some sort of petitional prayer where what we were finally led to in an extended season of prayer was very different from what we began to pray for. I may have begun to pray that a person's health or mortgaged house threatened with foreclosure or former apparently stable marital situation might be restored, when none of these so-called restorations were really the most important of his or her needs. Most of us have learned from experience, however, that if we stay with a season of prayer for long enough, the things we originally put forward in our prayer have been searched and often put aside, and a whole new layer of longings for the person or situation often emerges in their place.

Not only in intercession, but in all petitionary prayer, the same principles seem to operate. For seasoned veterans of Christian prayer, there is a total absence of fastidiousness about where or for what they are permitted to begin their prayer. They know the truth of the dictum, "You must pray as you can, not as you can't," and of the fact that whether it is their own personal needs or the needs of others that they enter into prayer, these needs, whatever they may think them to be, will naturally pour into their prayer at the outset. But there are always at least two provisos to be kept in mind. First, it is not where our prayers begin but where they end that really matters. This means that a season of prayer must be long enough, and the one praying must be open and malleable enough, to see his or her initially stated concerns refashioned. Jesus himself began his prayer in the Garden of Gethsemane with the request that he be spared the cup of death with which he was threatened. And yet he stayed at prayer long enough to have wakened his three sleeping companions again and again before the full yielding came. In our prayers for others it is often only after a time of wrestling during a sizable season of prayer that for us also the "not my will but thine be done" emerges and is accepted.

The second proviso is to learn to remember that all Christian prayer is to be offered in the name and spirit of Christ. In this wise scriptural prescription we find a winnowing and a cleansing power of separation that can swiftly sort out the self-seeking, manipulative elements in our prayer so that it may become a creative part of a truly redemptive action on the soul and the body of another. P. T. Forsythe once wrote a reassuring word about this fear of ours that our prayer may not contain what the one prayed for really needs. He wrote, "Our best prayer, broken, soiled, and feeble as it is, is caught up and made prayer in deed and power with God. This intercession prays for our very prayer and atones for the sin in it. This is praying 'for Christ's sake.'" If intercessory prayer is caring for another or for a human situation in the presence of God, and if it is our communion with God for others, then the divine presence may be trusted to lift it from our well-intended initial outbursts into a critically important thrust of love that may change the situation, even though the change may be widely different from the cry we entered with or from any of our expectations.

COSTLY INVOLVEMENT

A WORD IS ESSENTIAL on the costliness of intercessory prayer to the one who prays. Oliver Cromwell once declared, "We never go so far as when we don't know where we're going." And nowhere is this more visible than in intercessory prayer. For whether we intend it or not, to pray for another is to become involved in his or her life. For one who wants to avoid being drawn into costly involvement, intercessory prayer is to be shunned like the plague.

These personal costs to the one who prays for another are of two different species. The first is the willingness to assume the spiritual costs of entering into a measureless involvement in the caring for another. This may take many forms. When Jesus cried out "Who touched me?" at the moment that the woman with the chronic hemorrhage received her healing, he referred to the psychical cost to the one who has become vulnerable enough to engage in this service to others. There may not be one but many transfusions of "psychic blood" taken from the one who prays before the siege is over. It was a deep consciousness of these costs that led Evelyn Underhill to write with great frankness to her spiritual director Baron von Hügel that she did not believe she was strong enough yet for intercessory prayer. Von Hügel in turn assured her that when the time came for intercession she would know it, and before long she reported to him that she had begun to pray for others.

Apart from the psychical cost of this vulnerable involvement for others, in most cases to pray for others almost inevitably involves us in physical responsibilities for them, whether we meant to do that or not. The old Quaker who prayed for the health and strength of his young farmer son-in-law, whose farmyard was often wet and soggy, found himself drawn to send a pair of rubber boots to him for his protection. Less obvious physical involvement, if it is called for, may consist of time for visits, gifts of food, books, letters, and often many forms of physical support. These simply go with the ticket. If you care enough, nothing will be held back.

A further cost of very different character that intercession almost inevitably exacts is the searching of the life of the one who prays and the bidding that comes to that person for deeper abandonment in his or her own life. All too swiftly we discover that it is not what we have already given away to God that makes us suffer but a matter of what we are still holding back from God. And we find that it is harder and harder to ask for changes in others without a willingness to yield to God whole new areas of off-limits territory in our own life. In the end, our intercessions are likely to become more and more "thy will be done in Mary *and in me*." And intercession for another reveals its true nature in lowering the threshold to the divine entry in both the one who prays and the one who is prayed for.

AFFECTING THE LIFE OF OTHERS

I WANT TO SUGGEST a fascinating way in which we can test where we are in the matter of our faith in intercessory prayer and in our being able to accept the plausibility that our souls really are joined together in the being of God. This test also lets us see if we really believe that when we love someone in the presence of God, our prayer does make a difference and does lower that person's threshold to awareness of God's love and infinite caring. The test is simply to ask ourselves whether or not we really believe in the practice and efficacy of secret intercessory prayer. The word *secret* in this test is essential. Do you believe that secret intercessory prayer can touch another's soul in the being of God and can be used by God to affect the life of the other? If you find this plausible and can accept it, your faith in genuine intercessory prayer has passed the test.

The western world's implicit faith in the operation of the laws of science would seem to rule out the possibility of intercessory prayer. A century ago George Meredith insisted that we ought not to expect God to step in between me and the operation of God's laws, which Meredith assumed that science was uncovering. But today the ditch between supposedly unbudgeable physical laws and psychological, mental, or spiritual functioning is at no point as wide or as absolute as Meredith believed it to be. Those who know the mood of the great scientists themselves in our generation are deeply aware of their increasing humility in the matter of their own theories. In our own day they are inclined to describe their theories not as either exhaustive or irrefutable but rather as useful metaphors or models that make little claim on finality.

Archbishop William Temple never tried to diagram in detail the operation of the coinherence of the physical and the spiritual in intercessory prayer. He only sketched out its plausibility. But he was not intimidated by either his worldly friends or his own skeptical moments when special things happened that might be passed off as coincidences—special things that happened as a result of intercessory prayer. And he did not care very much whether you called them coincidences or what today would be called synchronicities. He gathered it all up in a wonderful remark. He said, "All I can say is that when I pray, coincidences happen, and when I don't, they don't." And that is, in the end, perhaps, all that need be said.

CARING FOR SOULS

WE MUST NOW TURN from these problems with which intercessory prayer confronts us and which we have tried to face with full honesty and ask ourselves something about the way it is actually to be carried out. I know of a pastor in a generation preceding our own, when each family in the congregation had its own pew, who used to go and sit in the pew of his people during the week and pray especially for each one of them and their families in that pew, in the very place where they were to sit on Sunday. It was a way of coming closer to them and of bringing them closer to God.

Certainly few of us are so collected that we do not require a list of the people and perhaps their most urgent needs set down in a book. And this book, if we are actively using it, will need constant revision. There are the "intensive care" pages where people need a kind of prayer that takes priority. But these do not replace the ones in less urgent need who may be at some critical point in their journey where my prayers would matter terribly. A Chinese proverb says that the finest mind is less reliable than the purest ink. Prayer lists are indispensable to one whose intercession has to reach out to many persons.

William Russell Maltby was another of my trusted guides a generation ago. His blunt honesty about the practice of intercessory prayer has some bits that for me are required reading. He says:

I found that to pray for other people is a thing that can not be hurried. It did not suffice, it was not real, to name a dozen names and ask God to bless them. Every name I found had to stand alone until it was the name of someone as real as myself. I found that sincerity required me to be deliberate—one friend at a time. I found that I could not think of any of these, my friends, in the presence of God without some change coming over my thoughts, some stronger sense of their worth before God, some deeper sympathy with them as hard toilers in a great sea, some spontaneous delight in their qualities. It did not mean that the critical mind was submerged in a wash of sentiment, or that those we pray for are idealized out of recognition. On the contrary, they are seen more clearly and individually as they are, but all of this fades from our mind when we look at others in the presence of God.

Each person must learn to shape intercessory prayer after his or her own taste. I knew an old Swedish saint who had drawn together dozens of small intercessory prayer groups that called themselves "Bearer Groups." They took their name from the New Testament scene of the people who took the sick man on a stretcher through a roof into Christ's healing presence. The members of these groups did not feel that they could heal others. But they could in intercession bear them to Christ for him to transform.

I have found that hands are a wonderful symbol of giving. When someone takes my hand sincerely or puts a hand on my arm or on my shoulder, there is something special about what this body language is trying to tell me about the caring behind it. In intercessory prayer I have often envisioned the nail-printed hand of Christ being laid upon the one I was praying for, and at the same moment the other pierced hand being laid on me. When there is bodily healing to be lifted up, again I sometimes think of those pierced hands of Christ being laid upon the person, perhaps even in the very part of the person's body that one longs to be restored to wholeness.

The words of the Lord's Prayer seem for me a most suitable way for me to enter this intercessory prayer in which I ask that God's will be done in Mary and in me, God's kingdom come in Mary and in me. But the caring that follows is marked by what W. E. Sangster, an influential British Methodist of the last century, put in one phrase, "Wait before God in quietness." Sangster goes on to say, "Only those who attend the whispers of grace can hear Him inly speak." And waiting in supplication in God's presence is what intercession is all about.

Forbes Robinson, the Cambridge don at the end of the nineteenth century in England, may give us our closing word. He said, "To influence, you must love. To love, you must pray." There is no form of prayer that is more obvious an act of real love than the costly act of intercessory prayer. Let us in our prayers for one another join those who with Christ bear the burdens of creation.

Sanctifying Time, Place, *and* People

RHYTHMS OF WORSHIP
AND SPIRITUALITY

by Don E. Saliers

H UMAN BEINGS are ambivalent toward holiness. We are drawn toward those qualities exemplified by a St. Francis or by Mother Teresa, or by communities who witness to the gospel under severe persecution. Yet we find such qualities disturbing, too far removed from the way we must live our daily lives. Something deep within our existence creates a restlessness for God, yet we live and move and work in a culture of technology, efficiency, and the tyranny of the literal. The hunger for holiness coexists uneasily with the practical atheism of our way of life. Still, the deepest language of the Christian biblical tradition claims that the created world itself already reflects the goodness of God but also groans in travail for sanctification and recreation. The time and place where these tensions intersect is the gathered church at worship.

Whatever else moves us to worship God, we come because of a sense, however hidden, that time and place and life need to be sanctified and recreated. The search for holy times and places is itself an expression of our hunger for the transformation of everyday existence. This occurs outside the church as well as within. Despite the many ways in which our natural religious needs may be compulsive or deceptive, Christian people long for times and places in which God is real, relationships are healed and restored, and the meaning of life is regained. Worship, even when dull and routine, holds out a hidden promise of transformation in the midst of change, suffering, and death.

The Christian community gathers to remember and to enact its identity as a people called to holiness. "Be holy in all you do, since it is the Holy One who has called you" (1 Peter 1:15, JB). Each ministry in and of the community is a call to sanctify life. Since all ministries are rooted in the redemptive presence and

234

activity of Christ in the world, the focal question is how best to enable the community of faith to grow up in every way into Christ. Such holy servanthood does not take place unless the church remembers deeply, experiences the grace of God concretely, and is empowered through word and sacrament to rediscover true identity and mission.

Human hunger for times and places of holiness is only a starting point. Becoming a holy people is the deeper issue for the church. Gathering to remember, proclaim, and celebrate the gospel requires levels of vulnerability to other human beings and to the mystery of God in our own lives. The sign of such a vulnerable life for others is called baptism. So all baptized Christians are called to journey into the rhythms of remembering, experiencing, and empowerment. Baptism into Christ is the initiation of these rhythms of liturgy and life. Let us reflect on these in turn.

RHYTHMS OF REMEMBERING: THE ALREADY BUT NOT YET

CHRISTIAN WORSHIP is the ongoing liturgy of Jesus Christ in and through his body in the world. As Jesus' whole life was to glorify the one he called Abba, so we are to glorify God. But in so doing, the paradox is that God the Holy Spirit sanctifies all that is human in us. As Paul reminds us in Romans 12 and elsewhere, our whole lives are to be offered as a holy sacrifice of praise and thanksgiving to God. Times and places of explicit worship are to form and express what our whole lives are to be, what Christ continues to work in our midst. Worship is something we must do together, not out of duty or habit or vague obligation but because it is the way God has given us to remember and to express life "through Christ, and with Christ, and in Christ . . . in the unity of the Holy Spirit."[1]

The adequacy of our worship, both explicit and implicit, depends upon remembering and celebrating the whole story of creation, covenant, redemption, and God's future for the world. This is why sanctifying time is essential to Christian liturgy and life. We are to be shaped in accordance with the whole biblical witness to what God has done, and to what Jesus said and did—precisely as the reality of what he *now* says and does. The liturgical year is an

---

[1] "Great Thanksgiving 6: A Common Eucharistic Prayer," *At The Lord's Table* (Nashville, TN: Abingdon, 1981), p. 23.

embodied way of remembering and acknowledging what God will yet bring to completion. Christologically expressed, the cycles of the church year enable us to keep time with Jesus and to enter into the whole mystery of God-with-us.

To sanctify time involves opening the treasury of who Jesus is and what he proclaims. The discipline of time reveals that worship, Sunday upon Sunday, invites a deepening awareness of the narrative of our own lives—for good or for ill. Uncovering the gospel in the rhythms of the liturgical seasons is thus a spiritual encounter for any who wish to take baptism seriously. To be "born anew" implies growing up, opening to the surprising work of God in and through us. So Advent/Christmas/Epiphany is the pathway of expectation and incarnate hope, of living in the tension between the "already" and the "not yet" of the kingdom of Christ in our lives and the world. With Lent/Easter/Pentecost, the mystery of participating in dying and rising with Christ is the essence of the journey. Opportunity to understand and to reorder our emotions, desires, and intentions is part of the very rhythm of incarnation— God's coming to us in intimacy and judgment, in dying and rising among us, redeeming us in time from time's sin and death.

Participating in these focal cycles of the Christian year provides the pattern of Christian spirituality and ministry. A prayerful discipline of time through feasts and seasons is itself a metaphor of our baptismal journey. Because all of us continue to undergo the changes of life—growth, suffering, passages of various kinds, and death—the liturgical year is never quite the same each time we move through it. Our very lives are constantly being reinterpreted into the story of God-with-us. In this manner, keeping God's time is never dull routine, nor empty ceremony as some may claim. Rather, it is a deeper walk with Christ and a journey into our humanity with God.

There is a central feature of Christian spirituality in all remembrance and retelling of the gospel over time. A permanent tension characterizes Christian worship and ministry. We acknowledge that the Messiah has come, ushering the new age and opening up a way into the kingdom of God. Baptized into Christ, we are called to be living signs of his rule and reign. Yet life goes on. Empires still rise and fall, the innocent suffer, injustice is rewarded, and inhumanity shows its face. Amidst the "already" of redemption from sin and death, there is unmistakably the pain of "not yet." The rule and reign of God has not fully come in human history, and the ambiguous evidence of holiness assaults our doubting hearts.

We live and serve "between the times." Any who attend to the anguish of multitudes of oppressed people or who listen to the disquieted voices within a local congregation know this. Racism, whether in Howard Beach, New York, or in Forsyth County, Georgia, reminds us of what is not yet. But this fact calls us to a holy witness and discipline. The church often recovers the prayer, "Thy kingdom come!" in the midst of experienced injustice and malevolence.

The continuing liturgy of Christ in the world still calls us to serve a broken, suffering world. The sanctification of time and place and human life cannot be possessed as a guarantee effected by worship, much less by baptism. No, Christ's liturgy plunges us into the concrete world of human experience. Just as Jesus Christ was humanity and divinity at full stretch, so our worship bids our humanity at full stretch before the divine. Authentic Christian worship gives time and place for learning how to live in hope.

Not only the year as the arena of sanctification but the week and the day as well are part of the discipline and discovery of holiness. The early church took the week, with the Lord's day at its beginning and ending, as the most significant liturgical cycle. Sunday, the day of creation and of resurrection from the dead, the "first day" and the "eighth day," was the recapitulation of God's history with the world. As did the Hebrew Sabbath, Sunday anticipated and even tasted the *shalom* of God yet to come. Christians celebrated the eucharist every Lord's Day as the pattern for orienting all other times, including the hours of daily prayer—sanctifying each day's labor and rest.

To be a part of a community of living memory is thus to be a recipient of that community's own ministry. To live in the pattern of celebrating Christ's advent and birth; his baptism and ministry; his life and teaching; his passion, death and resurrection; his ascending and life-giving Spirit, is to be sustained and nurtured both by what was accomplished in him and by what is yet to be revealed. There is a disciplined mutuality in which we participate. The symbols, the sign-actions of baptism and eucharist, and the hearing of God's word foster such mutuality. How rare is such a mutuality in service and such a "rendering holy" of time, place, and people! Yet it is the saving reality of the gospel hid from the eye of a pragmatic and self-sufficient culture.

The primary locus of common Christian identity is found in the equality and mutuality implied in baptism. We share a belonging to the mystery that claims us, who is both Alpha and Omega.

Thus, there can be no special spirituality for the clergy and another kind for the laity. Rather, particular gifts for worship and service flow from the one baptismal font and from the one Spirit who gives life to all. Together our times and places are sanctified by living through the whole story of God with us, rendering thanks and praise in all times and places, even as we struggle with the "not yet." Preparing to receive and to celebrate Christ in the assembly Sunday after Sunday invites a re-envisioning of the whole range of our ministries, beginning with our own need for a rhythm of serious study of scripture, prayer, the sacramental life, and works of mercy. Only by such remembering and awareness of the time between the times can we experience the mercy of Christ in our lives, our homes, our patterns of labor and rest, and in the social world of suffering as well as joy.

RHYTHMS OF EXPERIENCING: HOLY PLACES

THE SANCTIFYING of time cannot be abstracted from places we inhabit, for we journey in time and dwell in space. Just as in our own personal lives particular places become focal points of recognition and memory as well as pilgrimage, so the church has honored our need for places set apart. A meal with dear friends, a quiet retreat in the woods or by a lake, a grave site, a recital hall, a homecoming with "dinner on the grounds"—all these are memorial places that concentrate over time powerful accumulations of experience.

Particular places contain secrets to our history and identity. We desperately need holy places where accumulated experience carries the power to reorient us to what is essential to our humanity. In nearly every instance of significant human community life there is the receiving of that which cannot be contained in time and space precisely in the events and places "marked" by encounter: the Vietnam wall in Washington, the wailing wall in Jerusalem. In spaces of religious ritual and proclamation, of marriage and burial, of mourning and praise, the potential access to what is holy emerges.

Christianity does not sanctify one single place for God, for "our God cannot be contained in earth or heaven, much less in temples made by human hands." Because Christ has made every place and time a potential bearer of the holy, we can say that worship in a particular space prepares us for God's presence in all others. As the ancient hymn for Holy Thursday sings, "Where love is, there is

God."[2] Crucial to recognizing holy places in life are the explicit dimensions of place in our ongoing worship, spaces, as T. S. Eliot said of Little Gidding, where "prayer has been valid."[3] Rooms of worship, homes, the place of scripture, the font of baptism, the table of the Lord—these become holy by interchange between God and God's people. The sacred quality of worship does not come simply or directly from church buildings or from holy vessels in themselves. Rather, as Robert Hovda has observed, "sacredness derives from the Christian assembly and its liturgical action. It is the holiness of ecclesia in action that touches place, furniture, objects, and makes them special."[4] To experience worship fully requires us to perceive Christ in the midst of daily life, our places of work, and in the parabolic gathering and scattering of the church. We have stewardship over the rooms of worship and the elements of symbol, gesture, movement, raiment, furnishings, and song that invite and enable God's word and our response. The shoddy, the pompous, the trivial, and the sentimentalized have little power to evoke the power of God to sanctify. So we have responsibility for quality environments of prayer and proclamation and sacrament. In deepening the congregation's sensitivity toward authenticity and richness of Christian tradition; vitality in prayer and song; meaningful silence; and freedom of access to book, font, and table, we can indeed open ourselves in a more disciplined way to the beauty of holiness and to the incarnate modes of communication God chooses to use with us. Uncluttering our sanctuaries and encouraging a wider emotional range (from solemnity to great joy) means attending to integrity of materials, colors, quality of communion elements, vestments, movements, and other nonverbal dimensions of our experience. All these can become occasions for attunement to God's word and action among us. Worship is a school for learning how to refer all times and places and persons to God.

These points are well summarized in Marion Hatchett's phrase "The whole of life, of time, of space is sanctified, made holy, by setting apart particular events, moments and places."[5] In the most radical sense, God has already made things holy in the life, suffering,

---

[2] "Ubi Caritas" in *The Upper Room Worshipbook* (Nashville, TN: The Upper Room, 1985), #82.

[3] T.S. Eliot, "Little Gidding" in *Collected Poems 1909-1962* (New York: Harcourt Brace Jovanovich, 1970), p. 201.

[4] Robert W. Hovda, *Strong, Loving and Wise: Presiding in Worship* (Collegeville, MN: The Liturgical Press, 1983), p. 49.

[5] Marion J. Hatchett, *Sanctifying Life, Time and Space: An Introduction to Liturgical Study* (New York, NY: Seabury, 1976), p. 12.

death, and resurrection of Christ. Christ has renewed the holiness of creation. To uncover this astonishing reality, our worship must prepare us for deeper experience. Holiness is movement of life with God such that every time and place is touched with the fire of holy love and mercy. This is not a static possession of the church. But, as a people gathered for waiting silence, for prayer and song and bread broken, for wine poured out and for the waters of cleansing and the embrace of forgiveness, our lost capacities to experience God may be replenished. Disciplined remembering creates experience; and experience is made significant where space and its non-verbal languages manifest the holiness that transcends the literal, the efficient, and the trivial pragmatism of human invention. God alone sanctifies our times and places.

RHYTHMS OF EMPOWERMENT: LITURGY AND LIFE

IF OUR WORSHIP is to transform and shift the axis of our world, discipline and experience must combine. How we prepare to worship and how we receive anew our actual world in prayer are crucial matters. Faithful liturgy has the power to "cleanse our perception" and to reorient us to the foundational meanings of life with God.

In several local congregations with whom I have worked, the recovery of worship as the making holy of time and place has brought a new perception of corporate ministries. Several laypersons have spoken of coming to see that worship "rehearses" the attitudes and dispositions we should have with our neighbors in our public lives. Reform and renewal of worship in the twentieth century have brought a new appreciation for the *intrinsic* connection between praying for others and ministering to them. Thus the renewed role of intercessions—the "prayers of the people"—between the service of the word and the service of the table has become, for increasing numbers of laity, a time of making their common ministries audible. The same is true of sacramental participation when attention has been given to sustained teaching and preparation. Breaking bread together in the Lord's name opens up the meaning of breaking bread with and for a hungry world. When authentic and mature participation in worship begins to emerge, growth in holiness increases in the form of ministries to the wider world. As John Wesley so truly observed, there can be no scriptural holiness without social holiness.

The point of recovering worship as communal action that glorifies God in all things can make visible and audible the reality of divine reconciliation and healing as a pattern for common life. The very concept of acknowledging and praying that God's name be made holy and that God's will and reign come, is central to vital worship. But this in turn involves moving toward the neighbor and the wider world with the eyes of God. We are to move in the very direction God's compassion looks. Empowerment for common ministries to the world comes in relation to how much we are disposed to receive in word and sacrament. Long ago, St. John Chrysostom told the church to first feed the hungry and then prepare the table of the eucharist. The afflicted neighbor's body is a temple, he reminded his hearers. It "is more holy than the altar of stone on which you celebrate the holy sacrifice. You are able to contemplate this altar everywhere, in the street and in the open squares."[6]

There are rhythms here, too. At times we are literally compelled by what we do at table and with new Christians in baptism to go forth into the world, "sent in Christ's name." At other times, our attempts at social ministries confront us with more than we bargained for, with resistance, discouragement, and human complexity beyond our strength. Then the rhythm reverses and we bring our intentions and our burnt-out actions, our ambiguous failings back to the font, to the word and table. Too often we fail to accept God's sure provisions in the very rhythm of word and holy meal over time, of seasons of feeding and of being fed.

The radical equality made visible and palpable in baptism (cf. Galatians 3:26-28) wherein there is neither Jew nor Greek, male nor female, but all are one in Christ Jesus, is the source of our ministries. The vision of equality and justice in the social order is grounded here, even though we must admit that the sacraments have been and can be abused to reinforce social stratification. When we are confronted with the abuses of worship, we need the rhythm of repentance and healing. Tolstoy once quipped, "God sees the truth but waits." Perhaps it is that God has much more merciful patience with us than we can ever have with ourselves or with God.

Worship empowers for ministry in unexpected ways. The sacraments, when faithfully entered into, invite a transformed world to be inhabited and teach us that we are to behold the altar of God in the suffering bodies and hearts of humankind. The equality God

---

[6] Tissa Balasuriya, *The Eucharist and Human Liberation* (Maryknoll, NY: Orbis Books, 1979), p. 26.

confers through baptism is the root metaphor and healing stream of grace already flowing through the lacerated and oppressed world awaiting our approach. The whole narrative of God's ways with the world gives the community of memory and hope an unexpected foretaste of God's future to which we are bound with cords of mercy and righteousness.

Over time liturgy is the school of God's self-giving and the drama of our lives in miniature before God. The Holy Spirit, who gives life to all such worship, has never despised or rejected human discipline and preparation. So the journey toward holiness of time, place, and people may ask a few things of us. Consider five points that suggest some specific directions.

1. We can undertake more disciplined study of scripture in common over time, especially in preparation for the principal cycles of time. Study and prayer based upon the lectionary for Advent/Christmas/Epiphany and Lent/Easter/Pentecost will link common worship, devotional life, and the central themes of the gospel together for the whole community.

2. The more intentional use of traditional patterns of morning, evening, and night prayer within various groupings of a congregation and in our households will help restore a rhythm to the day. It will reacquaint us with the range and spiritual strength of the psalms and canticles.

3. We can develop times of solitude and meditation and open up more significant times of silence and reflection in worship. The lost art of meditation on the actual experience of worship may assist us in understanding at a more profound level what our general lack of attention causes us to miss in what we already pray and sing and enact.

4. With the clergy, the laity can take more intentional responsibility as sponsors for those to be baptized or for those who are renewing their baptismal covenant (confirmation), stressing the priesthood of all believers.

5. We can study and prepare devotionally for more frequent participation in the Lord's Supper, particularly in smaller groups and in one another's homes to restore the meal context to the sacrament.

The cycles of time and the sacramental sign-actions open us to life with God and neighbor in time and space. This is not a matter of doing "the same old thing." Rather, the baptized community itself is to open up to what God continues to lavish upon us all in Christ.

God's self-giving is a mystery hidden from the plain view of the world. It is counter to much that our North American culture shapes in us in our everyday times and places. At the heart of glorifying God is the empowering mystery of God working in and through all the rhythms of the church's life to sanctify everything that is human. In the happy phrase of Irenaeus, "It is the living human being who is the glory of God."

Sing *to the* Lord *a* New Song

by Susan Mangam, S.T.R.

HARRY has lost his dominance. His son has just taken over. It is hard to see the once proud little bantam huddle in the corner behind the hens. I am tempted to interfere, but past experience teaches me that these creatures will work it out for the best. They know how to be who they are. May I let them be chickens. After all, it is I, the human being, who need to learn who I am.

In many ways I only began to learn this lesson in my middle years. Memorable in this education is the day when I lay face down on the monastery floor during the chanting of the *Veni Creator*. Suddenly a powerful image of all creation rushed in through the soles of my feet, out the top of my head, on through the bishop and the altar beyond, and into the cruciform icon of Christ on the apse wall.

This vision is gradually revealing itself to be the image of God in each and every aspect of the creation. The God I once thought of only as the transcendent Wholly Other is becoming ever more present to me in the smell of the mauve earth after the frost leaves it, in the taste of the first sun-warm tomato, in the ground aglow with fallen leaves, in the silence of the creek when the ice closes it over. A wondrous paradox—the spiritual life is earthy.

COURTEOUS INTERCHANGE

AT THE HEART of my earthy existence is my participation in the cycles of mutual sacrifice that sustain all living beings. The poet Wendell Berry says, "To live we must daily break the body and shed the blood of creation." This is cause for great thanksgiving. But sadly, we humans tend to see ourselves as consumers only and not as sustainers of life, and blindly we violate this courteous interchange.

When I first moved to these mountains, I set up my wood stove and began cutting down nearby deadwood. Then I decided to clear out some young trees beginning to overtake the old orchard out back. It became a mindless routine of cutting, piling brush, stacking wood. Having just cut through one sapling, I stepped back to watch it fall. What I saw, slowly falling, was a beautiful, tall, straight black cherry whose silky skin was burgundy colored—the color of my prayer garment. And it came to me that in my trying to make the orchard conform to my ideas, I had acted carelessly and so had killed a part of myself.

We are facing a winter of great darkness and great hope on our planet: darkness, because Earth is critically wounded; hope, because we begin to be aware of our responsibility. Thomas Berry diagnoses the Earth's illness and prescribes a cure:

> *If the earth does grow inhospitable toward human presence, it is primarily because we have lost our sense of courtesy toward the earth and its inhabitants, our sense of gratitude, our willingness to recognize the sacred character of habitat, our capacity for the awesome, for the numinous quality of every earthly reality. . . . We need to present ourselves to the planet as the planet presents itself to us, in an evocatory rather than a dominating relationship. There is need for great courtesy toward the earth.*[1]

Healing the planet necessarily leads to self-healing, as I discovered for myself a few years ago, when I went to the Maine coast to camp in the quiet off-season. I wanted to breathe the salt air and do some drawing, but more, simply to sit on a rock at the meeting of land and sea and let the ocean give me perspective, heal me. It had always worked. But this time was different, for I felt no healing. I felt nothing. Distressed and fearing I had lost touch with the sea, my mother, I tried to draw. It came hard, as though something were wrong with me. Somehow I stuck it out, not knowing what was going on. Day after day I drew, and it seemed all darkness and chaos. Gradually, I began to come to myself and to listen. The sea was telling me I am no longer a child. I can no longer just demand, "You fix me and make me better." I was learning that the sea and I are one. This salty life-fluid of Earth is in my veins. By it I was baptized. Now I was being called to return this gift of life to the sea, my sister—to complete the cycle of courtesy. As I open myself to healing, Earth heals; as Earth heals, I heal.

---

[1] Thomas Berry, *The Dream of the Earth* (San Francisco: Sierra Club, 1988), pp. 2, 14.

TRANSFORMING POWER OF LOVE

A TREE BROUGHT ME face-to-face with my own destructiveness. Another tree, carelessly cut and fashioned into a cross, became by the transforming power of love the tree of life. By sacrificial love, every created being, from the tiniest atom to the farthest galaxy, journeys the way of the cross for the sake of new life.

The way of the cross is in each creature, faithful to its kind, participating in the cycles of mutual sacrifice. It is in the old rooster, faithful to how he is created, losing dominance to his son. It is in the rotting plant, the decaying body, returning to the soil to nurture future life. It is the path of life, death, and resurrection. The way of the cross is, day by day, to bear the burden of becoming who I really am—the person God creates. This is a process of dying to whatever blocks me from transforming love: carelessness, possessiveness, human arrogance—anything that separates me from any other being.

Thomas Merton was aware of the need to die to illusion—all that stifles the reality of God living in me—in order to become free "to enter by love into union with the Life that dwells and sings within every creature and in the core of our own souls."[2] Creation is the process of love's ever emptying into new life. In the beginning, love emptied into the void in the form of hydrogen. Hydrogen, by the transforming power of love, gave birth to helium. Through cycles of life, death, and resurrection; love poured into galaxies, our solar system, Earth; into water, air, and plant life; into reptile, bird and animal life; and love emptied into human life. All enter life by love because we are loved. In Jesus is the revelation of who we really are: love incarnate, in flesh and blood. In him the reality of every created being is revealed: "Christ is all, and is in all" (Colossians 3:11, NEB).

Jesus calls us to this fullness of life: "Unless a grain of wheat falls into the earth and dies, it remains alone; but if it dies, it bears much fruit" (John 12:24, RSV). Unless we humans enter by love into the Earth community, we have no life. This is true not only in the outward, material aspect but also in the inward, spiritual aspect of our being; for it is here, in the Earth community, that we live in Christ. Again, if we die to enslaving illusions—to all that separates us from the reality of God living in every creature—we are free to enter

---

[2] William H. Shannon, *Thomas Merton's Dark Path* (New York: Farrar, Strauss, & Giroux, 1981), p. 45.

by love into life eternally unfolding. By the way of the cross we come into communion with all creation—the body of the risen Christ.

And as one who was dead and is alive again, we behold all as gift. The air we breathe, the trees and rocks and waters, the living and the dying, what we eat and drink, this wondrous interchange—all is the gift of love outpoured. And our hearts overflow in gratitude.

We enter as a newborn into a holy communion in which each being unfolds a unique and irreplaceable revelation of God-love. Now, in the one and only response to love, we sing, in harmony with diverse voices, creation's song of thanksgiving:

I will thank you because I am marvelously made;
Your works are wonderful, and I know it well.[3]

NEW LIFE

YEAR AFTER YEAR in the springtime, I watch my neighbor's cows—watching for one who begins to withdraw from the herd and get that inward look And when she doesn't show up at the barn for feeding time, I search the pastures and woods. I suppose it is part curiosity, part concern, and still a bit of human arrogance that assumes she won't make it without me (though only once in all these years did a cow need any help in giving birth). Most times I find the cow already crooning and licking over a little, wet, glistening white-faced creature. I've learned not to get too close; mama can be quite protective. For a few hours, mama and baby are alone. The calf is scrubbed and scrubbed. It stands, falls, stands, and learns which end of mama is full of milk. Then, side by side, they begin their first journey together. Ordinarily they stop as they near the herd, and mama steps back and presents her child. One by one, cows come to greet the newborn with a gentle sniff.

On a cold, rainy morning last spring, big old "Gramma" didn't show up at the barn. After a long, wet search, I found her way down in the woods with her newborn. I stopped a way off. Gramma looked at me, sang that low sweet sound, stepped back, and presented him to me. Never before had this happened to me—this

---

[3] Psalm 139:13, *The Book of Common Prayer* (New York: The Episcopal Church, 1979), p. 795.

sacred ritual of infinite courtesy. And after I, on my knees in the mud, had joyfully caressed the new life, and Gramma and he were heading to meet the others, I thought, "I'm a cow!" No. Gramma and I know differently. But I'm no longer an intruder: I am one with them!

*   *   *

Now it is dark winter, the time of gestation, when year after year we await the coming of new life. A young woman about to give birth and her husband seek hospitality and find it, not among human society, but in a cave with cattle. After the child is born and has a time of intimacy with his mother, he is presented in the animals' feeding trough. He is greeted by lowing sounds and warm breath from gentle muzzles. And as the invisible forces of the universe commune with the visible, those humans who are in harmony with Creation—the earth, sheep, plant life; the heavens, stars, planets, cosmic life—come to this cave singing praise and thanksgiving to the God of infinite courtesy.

The Carpenter *and* the Unbuilder

by David M. Griebner

O NCE UPON A TIME there was a man living in a certain
kingdom who received an invitation from his king to come
to dinner. Something inside him was excited as never
before by the invitation. Something was afraid as well. Would he
have the right clothes to wear? Would his manners be good enough
for his lord's table? What would they talk about when they were not
eating? Above all, the man was frightened by the long journey to
the king's castle.

So what did the man do? Well, he spent one month deciding
what to wear and buying the clothes he did not already have. He
spent two months learning the rules of etiquette and practicing
them as he ate. He spent three months reading up on all the latest
issues faced by the kingdom so he would have something to say.

Finally, he faced the journey itself. By trade the man was a carpenter. He built small houses and extra outhouses and garages better than anyone else. After he had packed the clothing and food he
thought he would need for the journey, he had room for only a little more. So he decided to pack a few tools, enough to permit him
to build adequate overnight shelter on the journey. Then he started
out.

The first day he traveled through the morning and early afternoon, stopping only to eat a bit of lunch. Then he set about con-
structing a rough shelter to spend the night in. After a few hours
labor he had a small, safe, dry place to sleep. The next morning, as
he was about to start out again, he looked at the shelter he had built.
He began to notice places where it could be made better. So instead
of resuming the journey right away, he began to make improve-
ments on his little dwelling. Well, one thing led to another, garage
to kitchen to study and indoor plumbing, and so on. Soon he had
pretty much forgotten about the journey.

Meanwhile, the king began to wonder about the man. And so,
as kings are able to do, he arranged for another person who was also

traveling to the dinner to stop by and see how the man was coming along.

When he found him, the carpenter was living in his second house. He had sold the first one to someone, remembered the invitation, and moved on for a day or so. However, soon he had settled in and built a bigger and better house on the profits he had made from the sale of his first house. The carpenter was only too happy to invite the visitor in for lunch, but while he was content to accept the offer of food, the visitor preferred to eat out in the yard under a tree.

"Is there a reason why you don't want to come in?" asked the carpenter.

"Why yes," replied the other. "You see, I am on a journey to have dinner with the king of our land. It is important for me to stay on the journey. Perhaps, after lunch, you would like to come with me?"

"What you say sounds familiar to me," said the carpenter. "I think I too received an invitation to have dinner with the king, but I have been a little bit uncertain of the way."

"I know," said the stranger. "I was uncertain once as well. As a matter of fact, once I was a carpenter just like you. I too wanted to build safe places along the way to stay in. One day, another fellow on the journey helped me to learn how to unbuild instead of to build. He helped me to leave the home I had been living in and trust the journey itself. I was worried about following the right path. He told me that there were a number of paths that would lead to the dinner. The king had set it up that way, and the king had also set up warnings along the wrong paths. The important thing was just to continue to put one foot in front of the other with love and trust. I was also worried about what I had left behind. To this he said that the king had seen to it that everything worth saving would be at the castle waiting for me."

"What you say is certainly of comfort. It helps to know that you have been just like me," said the carpenter.

Well then, why don't we let go of this house and get on with the journey?"

"I don't know. Maybe. Can I sleep on it?"

"I suppose."

"Can I fix a bed for you?"

"No," said the visitor, "I will just stay out here under the tree. It is easier to notice the wonderful things the king has put along the way when you aren't looking out from inside something you have erected to protect yourself."

The unbuilder waited outside all night. The next morning the carpenter indeed had decided to resume the journey. Together they prepared to set out.

"Well," said the carpenter, "which way shall we go?"

"Which way seems right to you?" asked the unbuilder.

"I'm not sure."

"I'll tell you what. Let's just sit here for a few minutes and think hard about the king. Remember the stories you have been told about him. Remember how much he loves you. Remember how much you love him. When you have remembered as clearly as you think you can, consider the paths that lie before you and see which one seems to best satisfy your longing for, and remembering of, the king. Let your desire to be with the king become more powerful in you than your uncertainty and fear about choosing the right or wrong path."

Silently they sat through the morning in the carpenter's front yard. Slowly it began to seem as though they were already on the journey. As that feeling grew and grew, it suddenly didn't seem like any decision needed to be made. It just happened. With a deep sense of freedom they were off.

Many of the days went just like that, new steps out of silent beginnings and pure desires. They simply waited until the sense of journeying wrapped around even their waiting, and then they were off without worrying overmuch whether they were on the "right" path or not. In the stillness of their hearts they made room for the path and the path seemed to come to them.

Of course the carpenter still felt the need to build a home from time to time. The unbuilder made sure he understood what he was doing and then let him do it if he really wanted to. While the carpenter labored, the unbuilder, his guide and friend, would continue to practice the silent waiting in the yard under the tree, and soon they would unbuild yet another house and begin the journey again.

In the meantime the king kept the food warm, which he was very good at doing.

Index

The following is a guide to the articles in this collection, which indicates where they originally appeared in Weavings.

Desiring

Waiting

Discerning

Responding

WALKING HUMBLY BEFORE GOD
Beasley-Topliffe, Vol. V, No. 2 (March/April 1990)

FROM THE GREAT CLOUD OF WITNESSES
Hunsinger, Vol. II, No. 2 (March/April 1987)

COMPASSION AND COMMITMENT
Gutiérrez, Vol. V, No. 6 (November/December 1990)

BECOMING BEARERS OF RECONCILIATION
Bondi, Vol. V, No. 1 (January/February 1990)

MOVING TOWARD FORGIVENESS
Thompson, Vol. VII, No. 2 (March/April 1992)

INTERCESSION: CARING FOR SOULS
Steere, Vol. IV, No. 2 (March/April 1989)

SANCTIFYING TIME, PLACE, AND PEOPLE
Saliers, Vol. II, No. 5 (September/October 1987)

SING TO THE LORD A NEW SONG
Mangam, Vol. VII, No. 6 (November/December 1992)

THE CARPENTER AND THE UNBUILDER
Griebner, Vol. II, No. 4 (July/August 1987)